The Drama DIET

LISA STUART

PRAISE FOR THE DRAMA DIET

"I've known Lisa Stuart for many years and have been lucky enough to experience *The Drama Diet* up close and personal. Lisa has always been there for me – talking me through difficulties, helping me find clarity, and reminding me of my strength. She has an incredible gift for simplifying the complex and offering wisdom that truly lands – and now she's doing that for you, too. *The Drama Diet* is the perfect blueprint to detox from the chaos around you and reclaim your energy. With her signature wit and heartfelt honesty, Lisa helps you shed the emotional weight that keeps you stuck – so you can stop spinning and start showing up for your own life with clarity. You don't have to cancel the drama – just renegotiate the terms. And anything that costs you your peace? That's a firm *no deal*."

> ~ Patricia Kara, *Deal or No Deal*, author of *Dream On... Now Deliver!*

"Lisa's work is a breath of fresh air for every woman who's tired of being pulled into everyone else's drama. *The Drama Diet* is smart, soulful, and emotionally liberating – a guide to reclaiming your peace, your energy, and your power. If you're ready to stop managing other people's chaos and come home to yourself, this book will lovingly walk you there."

> ~ Sarah Pendrick, bestselling author of *Beautifully Brave*

"Lisa's book *The Drama Diet* takes you on a journey to not only discover your true self but also break through the limiting beliefs and stories holding you back. It empowers you to let go of the toxicity in your life and gives you tangible tools on how to do it. As a friend and someone who has watched Lisa's growth as a coach as well, it's inspiring! She shows you how to dance through the dark and into the light. Her vulnerability in this book and her method of *The Drama Diet* are helpful for any stage of life, and I'm so proud of her for sharing it with the world! Let's be real, we all have drama and need tools to not only handle it but release it! That's what *The Drama Diet* is! And her beautiful card deck is the perfect aesthetic, matched with easy everyday practices to enhance your journey! "

~Ali Levine, Certified & Trauma Informed Breath Coach & Author

"Finally! A diet we can all live by without any calories or caveats! Lisa Stuart has created a recipe for inner happiness and peace, and power with her clever and insightful voice, which deserves to be part of our daily intake!"

~Nancy Steiner, Steiner Coaching Solutions

Copyright© Lisa Stuart 2025

All rights reserved. No part of this book may be reproduced in any form or by any electronic or mechanical means, including information storage and retrieval systems, without permission in writing from the publisher. The only exception is by a reviewer, who may quote short excerpts in a review. For permission requests, please address The Three Tomatoes Publishing.

Published October 2025
Paperback ISBN: 979-8-9926661-6-8
Hardcover ISBN: 979-8-9926661-7-5
Library of Congress Control Number: 2025913848
For information address:
The Three Tomatoes Book Publishing
6 Soundview Rd.
Glen Cove, NY 11542
Cover design and Author Photo: Russell Stuart
Cover photo: Glenn Nutley and BP Major
Interior design: nycartdirector.com

DISCLAIMER

Dear Reader,

Thank you so much for picking up this book. It means a lot to me that you're here, and I'm genuinely honored to be a small part of your journey. I don't take your time or trust lightly.

That said, I want to be clear: while everything I share comes from personal experience, insight, and a genuine desire to help, I am not a licensed therapist, doctor, or mental health professional. This book is not intended to offer medical, therapeutic, or psychological advice of any kind.

If you are struggling and feel you need professional support, I strongly encourage you to reach out to a qualified provider. I'm a big believer in the power of therapy and a proud advocate for ending the stigma around mental health. We all deserve support, and you don't have to do it alone.

With love and respect,
Lisa

FORWARD

Let me just say this: *Lisa Stuart is that girl.*

You know—the one who somehow makes you laugh, cry, and rethink your entire life plan... all in the same conversation. And then texts you a hilarious meme and reminds you you're amazing.

When I had Lisa on my show, *The McCord List Today*, she lit up the studio with her fire, her fun, and her soul-level truth bombs. But honestly? That's just who she is. Whether she's in front of a camera, coaching high achievers, or writing this book, Lisa shows up real, radiant, and ready to *disrupt the drama.*

And *The Drama Diet*? It's her in paperback.

This isn't your typical self-help "just meditate more" fluff. It's a total mindset makeover wrapped in sass, science, and spiritual mic drops. Think of it as a soul smoothie—equal parts wisdom, wit, and "wow, I needed that."

Lisa breaks it all down: how to deal with energy vampires, escape the trap of other people's chaos, and finally stop auditioning for roles in dramas you didn't even want to be cast in. (Retire the crown, Drama Queen—you've got better things to do.)

This book is for the woman who looks like she's got it all together—but secretly feels like she's one group chat away from losing it. It's for the go-getters, the self-help junkies, the spiritual baddies, and the burned-out boss babes who are *so done* living in survival mode.

I know the heart behind these pages. Lisa doesn't just *write* about transformation—she lives it. And she'll lovingly, hilariously, and unapologetically help you do the same.

So if you're ready to drop the drama, detox your energy, and finally live like the main character *you actually want to be*—this is your moment.

Get comfy. Grab a journal. And get ready to meet the most peaceful, powerful version of *you*.

Xoxo,

Rachel McCord
TV Host, Speaker, Founder of The McCord List

TABLE OF CONTENTS

Preface 1

Introduction 5

Chapter 1 - The Outdated Checklist 9

Chapter 2 - Drama Dance 21

Chapter 3 - Squirrel Syndrome 37

Chapter 4 - The Drama Diet Cheat Sheet 55

Chapter 5 - Disrupt Part 1: Drama Magnet 75

Chapter 6 - Disrupt Part 2: Creative Director 101

Chapter 7 - Friending Fear 131

Chapter 8 - Deflate Part 1: The Deep Dissolve 153

Chapter 9 - Deflate Part 2: Dark Light 177

Chapter 10 - Detox Part 1: Surrendering to Chaos 199

Chapter 11 - Detox Part 2: Fall with Faith. Fly with Fear 233

Chapter 12 - Drama Diet Dessert 263

Continuing the Journey 275

Acknowledgments 277

About the Author 281

DEDICATION

To everyone who brought the drama – thank you. Without you, this book (and the plot twists) wouldn't exist.

To those who stood by me when I was knee-deep in the chaos– your love and patience helped me find my way to peace a little faster.

To me – for being a drama magnet and learning to flip the magnet by embracing the darkness and letting light shine the way. This was the catalyst for creating The Drama Diet, and it is an honor to share this gift with you.

And to you – for showing up for yourselves to dance with your drama but let love take the lead, so that you can live a life of peace, clarity and freedom.

PREFACE

So, there I was. Mechanically going through the motions, although I felt like I was moving through muck. I had a plastered smile on my face, knew the auto responses of what to say, and with a heaviness permeating through my soul, I carried on like everything was fine. Only it wasn't. *Insert name of choice you can relate to* was reeling into me. Depending on the day, it was either about something I did or something someone else did, and I was assigned to be a mediator to rectify the drama of the month. The details are not important. Nor are the identities of the parties. What's important is that I was sucked into the center of yet another drama filled situation. And I did what I usually did best. I suppressed my voice to keep the peace, despite the tornado of drama swirling around me.

Who placed me there, them or me? It really doesn't matter. *Drama doesn't take sides, it just recruits.* You're either a spectator or a participant. Either way, you're in the thick of it. And it doesn't feel good. You might think this was about a case I was arguing for one of my clients in Court. Nope ... this was just me ... dripping in drama.

I am a recovering Drama Magnet.

Yes, it's true. There was a time when I attracted drama wherever I went. When there was a chaotic situation, I was immediately drawn to it like a moth to light. And when I tried to pull away, I was immediately pulled back in. Was this intentional? No. Was it avoidable? Sadly, no. At least at the time. You see, I didn't know how to repel drama. I didn't know that when someone pushes my buttons, I can simply *move the buttons*. But I also wasn't one of those people who thrived on drama. You know the type ... whenever things seem to settle down into peace, they get all angsty and need to stir the pot. They get a kick out of drama. Why? Maybe it distracts them from their own life. Or maybe it distracts them from the true chaos that lies within.

And that's where I seemed to dwell most on drama. My inner chaos. My mind chatter. The self-sabotaging thoughts that ran laps in my brain, seemingly going nowhere but in circles. I must have run countless marathons in my head, usually competing against my own thoughts, and inevitably letting my fears take the lead. This was me attracting drama.

So what did I do? Well, I dwelt in the drama. But soon (and by soon, I mean over four decades ... yes, I'm dating myself), I got tired of being a drama dweller and learned how to flip the magnet. How to repel the drama. How to become a **Drama Ninja.** Yep. That's a thing.

That's when I remembered, *wait, I am the CEO of my life, the creator of my story, the gatekeeper to my happiness.* And with a deep breath, I inhaled courage, exhaled fear, and took charge of my power. Good thing, because the battery pack of my power was in the red. But since I declared this a judgment-free zone, I didn't beat myself up for allowing the *drama daggers* to stab me before I leaned into my power. Nor did I judge those around me for dragging me here, again. No one can be dragged to drama; we are all willing volunteers, albeit subconsciously.

It's truly amazing how, with the right tools, you can literally transmute the energy of *fear into love*, melting all the swirling chaos into droplets of past drama that simply wash away into nothingness.

But before I show you how, you may be wondering ... who am I, and how did I come up with *The Drama Diet?*

Hi ... I'm Lisa, and I am a recovering people pleaser, a quasi-reformed perfectionist, a mom, a wife, a daughter, a sister, a friend, an attorney, a speaker, a writer, a songwriter, a drama dietician, a life designer, a spiritual stylist, a workout enthusiast, a pseudo-vegan, a coffee, chocolate, and tequila lover. I'm also an overthinker, an over-analyzer, and partially neurotic. I believe you can have many labels, but I don't believe they need to stick to you and define you.

I have a love-hate relationship with journaling, meditating, and giving up sugar. I don't believe in judgment unless it's in a court of law. And even that can be challenged.

I believe that you can elevate your worth and fly, but that to F.L.Y., you must First. Love. Yourself. And in flying, you must fall, a.k.a. *fail*, a hell of a lot of times to succeed. I believe the most important relationship you will ever have is with yourself. I also believe that the *hardest* relationship you will ever have is with yourself.

As a lawyer, I believe the supreme L.A.W. is that *Love Always Wins.*

I believe that we all have a purpose, and that we know what that purpose is by what we desire. *Spoiler alert:* feelings of jealousy, envy, and comparison-itis are usually signs of the things we crave. I also believe that our life's purpose often tends to be something in complete contrast to what we believe we are supposed to be doing. They are generally things that require us to bravely move through fear.

I believe that fear is our friend, that it will lead the way to everything we want, and that we need to transmute that energy into courageous excitement. I also believe that fear is our greatest obstacle … that our mind tricks us out of things we want, that our emotions support that, and that our ego is satisfied to stay in a place of comfortable complacency, or even comfortable chaos.

I believe that we don't have to believe everything we think. And therefore, I believe that we don't have to believe everything we believe. *The Drama Diet* serves up many courses, and these are just a few preshow golden nuggets before we delve into the main *course* (pun intended).

In case you see a theme, I believe in the **law of duality**, and this book will take you on a journey of *light and dark* and demonstrate how we actually need *both* polarities to co-exist in peace. I'll show you throughout this book *how to navigate with fear but lead with love*. How embracing the dark side will lead you to a more peaceful and happy life. I know that's a mind bender, but remember, a magnet only attracts the opposite of its polarity. And you deserve to attract the life that you desire, despite your chaos.

So let me show you how.

With Love,
xo Lisa

INTRODUCTION

Endless Chaos.

Chaos has always existed since the beginning of time. I don't think anyone can pinpoint a time in history when it first emerged. The first sentence of the Bible states that the Earth was without form and there was darkness. This can be interpreted as chaos. Until light was created from darkness.

So we can comfortably assume that if the chaos has no retrospective beginning, then it has no foreseeable end.

It is constant. Just like gravity. If we didn't have gravity, we would float away. If we didn't have chaos, we would not know contrast. And it is the contrast that sets the borders defining what we don't want, so we can clarify what it is that we *do* want– much like the bumpers of a bowling alley lane that not only help keep my ball from going in the gutter, but more importantly, redirect my ball to the desired pins. Hey, you may call this cheating. I call it getting a little help towards my goal.

It's the concept of duality that keeps balance in the world. It's learning to live a life of harmony in spite of the chaos.

And I have finally figured out how. But as I stated earlier, I wasn't always like this. My basic instinct was to embrace drama like the permeating fiend it was and to play victim to it. Usually swept up in the frenzy of whatever symphony was playing at the moment. I fell prey to reacting to the music of choice. It took me many years of emotional turmoil, physical ailments, and mental anguish to realize that there must be a better way. A universal way to live a life of peace despite drama.

And then one day, I'm guesstimating around ten years ago, I said to someone, *"I wish I could just go on a Drama Diet."* The problem was that no such diet existed. *Yet.* So over the last decade, I developed *The Drama Diet*. It is a work in progress that I practice(d), working out the kinks through trial and error. Luckily for me, that was the time in my life when the drama really hit the fan! The universe truly has a sense of humor. It was as if it was taunting me, saying, *You think you have the drama antidote? Here's another hellish scenario for you to master.* And no matter how many times I landed flat on my face, often in a heap, crying on the floor, I would inevitably get up and challenge the universe back, shouting *Bring it on*!

And boy did it! It reminds me of those bop bags I used to love as a child. The inflatables with weighted bottoms, that, no matter how many times you punched that thing down, it would bop right back up. Eventually, I learned my *Drama Ninja* skills on how to do a one-two punch back so that I was always a step ahead of the drama, ensuing the peace.

But let me tell you, no matter where you are on the spectrum of drama, if you practice the tips and techniques herein, I truly believe that *The Drama Diet* will help you. Everything in this book is based on my own experiences. *I don't preach what I haven't actually practiced.* I know what worked and what didn't.

I didn't take courses to teach you fluffy mantras and sparkling words of wisdom. I have been in the trenches, doing the hard work, digging up the internal muck that accumulated over the years, and have come out the other side. Definitely not unscathed. I've even got the war wounds to prove it. But I earned those scars, and they are reminders to never give up on yourself. Or your dreams. They're waiting for you to grab them. You may have to go through a military grade obstacle course to get there, but believe me, it is worth it. Hey, no one said facing drama like a ninja was gonna be pain free. But it will definitely show you how to be drama-free. Or at least *drama lite*. And that's something.

The Drama Diet

So, I hear you scratching your head, what exactly is *The Drama Diet*? Is it another trendy diet-of-the-month? Is it going to help me until I plateau, and then leave me stuck in the same situation? Is it going to fill my head with fluff while emptying my bank account? Not at all. This is in no way a fad diet. It is a lifestyle change. A sustainable way of living. Ever evolving with each set of circumstances you encounter. Let me explain.

We all carry extra weight on us. And no...I'm not talking about the pounds that may have you reaching for Ozempic. I'm talking about the pounds you carry around of other people's opinions, judgments, and unattainable expectations. *The Drama Diet* is a weight loss system to shed the weight of all this and more.

It provides **recipes** on how to deal with external factors such as energy vampires, re-evaluating relationships, guilt trips, boundary borders, and people pleasing.

It's also designed with **exercises** on how to lose the heaviness of your internal drama such as limiting beliefs, mind chatter, self-sabotaging thoughts, and negative self-talk. You know, the ones that love to grab your attention at 2 a.m. and keep you awake so that the *dark circles* under your eyes in the morning match the *dark thoughts* that *circled* your mind all night.

*Bonus: Following *The Drama Diet* may lead to saving money on under-eye concealer.*

It's a roadmap to where you want to go, no matter what cave or hole you find yourself stuck in. *The Drama Diet* will guide you on how to crumble the patterns of outdated stories and beliefs that have been holding you back and keeping you stagnant. This book will provide step-by-step tools on how to chisel away what doesn't serve you so that you can return to the core of who you are authentically, unapologetically, and vibrantly.

The roadmap of this book

Chapter 1: Why you need to rip up the outdated checklist and other confessions from a recovering drama magnet.

Chapter 2: Defines drama and explains how we need to dance with our darkness.

Chapter 3: Explains how avoiding drama has inflated the problem.

Chapter 4: Breaks down the *3D Drama Diet Formula* and all its components.

Chapters 5-11: Dives deep into dissecting each component of the formula. Each chapter starts off with a *Case Law* to provide an overview of the chapter's theme. At the end of each of these chapters you'll find Recipes, Exercises, and Drama Diary Journal Prompts.

Chapter 12: Provides a recap and other goodies.

Each of the chapters can be read in order or not. My intention is that they all stand on their own and you can turn to any one you choose depending on your needs, curiosity, and purpose. Feel ready to jump around. In fact, *feel free*, period. This journey is about freedom.

At any point along your journey, you will have access to pinpointing the exact spot on the drama wave that has swept you up to make sure you have a smooth ride, instead of having the drama wave crash down on you. Use the tools in this book to help you ebb and flow with the rhythm of life.

Happy reading.

1

THE OUTDATED CHECKLIST

Before we can jump into *what The Drama Diet* is and *how* to effectively implement it, we need to break down the elements leading up to *why* we need *The Drama Diet*. *Why* we want results.

As a practicing lawyer, I expect results. In evaluating cases, I weigh the pros and cons and do what I can to tip the scales in my favor to get good results. Imagine the scales of justice as a metaphor for the law of duality. When one scale has too much pressure, it will be weighed down, and the opposing scale will lift. These are like the pros and cons of life, weighing each decision, each thought, each action taken (or not taken). To maintain internal balance— which is what we are all seeking— we need to find the right ingredients to tip the scale in our favor despite how out of balance our external world may be.

The Drama Diet provides tools to mix the right ingredients no matter what life recipe you are dealing with. And, as with any proper diet, what you gain tends to outweigh what you lose (no pun intended). So when you eliminate the internal and external factors that no longer serve you, you will gain so much more.

> DISCLAIMER: Side effects of the Drama Diet include owning your worth, gaining clarity from chaos, feeling lighter, freer, and in control of your happiness. You will learn how to flip the magnet to repel drama instead of attracting it. In other words, finding the sweet spot of inner peace while keeping your mojo and power. But like anything worth having in life, in order to maintain ease and freedom, you must be consistent and mindful. And if you fall off the proverbial mindfulness wagon, you can jump back on at any given moment without shame or guilt: two wasted emotions that sap your time and energy.

I had to put in a disclaimer. You see, I've been practicing law for over 25 years. Holy sh*t, it's been that long. Which means I have a ton of experience witnessing a lot of drama in my profession. As a personal injury attorney, I am also a sort of therapist to my clients. Every case involves some form of emotional component requiring compassion, empathy, and clear direction. And as a litigator, it is my job to advocate fiercely for my clients.

And this made me think, *"If I advocate for them, who advocates for me?"* (Having a Superman moment here … *"If you've got me, who's got you?"* #IYKYK.)

It was so easy for me to fight for my clients' worth. *Literally.* The only way to get compensated in civil law is to put a monetary value on the damages. In other words, *what is the case worth*? But when it came down to my life, many times I didn't feel that I deserved certain things. Funny enough, I was fairly confident.

But what I did not lack in confidence, I lacked in self-worth.

And that is a horrible place to be because a confident exterior tends to hide an unworthy interior filled with limiting beliefs. Add a dose of perfectionism and a wallop of people pleasing and voila, you can picture the *L.O.L. Life Of Lisa*. Pre-Drama Diet.

Imagine this if you will. I was:
- Consumed by worry (*carousel of thought loops in my mind*).
- Never feeling good enough (*perfectionist junkie*).
- Procrastinating for just the right time (*getting stuck in analysis paralysis*).
- Affected by other people's opinions (*burdened by judgment*).
- Never wanting to cause drama (*always the people pleaser*).
- Riddled with mom guilt (*hashtag mom fail*).
- Pulled in multiple directions (*the juggle is real*).
- Not living my authentic purpose (*oooh this was a big one … following someone else's checklist*).

And on … and on … and on.

It was all fear-based. Fear of failure. Fear of judgment. Fear of what I would be losing. Fear of *who* I would be losing. Fear of embarrassment. Even fear of shining. Yes. "Who am I to do this?!" Imposter syndrome was at the top of my list. I wasn't ready at the time to accept the duality concept of "Who am I *not* to do this?!" I was light years ahead in my accomplishments and years behind in my self-love. Always chasing the next goal before my limiting beliefs caught up with me. Which they inevitably did. Can you relate?

My life looked perfect on paper. Married with kids, great family and friends, a good career, vibrant social life, involved in charities and boards, always making time for exercise & shopping, and girl time was a non-negotiable. I had checked everything off the list– *The Checklist*.

*****

You know *"The Checklist"* – it's the preconceived list we are conditioned to believe we need to fulfill. Did you also get a copy of *The Checklist* during your life?

The funny thing is, I'm not sure anyone really knows who originated *The Checklist*. As it has gone through many revisions throughout the years based on societal norms, familial expectations, religion, and even social media. But the premises are all the same. Conform to *The Checklist* or you risk being judged, shamed, excluded, or even canceled.

You see, I used to believe that in order to have the "perfect" life, I had to check off all the boxes on *The Checklist*. And then, as if I were in some personal race, I tried to check off as many of the boxes as I could in record time. By the time I was thirty, I was married with two amazing boys, and in my sixth year as a lawyer. Then, in my thirties, I went into overdrive. As a working mother, I tried to do it all because ... isn't that what everyone is supposed to do?! Balance work, family, social life, keep yourself in shape, volunteer for charities and fundraisers, keep everyone around you happy, and try to keep your sanity! All the while with endless energy and

The Drama Diet

abundant appreciation. Then get up and do it all over again. *The hamster wheel of The Checklist.*

But I added an extra ingredient–*pressure*. I lived my life in a pressure cooker and felt that every minute had to be accounted for, or I was wasting space. And as a perfectionist junkie, I felt that I had to be the best at everything, or my value would decrease. But just like anything that succumbs to excessive pressure, something always has to give. In my case, it was my health— mind, body, and emotions. I was completely depleted, stressed, and pulled in a million directions. Yet I wore it as a badge of honor. I prided myself in "doing it all" and felt that if I wasn't, then I wasn't "good enough." I mistook being busy for being productive. I believed that the busier I was, the more accolades I would receive, thus validating my worth. I would push myself to the edge. Get depleted. Refuel. Then go full throttle ahead. Again.

And so the cycle perpetuated, causing drama on repeat. With no pause button until I crashed. Completely unsustainable. But at the time, I accepted it as the norm. I thought it was normal to sacrifice your well-being as long as *The Checklist* was getting completed. I thought it was all part of the process called "your ideal life".

Sometimes drama comes wrapped in Chanel and Tiffany diamonds. Who said drama can't come in the form of your perfect life? Then it creates internal drama. And while on paper my life looked great, inside I was suffering. I was burnt out, my health suffered, my wellbeing suffered, and I always felt like I was missing something, as though the "real" me was burning to come out but didn't fit into a pretty Tiffany box. I was suffering from a bad case of comparison-itis. I always felt I wasn't living up to my standards if I wasn't where "so 'n so" was, not taking into account all that I had already accomplished. Many times, I shoved my dreams aside so I could live up to other people's expectations.

I was trying to win a race I didn't even sign up for.

And it was exhausting, draining, and completely unrealistic. Sound familiar?!

Yet that was the standard I lived by. I didn't know that I could take back the pen to my life and write my own script. I hadn't yet learned that I was actually the star of the movie of my life and could at any point create a life beyond my wildest dreams.

I didn't understand that once you decide to change the story of your life you will realize you always held the pen.

I often had willingly, and unquestioningly, handed over the pen to my life for others to write the script ... star as lead roles ... and direct the trajectory of my life. Many times, I thought that they knew better. I didn't always fully trust my judgment. The day I decided to take back the pen to my life and write my own script was the day that everything changed.

See, once you tap into your own light and realize the power that you harness, you become unstoppable. Everything in your life shifts. For the better. But this requires doing the inner work. I mean the deep, deep, *deep* inner work. First, you have to tear everything down. But nobody told me this. Nobody told me that once you choose your voice over others, things don't just magically fall into place or neat little Tiffany boxes. No ... instead everything falls, no, **tumbles** around you like *boulders* that were once on your *shoulders,* pounding to the ground. From there, all that you knew then **crumbles** into shards of your pre-existing life that no longer serve you, creating chaos and disorder and ... you guessed it ... more drama.

Wait, you say, *isn't the whole point of taking back your life to eliminate the drama?*

Hell yes! But this is where things get real. And as much as I have a sweet tooth, I don't sugar coat things. In order to create and cultivate the life you have been waiting for, you need to rebuild with new construction. And with **construction** inevitably comes **destruction**. Again, it would have been really nice if someone had told me this ahead of time. But they didn't. So, I am telling you because I had to learn it the hard way. Again. And again.

Because I was inevitably using the same broken blocks glued together to build my new life instead of courageously using a new blueprint for a solid foundation.

I was trying to reconstruct my new life with the fragmented pieces of my old life. And that simply wasn't working. The glue was just a shield to protect me from what I was avoiding –facing my truth– acknowledging what I really wanted in life.

Don't get me wrong. I was relatively happy. But I always felt like something was missing, something that I couldn't quite put my finger on. It was gnawing at my soul, like a void I could never fill. I inherently knew there was a deeper desire within me that had to get satiated. Every time the feeling would creep up on me, I would shove it back down, deep into the recesses of my core, and shake it off. It was easy to hide something that I couldn't even identify. I wasn't really sure *what* I wanted, which made it even more confusing.

And worse, I felt guilt and shame for even entertaining that there was more to be had in life because I had so much to be grateful for. All the boxes were checked on the proverbial checklist. How could I be so selfish? How could I not be satisfied with the life I had? How could I possibly be greedy enough to ask for more?

But eventually, the feeling grew stronger and louder. It became harder to ignore that indescribable gnaw in the center of my core. There was no denying the void inside me, one that was growing wider by the day. Until eventually I felt as if the Grand Canyon was stuck inside my soul, trying to pry me open to a world I wasn't yet ready to enter. But I didn't know how to articulate into words what it was that I was feeling. Nor did I feel I had permission to pursue an uncharted road to follow a burning desire inside of me that I still couldn't identify. So I stayed trapped in my "perfectly curated world" trying to satisfy expectations placed on me by others, and myself. It was the people-pleasing, perfectionist in me, and I wasn't going to let her, or those around me, down.

That "thing" I couldn't identify was living my authentic self.

Eventually, I realized that there is no one-size-fits-all blueprint for life. What I wanted didn't fit into any pre-existing box. I had to learn to design my own life, even if it deviated from *The Checklist*. And it was the hardest thing to do. Because in designing my own life, I had to first unravel the life that I built. I risked tarnishing the image I created for myself. I was held back by the fear of how others would perceive me if I changed into the person I always knew I was. But with painstakingly slow action, I allowed my life to unravel. And I knew that once I pulled that thread, there was no going back.

R.I.P. up the outdated checklist. Rest In Peace.

It was when I decided to take the pen back to my life and rip up that outdated checklist that everything changed. When you R.I.P. up the list, you're telling your old self to *Rest In Peace*. You are essentially rebirthing your worth, like a phoenix rising from the ashes.

But it took writing many versions of the script, many drafts, and many changes. But that is life, ever evolving. And either we try to catch up with it or it has to catch up with us. And I prefer the latter. That is when you know you are a trailblazer, when the path before you has no footprints.

*****

I was patiently waiting for somebody to give me permission to live my dream and find happiness. But nobody was giving it to me. I had to give it to myself. And with self-permission came self-worth. And that was a journey in and of itself. The 1.0 version of me handed over my worth on a rose gold platter for others to validate.

The Drama Ninja in me says save validation for parking tickets.

Now, I advocate for people to rip up their outdated checklist that someone else dictated and write their own! If you're reading (or listening) to this book, and you're waiting for that permission, *consider this it*. Not that you need my permission. But maybe my story will inspire you. Or perhaps my support will encourage you.

I often felt that most people had it all figured out. So, it was eye-opening to discover that I wasn't alone. I realized throughout the years, both in my professional and personal life, that this was a universal theme – that most people feel held back by fears of drama and judgment. That they too get caught in the repetition of the hamster wheel and don't know how to stick a cog in it, lost on how to disrupt the pattern, wondering if that's even possible.

I was also astonished to learn that, statistically, approximately 80% of our thoughts are negative. Truth be told, mine were probably hovering at the 97th percentile. This makes sense since statistically, 90% of our thoughts are the same as the day before. And with humans producing approximately 50,000 thoughts a day, having at least 40,000 of my thoughts be negative, day after day, it dawned on me that I was the problem.

But I also recognized that if I was the problem, I could also be the solution to the problem. I could *train my brain* to think new thoughts. So then why was that so terrifying? Was I truly comfortable in my own chaos? Was I scared to trust myself and step into my power? Did I not trust my internal navigation system? Yep. All of the above.

So I weighed my options –*cue the scales of justice*– live in fear or live *despite* fear.

I chose the latter. You see, I had no choice but to be the solution, as nobody was coming to save me. My reality was only getting more solidified the way it was. I had to make drastic changes and take full responsibility for my life if I wanted things to change. Be accountable for myself, the good, the bad, the ugly.

As much as I dealt with chaos, conflict, and confrontation in my professional life as a lawyer, I shied away from them in my personal life. I would rather have kept the peace than face the music. The thing is, the music is always playing, no matter how hard you try to drown out the sound. But when keeping the peace for others took too much of a toll on my inner peace, I had to put on my big girl pants and face the music head-on.

And while the road ahead wasn't quite visible yet, my destinations were. And I began to believe that with courageous action, I could turn my dreams into reality. And I did.

After a painful divorce, years of releasing outdated stories and beliefs, overcoming adversities to marry my soulmate (twin flame) against unimaginable odds, having a daughter in my mid-forties (the magic of manifestation and divine intervention), pursuing my passion and living in my purpose, I have a burning desire to help you, and countless others, live the life you deserve. I want to shout from the rooftops that it is possible. Look at me. *Learn from me.* I did it! Limiting beliefs and all.

I discovered something in doing so—*don't fear the drama.* You need to embrace the dark side in order to shine. The darker the night, the brighter the stars. Once I learned to embrace drama head-on, I was able to convert my mindset around the fear of drama. The old adage is true – everything you want is on the other side of fear.

Through my own process, discoveries, breakdowns, and breakthroughs, I found a new truth that helped me flip the drama magnet in my own life.

> By learning to embrace and detach from chaos I was able to create inner clarity and peace.

Doing so required me to face the darkness and the drama I had allowed into my life. I had to take responsibility for my happiness, one decision and one boundary at a time. And it took work. Daily focus. Internal willpower. Mental strength. Emotional clarity. And a burning desire.

So with one shaky stiletto in front of the other, I stepped bravely into my authentic self, wobbling along the way, but always finding my footing. It felt like I was on a tightrope, trying to balance my past self with my future desires. But I was learning how to *navigate with fear* and *lead with love*.

I was becoming a *Drama Ninja*.

Before you move on to the next chapter, take *The Drama Diet Test*.

The Drama Diet Test

Where do you generate the most drama in your life? Take the following test to see where drama is testing you most. Rate each item from 1-10 …

1 being the lowest level of drama and 10 being on high alert, entering the toxic zone of drama overload.

Once you've rated it, see where the highest numbers fall. Keep this in mind as you continue through this book. And remember, the drama always changes, so come back to retest and reassess as much as needed.

The Drama Diet Test

Rate your answers from 1 to 10. 1 being the lowest level of drama.

1. Do you find yourself feeling energized or drained after spending time with friends and family? Think of specific people. Choose those you surround yourself with the most.
Rating _____

2. Do you wake up in the night with anxious thoughts circling your mind like a carousel?
Rating _____

3. Do you find yourself constantly telling your brain chatter to shut up?
Rating _____

4. Are you consumed with self growth but still feel like you're stuck with your wheels spinning? Not sure which direction to go in, or even how to get yourself out of that spot?
Rating _____

5. Do you get a physical reaction like a pit in your stomach when you have a gathering or event with certain people you know you have to face?
Rating _____

6. Do you feel like you're always being judged and talked about?
Rating _____

7. Do you sometimes find yourself judging yourself?
Rating _____

8. Do you have a fear of judgement? Fear of failure? Fear of success? Fear of unworthiness? Fear of lack? Fear of the truth?
Rating _____

9. Do you compare yourself to others and feel twinges of jealousy?
Rating _____

10. Has comparison-itis got your confidence?
Rating _____

2

DRAMA DANCE

> The dance between darkness and light
> ...is not always so black and white.

I remember being immediately drawn to the character *Indiana Jones* the first moment I saw him on a massive movie theater screen. He was running from a giant boulder that was chasing him as it rolled, while I watched helplessly from my seat, biting my nails. And in true Indie fashion, he escaped the drama with seconds to spare, leaving the audience to pry open their fingers that were digging into the arm rests they were gripping onto for dear life (or worse, out of the arm of the person sitting next to them, no doubt leaving nail marks.)

If you haven't seen the classic *Raiders* series, stop reading now and go treat yourself to hours of action blended with humor. And that is like life. The *drama* (*action*) needs to be infused with *lightness* (*humor*). It not only diffuses the tension, but it also makes us feel better. And throughout this book, I will harp on this concept that I cannot stress enough – the way you feel is *paramount* to the peace and happiness in your life. (OMG! It was only *after* I wrote the last sentence that I realized that Paramount Pictures actually distributed the first four *Indiana Jones* movies. True story. Can't make this up. Gotta love synchronicities. They're winks from the universe confirming how aligned we are.)

So now, whether or not you've seen the *Indiana Jones* movies, I want you to do the following exercise. Close your eyes and imagine the one thing looming in your life right now that is causing you the most stress. That pressing feeling blocking your joy and ease.

What is Causing You Stress?

- Is it a toxic relationship?
- That argument you had with a family member?
- The weird energy that you felt with a friend?
- The back stabbing you experienced at work?
- Or the promotion that passed you by?
- The struggle you have pursuing your passion?
- The limiting beliefs that let life pass you by because you haven't given yourself permission to go after your dreams?
- Is it the utter fatigue of raising small (and older) children that is draining your energy and depriving you of "me time"?
- Is it not being able to make a decision for yourself without hurting someone else?
- Is it being unable to say "no" to someone when all you want to do is say "yes" to yourself?
- Is it the jealous feeling from seeing someone you know get exactly what you wish you went after, but didn't have the courage?
- Or is it a feeling that you've outgrown a situation or relationship but don't know the next step to take?
- Is it not being able to live your truth without disdain and judgment?

And if none of these scenarios apply, then insert your own.

Once you've selected the *drama of the day* and your eyes are closed, I want you to picture that the drama is a giant boulder chasing you and you are desperately trying to run away from it. How does that make you feel? Does your heart beat a little faster? Do your palms feel a little sweatier? Does your jaw start to clench, and your gut start to tense up? Notice the physical sensations that come up for you.

Next, I want you to imagine the worst thing that can happen. I want you to envision that you have stopped running, but the *boulder of drama* is still chasing you, picking up speed, gaining momentum, and ready to pummel over your tense body. Now ... *visualize that it does*. Yes. *For reals* (as my daughter says.) I want you to imagine how it *feels* for the drama to literally wash over you, bearing its heavy weight, and pressing into areas of your body where you hold stress.

Before you ask .... No. I don't want you to actually experience any life-threatening pain. Only the anticipated pain you think you will feel from the crushing weight of the boulder. But in fact, you come out ... okay. No, better than okay. I want you to imagine that while the boulder was rolling over your body, rather than **compressing** you, it was **decompressing** your fear, your anxiety, and your tension.

Then let the boulder roll off into the distance, where you watch it disintegrate into dust, blown away by a gust of wind.

Take a second. Reassess. Open your eyes. How do you feel now? Do you feel like you've been crushed? Or did that boulder release something in you? Chances are, you feel unexpectedly lighter. Did the drama go away? In a sense. Maybe the drama itself did not necessarily go away, but the stigma around it may have dissipated. And that is because much of what we fear tends to be anticipating the worst.

> Creating scenarios in our heads of what could go wrong. Reliving experiences as if they were on syndication.

But unless a different approach is taken, the drama will be

back. And the temporary reprieve from it will be a fleeting moment of the past. Why? Because *drama never dies*. It just transforms into various shades of drama. Drama is a permanent resident of our existence. Always has been. Always will be.

So, what exactly *is* DRAMA? Let's dissect it.

DRAMA is CHAOS.
Constant, endless and eternal.

- It's instability.
- It's shade.
- It's the uncertainty of change.
- The terror of the unknown.
- The bottomless pit of *what ifs*.
- The turmoil of guilt.
- The tornado of opinions.
- The onslaught of judgment.
- The carousel of limiting beliefs.
- The attacks by others.
- The hidden shame.
- The friction of relationships.
- The duality of conflict.
- The toxicity of negative energy.
- The uneasiness of unrest.
- The fight between what we want to do and what we "should" be doing.
- The racing thoughts of our minds.
- The poisonous words of others.
- The backstabbing talk behind our backs.
- The ego voice in our heads.
- The *mean girls* in our lives.
- The unvalidated meaning we attach to others' actions and words.
- The struggle of ignoring our inner voice.
- Drama is the contrast we resist.
- Drama suffocates the act of surrendering.
- Drama is fear perpetuated.

DRAMA ... in its simplest form ... is DARKNESS.

Drama disguises itself in relationships, in thoughts, in emotions, in habits, even in perspectives. It morphs and evolves depending on the circumstances of our lives. It pretends to be a friend when really it's a fiend. An energy vampire. It keeps us addicted to it by creating excitement and entertainment. It keeps us distracted. *And distraction leads to inaction.* It keeps us stuck. It keeps us up at night. It causes physical symptoms. Emotional trauma. Mental anguish. Spiritual turmoil.

It simply is the darkness to our light.

This book will show you how to be the flame that will *burn* the drama and light up the dark, how to extinguish the present chaos from your inner peace.

But in order to "extinguish" drama, it is important to "distinguish" drama.

Drama, at its root, is twofold. It presents itself in two ways—**internally and externally**. Everybody has some form of drama in their life. Either external or internal. And if you're anything like me, then you've got both. And then some. And if people tell you their lives are "perfect," you know there are some shady skeletons they're just not willing to face. But skeletons resurface no matter how many times you try to shove them in the overstuffed closet of perfectionism. What you try to hide, *even from yourself*, has a way of causing havoc within if you don't do the work within.

*****

Speaking of going within, let's talk about INTERNAL DRAMA.

We've all been there before. Attacked by self-sabotaging thoughts. Held back by limiting beliefs. Spiraling down the rabbit

The Drama Diet

hole of our mind, riddled with negative self-talk. Yep. That's internal drama. It fuels our unvalidated worries and feeds off our irrational fears. You know, the ones that keep us up and play on repeat in the middle of the night. The ones where we wake up with circles under our eyes to match the carousel circle of thoughts. It's the internal drama that holds us back.

Have you ever had a desire that seemed so tangible in your gut, but your mind kicked in and told you all the reasons why it won't work? You know that voice in your head that tells you it's trying to keep you safe so you won't fail, mess up, make a fool of yourself, [*insert your favorite limiting belief*]. That inner voice that you hear, the voice *loves* to stir the pot! Daily! And it keeps adding its reasons why you can't and shouldn't pursue your dreams and goals. It's the recurring voice in your head that tells you that you can't, that keeps you comfortably safe rather than courageously curious.

> That voice disguises itself as protection, but it's really just your ego self-protecting "its ego" from getting bruised.

It would rather "play it safe" than take a leap of action. Your ego stockpiles guilt, lack of worth, self-judgment, fear of failure, fear of success, fear of others' opinions, fear of judgment, and fear in general. And don't be mad at it. The ego is just doing its job. But it's time to fire the ego and hire your higher self. The one that's truly in charge. That's an inside job, but you still have to face the outside world.

Which leads to EXTERNAL DRAMA.

*****

External drama is exactly how it sounds. Drama that swirls around you and manages to pull you into the tornado of chaos. It's the unsolicited opinions from others, unrealistic expectations from others, judgment from others, blame from others, shame from others, guilt trips, the need for other people's approval, and the disappointment from others when you can't meet their irrational needs. It's people who cross the boundaries without permission. It's people who cross the relationship borders without a valid or *validated* passport.

Think of a time that you were around someone, or a group of people, and you left feeling depleted as though the experience just drained the energy out of you, and you needed to replenish yourself and raise your spirit. FYI, that is not the sign of a healthy relationship. Those people, or rather, *energy vampires*, sucked your soul … literally. They invaded your space, quashed your spirit, and fed into your insecurities because …. honestly … you let them. But you can, and will, change that.

> Haven't you learned from watching movies that vampires can only enter your habitat when you extend an invitation to them?

External drama means that subconsciously, we are *inviting* this energy into our lives.

So why do we do this? Why do we allow drama to permeate our lives? Why are we such *drama magnets*? Are we conditioned, or is it something else? I don't think there's one answer, but in my case, it boiled down to not knowing how to stay in the moment, instead of straying to the dark side.

I didn't know how to tune out the incessant chatter in my head that cast doubt on my very dreams. I didn't know how to drown out the outside chatter that was judging my life choices. I didn't know how to filter out fear and move forward with freedom. And I certainly didn't know that I could *flip the drama magnet* to repel drama. But what I did know was that at the time, it was a matter of not having the right tools.

The Drama Diet

And I was determined to change that. I decided to find the right tools. I couldn't change my life alone. *I needed reinforcement.* And it came in many forms. Books. Friends. Music. Tequila. Podcasts. Chocolate. Exercise. Meditation. Netflix. Journaling. Saging. Psychics. Therapy. You name it. I was able to find quick fixes, but no long-term, sustainable solution. No matter how many times I tried to cast out the drama, it seemed to find another entry point. *Drama magnet.*

Then, somewhere along my journey, I started to notice a common theme strung throughout much of the self-development industry that was boilerplate. Most of the gurus and self-help experts were focusing on the positive in life, ignoring the negative. In other words, we aren't allowed to feel sad; we have to feel grateful. We have to turn our frowns upside down. Count our blessings and squash down the negative feelings rising from our core like bile.

I was following all the standard advice out there. And as much as I tried, this just simply didn't work for me. How could I pretend everything was rainbows and sunshine when it seemed that there was a looming tornado around every corner I turned? I just couldn't ignore the hot pink elephant in the room anymore. I realized I needed more. I needed something tangible.

Something that appreciated the shadows instead of trying to meditate or sage them away.

Something that allowed me to thrive *despite* the negativity that persisted. *Something that understands how to integrate all polarities in my life and alchemize it to free myself from my drama shackles.* And then it hit me like a wave of clarity.

Darkness. The common denominator of drama is darkness. And darkness needed to be addressed.

It dawned on me *like the morning light after a dark night* that this was the missing piece. The one thing everyone was trying to transcend and rise above was the very thing that needed to be included. *And embraced.* We need to *inhale darkness and exhale light* instead of the opposite, that's taught. You see, most of what is out there focuses on the positive, rather than *embracing drama in a positive way*. Focusing on the positive is a good idea *if* you first face your shadows. Embrace your shadows. Accept your shadows.

But a lot of teachings don't address this, and that has created a big problem. *It allows a stigma of shame around our shade.* It reinforces the notion that if you can't rise above the darkness and spread light, you are tainted. It makes you feel like you've failed if you don't walk around with rose colored glasses all the time. And when you feel like your life is spinning out of control, who wants to sit on a mountain and meditate?

Or spread sunshine when all you want to do is throw drama daggers at the shade?

In a world of duality, this has left a gray area. It highlighted a gap for people who need to learn how to bridge the light with the dark to live an authentic, vibrant life. How to integrate the duality of contrast.

But don't worry. I got you.

I used to think that to feel free, I had to knock out the negative. Shut out the darkness. And that meant that anytime I was feeling good, if a tiny bit of shadow started to cover my sunshine, it would immediately affect my mood. Making my happiness contingent on everything being perfect. Trust me, that is not a sustainable way of living. Not everything is going to be perfect all the time, and I had to learn to be ok with that. No, I had to learn to accept that, embrace that, and *dance with that*. Clouds and all.

> Our shadows form our fears.
> Our darkness forms our limitations.
> Our drama dictates our lives.

And this got me thinking. Why can't we navigate with our shadows, despite our shadows, and in partnership with our shadows?! I mean, it's not like they're ever going away permanently. So why not bring them along, train them to be quiet in public, and keep an eye on them so they don't go rogue? You know, put a leash on it. If we can learn to navigate *with* the fear, we can ultimately learn to bridge the light with the dark.

DANCE WITH FEAR...
but
LEAD WITH LOVE

Most often, drama leads. But when you learn to lead with love, you can take drama for a spin on the mental, emotional, and spiritual dance floor and dip your dramas away. Learn how to dance with drama. How to spin fear into love. How to twirl the chaos into clarity. How to pivot from negativity while remaining grounded, graceful, and genuine.

How to Dance with Duality.

But first, we must know with whom we are dancing. Who is our partner on the dance floor of life? To do this, we must understand the *antithesis of drama*. We must know what we are dealing with on the other side of the spectrum. *Light.* Light is the antithesis of drama. And what light is, at its very essence, is pure love.

The antidote to drama is love.

And the most potent ingredient of love is *self-love*. Contrary to popular belief, self-love is not selfish. It's essential. It's being self-invested, self-trusting, and self-compassionate. Let's quash the outdated notion that loving yourself first equates to being self-absorbed. In *Chapter 9*, I will delve into why *not* loving yourself is selfish to others. How it deprives others of your best self and shortchanges them. Talk about a *drama pivot*. It's all intertwined.

Woo Woo alert. I'm coming out of the *spiritual closet* for a moment.

Once you learn that your outer world reflects your inner world, and therefore your inner world creates your outer world, you've got the secret sauce to the manifestation recipe.

And it all boils down to *love*. When we tap into the energy of love, we feel we can do anything. That anything is possible. That nothing is off limits. That is because love is the greatest power. Love holds the energy of the highest frequency. And everything is energy. Everything has an energy gauge that quantifies the level of frequency it's vibrating at. Energy dictates what we attract into our lives and what we block from our lives. When we lean into love, we open ourselves up to attract more of the same energy. *It's the law of attraction*.

And in the same vein, the brighter we shine, the more we attract the insects drawn to our light. The higher the vibration, the faster we attract the energy vampires seeking to suck our vibrant energy. The greater the light we emit, the greater the chance of attracting the fear-based thinking from our ego that thinks it's protecting us by wanting to dim our light for fear of failure or judgment. Again, the *law of duality*. For every yin there is a yang. And as a lawyer, I love interpreting laws.

Without the darkness, we couldn't see the light.
Without light, we'd never see the shadows.

One can't exist without the other. *So if love is the epitome of light, then fear is the epitome of darkness.* And drama stems from fear.

Fun fact: Did you know that love and fear cannot exist in the same space? Although one can't exist without the other, only one energy can override the other at any given time. One must lead. One must be in charge. One must overpower the other. You're either leaning into fear or leaning into love. You can't do both simultaneously.

Try it. Try tapping into a lower frequency of anger when you have just gotten a promotion at work. Or vice versa, try loving on your partner when you want to wring their neck for forgetting to pay the cell phone bill and you can't get access to your lifeline. Can you feel those different energies?

One seems to take over your soul and shove the other competing energy out.

So which one wins? Which energy takes the lead? The one that's in control in the moment. But you can change this. You can control this. At any given moment, you can evolve into love.

Scan the QR code to view the video.

https://lisastuart.com/qr-codes/1

But to alchemize drama into love, you need to dip your toes into the very thing you are avoiding. *The drama dip.* Then you can do an energetic tango and dip your drama away. Rose, thorns, and all. The trick is to focus on the rose and keep the thorns at bay so they don't prick you.

The dark and light exist simultaneously, as it takes one to recognize the other. Law of duality. It takes knowing what we don't want to know what we do want. And vice versa. It takes two to tango. And I love a good dance analogy. So let's dance.

The Drama Dance - *Dancing with Darkness*

Chaos. We were never meant to control it. *We were meant to dance with it, so it doesn't control us.* We know when the drama controls us because it takes the lead in the dance of drama. I call it the dance of darkness. The dark-light dichotomy. We must address the shadow aspects of ourselves to gain control back. To reclaim outer freedom and inner peace. And this is where people get trapped. They don't understand that it's not a matter of getting rid of fear, it's a matter of keeping it.

Only by facing your biggest fears, and dancing *through* them, even awkwardly, *even with two left feet*, will you ever make it through the dance to the end of the song.

So how do you dance with drama? Drama likes to lead and have you follow its lead. *You* need to take the lead. Learn the steps. And don't let drama step on your toes. Nudge it in the direction of where you want to go. Once you do, you will be able to anticipate the moves and stay one step ahead.

> You can lead the drama where you want it to go rather than letting drama lead you in your life.

Take charge.

But you need faith in yourself, belief in your abilities, and practice. Lots of practice. And don't hold on so tight that you lose your grip or focus. It's a dance between holding on and surrendering. Acting and releasing. Channel your inner *Elsa* and *let it go*.

As long as the music is playing, there is a drama dance to waltz to. Or even shuffle to if you're dragging your feet. Of course, the dance always changes depending on the music being played. Life is a symphony of many songs that make up the emotional components of our lives. When life plays a romantic song, love naturally leads. When life plays a country song, a cloud of sadness may overshadow us. When life plays a pop song, we burst with joy. When life plays hip hop, well, we're all partying on the dance floor. And when an ominous song is playing, you know it, fear takes over.

But don't fear. I concocted a *3F Formula For Fear*. When fear rears its ugly head, imagine the *Indiana Jones* boulder of doom and …

Face it. Feel it. Free it.

Face it: Stop. Turn around. Face the growing boulder of fear.

Feel it: Let the unbearable, crushing weight of it roll over you.

Free it: Surrender to it. Release it. Watch it roll away and dissipate. *Let it go.*

Another F solution is to Flip it. Let's take the boulder building momentum and *flip it* so it's traveling in the opposite direction. Away from us. Pummeling over all the blocks and obstacles that get in our way.

There's also *Friend it*. That's a big one. And *F*ck it*. Well, that one is a last resort, but it's not what you think. *Chapter 7* is dedicated to all things fear. And I delve into all the ways we can address fear with the letter F. Clearly there's no shortage on how to deal with fear. It's like a *fear fest*.

Now, when fear walks through the door, don't shove it out the door. Dance with it. But *you* take the lead … don't be led by fear. *Lead with love. Only one energy can lead in the dance of duality.* So make a choice. Will you lead with love? Or with fear? With light? Or with darkness?

Even the most seasoned dancer has to practice to align with the musicality of the notes being played. But with practice, they learn to take the lead in the dance of life.

**They dance on the spiritual edge.
Teetering between love and fear. Light and dark.**

Ask yourself right now. Does avoiding the drama feel more comfortable than actually facing the music? If you said yes, remember this. The attitude of avoidance is an ominous song that is playing. Don't fall prey to reacting to the music of drama.

Dust off your dance shoes, learn the steps, **and take the lead.**

I'll see you on the dance floor.

3

SQUIRREL SYNDROME

Distraction Leads to Inaction

Life is like a treadmill. People are often so busy chasing things that they never actually get there. They just run on a loop, over and over, only to repeat it the next day. Some are chasing happiness. Some money. And others, love. Some are chasing fame, power, or success. Don't get me wrong. Wanting things is not bad. But chasing things is like a dog chasing its tail. So determined to get there and just out of reach.

> In the act of chasing, you are always trying to catch up to something, instead of allowing it to come to you.

And once we think we finally got there, we inevitably want more. You know the feeling. You've had your eye on the latest designer bag. You *just know* that once you have that eye candy dangling from your arm, you'll feel complete. But that only fills the void temporarily. Until the next conquest comes along.

It's the notion in life of *making it* or *getting there* when really all we are saying is that we are not happy or satisfied with **where we are now**. We know that gratitude allows for more abundance to enter our life. That energy flows where our attention goes.

But … I was grateful in my former life *and still* unfulfilled. It was an **emotional oxymoron**.

Grateful yet greedy for more.

So despite popular belief, gratitude only got me so far. *I learned that gratitude is an attitude for complacency when you lack the courage to change your life.* You need **gratitude** and **grit**. The appreciation for the now and the desire for what is next. But now I digress. *Squirrel.*

When you are chasing something, stop and ask yourself, *what am I running from?* Because inevitably, with the **law of duality**, *the chaser becomes the chased*. And somehow you can get so caught up in what's dangling up ahead that you never stop to cut loose the heavy baggage you've been dragging along with you!

Remember the *Indiana Jones* boulder exercise in the previous chapter? That applies not only to current drama but also to past drama we haven't released. You know, the ones weighed down by an anchor that's tethered to us. Those boulders of the past we lug around need to be addressed. Otherwise, we will always be running, while the pressure weighing us down becomes unbearable.

That's the treadmill of life. Running on a loop without a different outcome. And that's what I was doing. Always running. Always busy. I wore being busy like a badge of honor. It didn't win me any awards. But I did earn first prize for constant fatigue and burnout. I hadn't realized yet that busy doesn't equate to being productive. Two very different concepts coming from competing energies.

One fills you up, the other drains you.

Who knew? My mother did. Her ringtone for me was literally a busy bee because she said it reminded her of my chaotic schedule. Which just goes to show that moms know best. Someone please remind *my* kids of this.

I realize now that being busy was distracting me from what I didn't want to face in my life. Busy shielded me from feeling it. I could deflect the pain. The pain of my family breaking up, feelings of unworthiness, not following my deepest desires, feeling stuck, not listening to my own voice, and not expressing my authentic self. But eventually, the time comes when you need to take a break from chasing, and that's when everything catches up with you. The feelings, the avoidance, the denial. It all came flooding over me like a tidal wave crashing over my body. And it presented itself in the form of stress, causing physical depletion, emotional turmoil, even sickness, resulting in surgeries. Yep. Fun times.

Tying it back to the treadmill analogy, running on the treadmill was a savior for me. The pounding of my feet on the rotating band seemed to drown out the constant noise in my head. That, and whatever song of choice I had in my earbuds. Typically, Muse. Or Pink. I do realize now that running on the treadmill, going nowhere, was mimicking the hamster wheel of thoughts in my mind.

"Don't you ever do exercises that don't require your blood, sweat, and tears?" my trainer asked.

"Nope. Because if I don't feel like I've gotten to a point of depletion, was it really a workout?" I justified.

"Try slowing down, Lisa," he advised.

I didn't want to. It was a nice distraction from the stress in my life. When I slowed down, that's when I would think. That's when I would feel. That's when I would stress. I wanted to avoid that. I wanted to numb out, and adrenaline was the fastest way I knew how. I didn't just like to work out. *I needed to work out.* It was my therapy. Easily accessible and a lot more affordable than real therapy. And let me tell you, a hell of a lot cheaper than retail therapy. Which I also indulge(d) in, but we won't go there.

When I exercised hard, that's how I got my stress out. Taking a leisurely walk meant that everything slowed down, and the mind chatter would speed up. I would have to contemplate ... think ... go into *analysis paralysis*. That's when everything I was avoiding came to keep me company. Either then or in the middle of the night when I had nowhere to run or things to keep me occupied. Ugh. You can't escape from your mind, nor should you. You must face it head-on.

The quieter it got, the louder it became.

Until the silence was deafening with all the chaos swirling internally. I didn't notice it when I was busy. It didn't bother me when I was running around. It wasn't that I filtered it out. It's that it presented itself in the form of white noise. So I kept running. Like *Forrest Gump*.

But all that running did have a silver lining. First, I completed a half marathon on my thirty-sixth birthday. That was a feat I was proud of, and I can say in full honesty that I will never do it again. But mostly, I realized what I was running away *from*. *I was running away from myself*. The burden of what I didn't want to face. Running towards a perfect picture of what I thought I should be. What was expected of me, from me, by me, and to me. It was the beginning of the death of my old self and the *rebirth of my worth*.

It was a long, hard process of deconstructing the blocks that built me so I could chisel away the residue of limiting beliefs, judgment, and external expectations that had hardened over the years, settling in my core like plaque, blocking my true essence.

I was ready to make an appearance in the script of my life, not as a supporting role, but as the star of my story. The genre: *Drama Free*.

The question now becomes, how do we interrupt the running so we can stop and figure out what it is we are running from? What is it that we truly fear? Bear with me. This question spawns many different answers intertwined with a lot of reflection, all of which are addressed throughout this book. Again, it's the **law of duality**. The dichotomy of what we are chasing and what is chasing us.

This reminds me of a recurring dream I had growing up. Or rather, a nightmare. I would dream that I was being chased, but when I tried to run, my legs felt like lead. They were so heavy that each step felt like an eternity. And the harder I tried to move, the slower I would go. All the while, whoever or whatever was chasing me was constantly getting closer. I could feel it even if I couldn't see it. The funny thing is that I was never caught. And I never saw what or who was chasing me. But I would awaken from the dream feeling pure terror running through my body. And it always took time to shake off that feeling. Am I the only one who would have recurring nightmares? *Why couldn't I have the one where I showed up at school with no clothes?*

So what did it all mean? I'm not exactly sure, as I never had anyone try to interpret it. But I can make my own deductions looking back. It felt as if I was trying to control a situation (*my movement*) and the harder I pushed ... the more resistance I was pushing up against! The looming sensation of something out to get me in my dreams is so prevalent, even today. I can still recall my heart pounding so fast as I used every ounce of energy only to move millimeters. Maybe it's a metaphor for my fears overcoming me. Perhaps it's a manifestation of feeling trapped and not being able to move forward. Or it could have been my past catching up with me and weighing me down, literally, so that I couldn't move forward into my future.

Maybe it was not letting things go, so that when I closed my eyes at night, they came to haunt me. You know ... regrets, decisions, uncomfortable conversations, failures, disappointments, losses. All these things clung to me like lint on a sweater. I just needed to clean the lint, clear the filter of my mind, and surrender those old stories.

The common denominator in my dreams was that I always survived. I would wake up from the dream, usually in the nick of time, knowing that *the thing* was inches away from getting me. Very *Indiana Jones*-esque. I like to think that on some subconscious level, my higher self was protecting me. That no matter how close my ego got to the flame of fear, I knew how to wake up from that illusion and snap back to reality.

And that's all it really is. Us trying to wake up from the illusion of fear. Fear is just an illusion.

F.E.A.R. – False Evidence Appearing Real

Maybe you've heard this before. Maybe it's a new concept. But the truth is that most of what we fear never comes true. *Yet fear is one of the greatest distractions in life.* It justifies our inactions, pretending to keep us safe when really, we need to move through that very fear. We need to move from distraction to action. So let's start by identifying the distractions we need to eliminate.

The Squirrel Syndrome– from Distraction to Action.

Drama is a huge distraction. It comes at us externally from outside triggers, people, and situations. Think everything from a broken nail to judgment to an unfathomable pandemic. There is no shortage of chaos, and it doesn't discriminate who it hits, nor the magnitude of it.

It comes at us internally from the whirlwind of thoughts and chaos swirling within our souls. It breeds off our insecurities, feeds off our fear, and multiplies with water (no, that's *gremlins*… aging myself here in a major squirrel moment….) But really, it does multiply with anxiety.

> The amplitude of anxiety is directly correlated to the magnitude of drama in our life.

The **Squirrel Syndrome** is designed to keep our attention on something distracting. More importantly, *it takes our attention away from what we need to be focusing on.* It distracts us with shiny objects, so we don't have to face the darkness. It covers the darkness. Like a brown diamond that has been synthetically processed to look clear. It may appear clear, but the dark color is still hidden in its elements.

Distraction also comes in the form of a quick fix. Numbing out on alcohol, numbing out on Netflix, going down the rabbit hole of social media. Everything from drugs to shopping. The squirrel is the magic potion of life that will cure any ailment. Temporarily of course. But really, it's just a band-aid covering an open, festering wound. Because the drama is always there. It's just waiting for a moment when you let your guard down to seep into your pores. And no band-aid can conceal that. Or heal that.

Distraction is denial. The squirrel is in denial. It retorts that *everything's good ... just focus on the positive and let the rest roll right off you*. The squirrel distracts you by wearing rose-colored lenses, putting up two fingers for the peace sign, and preaching "love 'n light." At this point, you may feel you want to put up another finger for the squirrel and tell it exactly where it could shove its "love and light!"

No more shiny object syndrome. The "look over here at this sparkly gem of advice and you too will sparkle, not sweat, and radiate rainbows" attitude comes at a price. At what cost? At the cost of exploding.

When you can't admit all your faults, all your demons, your vices, your shadows, your dark side ... you are suppressing a part of you that completes the whole of you.

Read that again.

We're allowed to feel angry. We're allowed to feel sad. We're even allowed to feel envious. We don't need to push those dark emotions down because *they're not dark emotions*. They are part of the rainbow spectrum of how we're supposed to be. How we are allowed to feel. The very fact that we feel something gives it truth in the moment. It gives permission to *not* be in a good mood. It doesn't need to be justified. We could be neutral, even flat, and that's ok. We don't need to sparkle all the time.

And speaking of sparkling, sometimes distraction comes in the form of the shiny objects we want in life. The marriage that couple has. The car he drives. The vacations she goes on. Think of the shiny red apple from *Snow White*. Deceivingly delicious. Not everything is as it seems. We think that once we *get that* we will *feel* happy, loved, and secure. The grass-is-always-greener syndrome. A classic case of comparison-itis. But that's just a temporary moment of elation until the air fizzles out of the bubble of distraction and we come down off our high.

That is, until we crave the next fix.

That's the cycle of distraction that leads to inaction. It diverts your attention from what you need to focus on. It keeps you *addicted to the drama*. Maybe you need that spice in your life so you can feel better about yourself. Or maybe the distraction of someone else's woes keeps you from dealing with the issues in your own life. No judgment here. Just stripping it down to the basics.

Are you a *Drama Magnet* or a *Drama Addict*?

Here's the difference. **Drama Magnets** attract drama like flies to honey. **Drama Addicts** thrive on drama, they feed off it like mosquitoes or vampires –*energy vampires*– to blood.

But let's break this down even further. **A Drama Magnet is actually a Drama Addict in disguise.** Yes, you heard me right.

You see, you can be addicted to the drama either consciously or subconsciously.

Drama either *feeds you* or *bleeds you*.

There are essentially two types of **Drama Addicts**.

Type one: It *feeds* your desire to stir the pot. You thrive on drama. It fills your void. It makes you feel better. Temporarily. It places you on some self-appointed pedestal. It distracts you from your own life. This is the **conscious addict**.

...OR....

Type two: It *bleeds* your time and energy. It steals your peace and joy. It disrupts your momentum like a bike tire hitting a small rock, throwing you abruptly from your seat. This is the **subconscious addict**. Drama Magnet. In my case, *I was donating blood to the drama bank on a weekly basis!*

Sometimes it's a hybrid of both types.

In any case, what if you took the approach that before drama *feeds you* or *bleeds you* ... drama first *needs you*.

Like a host. To carry it. Give it life. So, it can pervade your cells. Invade every inch of you with its long tentacles. Take up space. Reside in you. Drama needs you to define it. To shape it. To amplify it. To elevate it. To put it on a pedestal. In the spotlight. That's where drama shines.

But if you know this, you can maintain it. Contain it. Train it. Drain it of its power. Think of drama as nothing more than a lump of solid in your life that you can mold like clay. You can't get rid of it, but you can transmute its form. Instead of putting it *in* the spotlight, put it *under* the spotlight, shine a glaring light on it, and call it out for what it is. *A distraction.*

So, what to do? We already touched upon the **Drama Dance**. How it's imperative to embrace our darkness and integrate it.

Navigate with fear but lead with love. Shine your light.

But let's step into the shade for a moment.

Shadow work is key to embracing love. Carl Jung introduced the idea of the shadow aspect of self, explaining that the shadow is comprised of the unconscious part of us we have yet to acknowledge. *Hello there, darkness … we meet again.* Let's get reacquainted with our dark side. Full on *Darth Vader* mode and all. Seriously. If we are going to change our lives, we can't ignore the nitty gritty inside of us that needs attention. No more diverting our attention from what needs to be done. No more distractions to cover up what we are avoiding. The *Squirrel Syndrome* days are over.

Don't be a squirrel. *Be a groundhog.* Look for your shadow. Invite the darkness within to come out and play in the sunlight. Suppressing it will not make it disappear. That's like the young child who covers her eyes and says, "Now I'm invisible, because if I can't see you, then you can't see me." The darkness sees us no matter what. It's we who choose not to see the darkness. It's much prettier to see the shiny objects and light. To pretend we don't hurt. To swallow our pain. To put on a good front. To put out a good exterior. To blend in with the outside noise. To suppress our burning urges of passion. To quash our big dreams. To justify our complacency. To hide what we deem are our bad parts, so we only illuminate our good parts. This is cherry-picking at its best. And cherry-picking season is just that. A season.

Maybe this is the season where you've had enough. The tides have changed. You don't have to wait until you hit rock bottom to decide to change the trajectory of your life. You can address it today. Now. This is the day you say no more to letting drama take the lead. When the darkness wants to snuff out your light, channel your inner *Arya Stark* and declare, "Not today." And then repeat that daily. It's all in the repetition. It's not a one-and-done.

So, in true squirrel fashion, let's switch gears.

My husband calls me his ADD queen. That's because we could be in the middle of a conversation on one topic, and my mind suddenly flips to a completely different topic mid-sentence. When this happens, he generally laughs and says *squirrel*. That's because of an inside joke when I literally stopped mid-sentence to yell *squirrel* because I saw … a squirrel. I know. I'm even SMH.

It's not that I can't stay focused on the topic at hand. It's that I get constant and frequent downloads of inspiration that spark thoughts on other topics. This shows the multiverse that exists in my brain, with thoughts scrambling all over each other, fighting to get to the forefront. And whichever is the most powerful thought wins. No wonder I was trying to drown out the noise with running when my thoughts got too loud.

But that is how I imagine our minds working overtime. Thoughts racing around in our heads, all trying to cross the finish line. Whichever thought gets there first overtakes the others. Kind of like sperm racing to implant the egg first. Until something inevitably interrupts those thoughts, throwing the race a curveball in another direction. That's how I envision the highway of our brains. And that's how I know we can redirect our minds and re-route our thinking. Traffic jams and all.

But sometimes when an outside stimulus abruptly changes the trajectory of our thoughts, we get thrown off course. And this affects our mood. Did you know that our emotions fluctuate up and down depending on the external circumstances? *That is because we allow outside forces to dictate our internal responses.*

And in keeping with the law of duality, while external factors dictate our inner emotions, *our inner emotions dictate our external actions*. Either moving us forward or holding us back. They can distract us with feelings of inadequacy, uncertainty, and our old friend, fear.

And guess what else dictates our emotions? You got it ... our thoughts. It comes full circle. Our emotions are a direct reflection of our thoughts. And where do you think our thoughts come from? They come from a folder filed away in the back of our brain called the *"subconscious mind,"* where it retreats to and recovers prior reactions we had to similar situations.

That folder also contains all your self-sabotaging thoughts, as well as a plethora of your run-of-the-mill limiting beliefs that are "supposed" to keep you safe. And while they keep you safe to the confines of your comfort, they also prevent you from taking calculated risks. And it is those very calculated risks that propel you forward in the progression of your desires.

So, in essence, the *safety of your thoughts* is preventing you from living your life fully. It's like the parent who gives the high schooler a curfew of 10 p.m. when the event starts at 9 p.m. The party's just getting started, and you're driving away with your face pressed against the glass, missing out on all the action. Not cool.

Let me give you a concrete example, as the attorney in me is all about the evidence. A drama-provoking situation occurs and what is your first reaction? Probably *OMG* or *WTF.* Those two are pretty much the auto-response reactions most people have. So now your brain goes into overtime trying to make sense of what just whacked it out of balance. And on autopilot, it wants to course correct.

What does it do?

It goes to the most *thought of thought.* You know, the one that consistently crossed the finish line first in your brain. It doesn't have to work hard to find the thought because it's hard-wired, probably programmed at a young age. Desperately needing an upgrade. Like a smartphone. If it's stuck in 2012, it'll revert to those thoughts.

Your brain has an *aha* moment to the drama stimulus, triggering a reflexive response. Your brain reverts to its emotional shield of choice– usually the knee-jerk reaction you typically feel in such situations. Your subconscious retrieves the last file used in a similar situation and relays it to your brain, *these are your go-to thoughts for this set of circumstances.* Then the thoughts communicate with your emotions, *these are the feelings you're used to eliciting from these types of thoughts. Let's go dwell there.* **Drama dweller.**

Your thoughts emit an emotional response, a feeling that surges through your body and pulses through your veins like poison. And it is a familiar feeling, an automatic coping mechanism you've ingrained in your memory from before. So why do we do this? Why subject ourselves to venom? The subconscious thinks it is protecting us from danger. It doesn't know any other way. **It would rather revert to the *known* response than challenge itself to find another path.** Don't worry. We will change this *thought process* in **Chapter 5**. But in the meantime, there is another way to shift the way you feel.

Come play in my **Spiritual Sandbox** for a moment. I'll even bring shovels to dig up some golden nuggets. Did you know that at any given moment you can change how you feel by changing your emotions? How? By changing your energy. And we know that everything is energy. And it's the energy of thoughts that runs through our bodies and translates in the form of emotion. And do you know what emotion is?

E-motion is *Energy in Motion*

E for energy. And that energy in motion runs through your veins emitting all sorts of feelings. And when that energy stays in motion, it does its job, it runs its course, and it gets released. In your body, through your body, and out your body. Like *face it, feel it, free it.*

But it's us who keep the emotions stuck in our bodies.

Did you know that all emotions are only supposed to run through your body for roughly 90 seconds? I didn't make it up, it's a scientific fact. Brain scientist Dr. Jill Bolte Taylor brilliantly articulated that when a person reacts to a situational stimulus, it creates a 90-second chemical process throughout the body. Any emotional response beyond roughly 90 seconds is due to the person restimulating that emotional loop. Can you even fathom that emotions have an expiration? It really changes the perspective on how we humans can get a handle on handling our emotional well-being.

When we don't release that energy after that approximate minute and a half, we hold onto it in our bodies.

Clinging to the energy like a codependent relationship. The stagnant energy, getting tired of us squeezing so hard, starts to look for a comfortable place to settle in. *Comfortable for the energy, not for us.* Insert stiff neck, gut pain, pounding headache. It can erupt in physical manifestations where the energy gets stuck in your body. And don't forget the emotional agony. Feeling out of sorts, antsy, not aligned.

The emotion *energy in motion* is meant to run freely through your body like a squirrel on a mission. Then released. But for some reason, we humans love to hold onto our emotions. Always pressing replay on the thought loops in our minds. Going nowhere but stuck in a moment in time. Which, by the way, keeps the emotions alive in our bodies like guests who overstay their welcome because we keep inviting them to stay longer. Constantly lavishing attention on them. *Feeding the drama with our home-cooked thoughts.*

And we know that emotional turmoil is a form of drama. Change your thoughts, transmute your emotions, and diffuse the drama. But if you can't get the thoughts off replay, you can still move the energy through your body with other forms of exercise. *Movement. Breathwork. Dancing*. If you can't get the guests out, then at least throw a dance party to lift your mood. Pirouette that energy out of your body. Throw a positive spin on it. Literally.

Wayne Dyer is famously quoted for the following phrase: *Change the way you look at things, and the things you look at change*. I'd like to piggyback on that and say:

> Change the way you look at drama,
> and the drama you look at changes.

It's all about perspective. Crank the prescription on your lenses to look at drama in a positive way. Drama is positive in the sense that it's driven by fear. And fear is your friend. It navigates you. By highlighting where you *don't want* to go, it shows you where you *need* to go. As you know, **Chapter 7** is dedicated to all things fear, and I explicitly filter out the type of fear that will cause you real harm. When I say move through fear, I'm talking about the irrational fear that holds you back.

The irrational fear that seems *rational* to you because of, well, your fear.

When you suppress what you have to face, you think you are moving forward because it feels like you are leaving the drama behind. But just like a boomerang, you only go forward so far until you ultimately get pulled backward. Law of duality.

Don't suppress fear. Address fear.

Remember the *Indiana Jones* boulder of drama analogy? It's the same about not addressing fear. The longer it takes to address fear, the more it builds. Like a snowball gaining momentum, growing into a greater and larger snow boulder. How long do you think you can keep running from it? Isn't it exhausting to imagine the energy expended from the endless running from fear? But I don't have to imagine it. I lived it. That's why I created *The Drama Diet*.

But the squirrel never got the memo. It would rather look at the shiny distractions. So, the squirrel never stops running. That could be one theory why it only has an average life span of six years. *It's afraid of its own shadow*. It turns stiff as a statue when confronted with something fearful. In contrast, maybe that's why tortoises live for so long. They're too slow to run. They can't run in circles chasing their tails. They can't outrun their shadows. They have no choice but to face whatever they're confronted with. And they live long lives, possibly outliving their fears.

As much as I try to make light of the dark topic of drama, avoiding it can actually be detrimental to your health. It attaches its tentacles to every aspect of your life - *mentally, physically, emotionally, and energetically*. It's vital to your wellbeing to clear out the stressors in your life. And if that's not possible, then learn how to respond to them in a positive way. It literally can affect your health.

In **Chapter 11**, I dissect how it's important to be a *Conscious Consumer*. How what you consume physically, mentally, emotionally, energetically, and *mindlessly* directly impacts your life. I will discuss how facing drama is not the same as *consuming* drama.

> Avoiding drama is essentially consuming drama.

If you're a **Drama Addict**, either consciously or subconsciously, and you're not facing your shadows, it could have a profound effect upon the quality of your life. And it all starts with telling your inner squirrel to turn around. About face. Be willing to step into the drama. Confront the uncomfortable. Look fear square in the eyes and have that tough conversation. Send that email. Take the first step. Do the thing you're afraid of. When you *act despite fear*, you release something negative from your life— physically, mentally, emotionally, and spiritually.

It's time. And time is ticking.

If not you, *who?* If not now, *when?*

It's time to take action.

It's time to slow down the chaotic frenzy in your life, chasing your tail like a squirrel.

It's time to divert the shiny distractions and dance with your darkness.

It's time to get the recipe for a drama-free life. The next chapter is the secret sauce. It's the blueprint for *The Drama Diet*. It explains the **3D Drama Free Formula** that sets the tone for the remainder of the book.

It's time to go on a **Drama Diet**.

The Drama Diet

4

THE DRAMA DIET CHEAT SHEET

The 3D Drama Free Formula

Now that you have a little backstory as to why I created *The Drama Diet,* how it's important to embrace the darkness and dance with your drama, and who it can serve, let's move on from the appetizers and serve the main course.

> To release negativity that weighs us down we have to go on a Drama Diet. It helps us let go of toxic baggage. Feeling light and free, you should try it.

The Drama Diet

Here's the 3D formula for the Drama Diet:

Disrupt. Deflate. Detox.

Done.

First you have to disrupt the drama.
Next you have to deflate the drama.
Lastly you have to detox the drama.

Once you have mastered this *3D Drama Free Formula,* you will officially become a **Drama Ninja**. Outfit not included. But you *will* be able to identify *oncoming* and *incoming* drama before it has a chance to penetrate your peaceful bubble of protection. You can sneak up on drama in a sleuth-like manner and stop it in its tracks and it'll never see you coming. But it's a practice you need to hone every single day. *Ninja skills.*

Disrupt the drama. Deflate the drama. Detox the drama.

Interactive scenario

I want you to physically do this with me. Eliminating drama is not just something you do silently, in your mind. It takes physical work too. Think about it. When you accept the negative energy of others *or yourself,* it directly impacts your emotions and is a total brain drain. When you allow others, *or your own thoughts,* to drain your energy, it affects you physically, causing fatigue, anxiety, insomnia, and other manifestations of physical symptoms. The drama pulses through your veins, consuming your *mind, body, and energy in motion (e-motion).* In the same vein, preventing drama from permeating your peace is also a full-body integration. Let me explain.

I want you to visualize a ball of drama-filled energy coming at you. Put your hand up in a *talk-to-the-hand* position as if to say **STOP** to the drama, and envision the ball hitting against your hand, disrupting its momentum. Stop the drama in its tracks. *Stun the drama system.*

Then take your open hand and close it so that all four fingers connect with your thumb. As if you are grabbing that ball of energy and squeezing all the air out. Like deflating a balloon. Imagine your hand opening and closing in a *blah, blah, blah* mannerism. Just close the gap on your hand to deflate the drama. *Suffocate it from the air that breeds it.*

Now, once you have deflated the drama, and your hand is closed, I want you to envision flicking that drama away, as though you're flicking an annoying bug off your sleeve. (Sorry for all you insect lovers.) If you remember table football, you will know exactly what I'm talking about. *Deflect that drama like you're repelling a bad hair day.*

>**Disrupt** - *Stop. Talk to the hand.*
>**Deflate** - *Shrink. Squeeze air out of the balloon.*
>**Detox** - *Flick. Bye-bye bug.*

Scan the QR Code to watch the video.

https://lisastuart.com/qr-codes/2

It's that simple—yet hard. And if my description was accurate, you should be having fun right now practicing the hand maneuvers. Try it this week. Use these hand gestures regardless of which hand gestures you're triggered to use.

There's a reason I'm having you connect hand gestures to thoughts.

When you involve all parts of you, *connecting your thoughts to physical actions*, it activates something. It stamps something into your response memory. It connects words and feelings with a physical act. It sets into your system. It ingrains something in your subconscious. It travels from the brain to the gut (*where the emotions dwell*) and acts as an alarm to alert you when you need to be proactive. Just when you need to recognize the drama and address it.

Sometimes when I'm confronted with drama, my hand automatically reverts to these maneuvers before my brain even kicks in. *Muscle memory*. And then, like reverse osmosis, it triggers a signal to my brain to stop it from going to the dark side just by the physicality of my hand movements as if on autopilot. It's subconsciously integrated. And it's a fully integrative experience. And that's truly what it comes down to.

Controlling the drama so it doesn't control you.

Sidenote: You may have noticed that the **3D Drama Free Formula** overlaps a bit with the **3F Formula For Fear**. But there is a difference. For clarification, the 3D formula *incorporates* the 3F formula, which will be elaborated upon in **Chapter 7**.

"Ok," you ask, "how do you know this formula will work?"

Well, for starters, it worked for me. And as an attorney, I'm all about the proof, the evidence, the trial period, and the verdict.

"That's cute," you say, "but how do you know this formula will work for *me*?"

I get it. You've gone down every road. You've journaled. You've meditated. You've hired coaches. You've made big changes. You've soul searched. You've saged, lit palo santo, and burned intention candles infused with crystals. You've written letters and lit them on fire. You've plunged into an ice bath and sweated it out at hot yoga. You've done breathwork, Reiki, sound bowls, energy healing, cleared your chakras, and possibly, after all this, cleared out your bank account. Yet despite all that, you can't seem to escape the drama. It's like a looming dark cloud that constantly hangs overhead. It literally wants to rain on your parade. And there's no umbrella in sight.

You may have tried setting boundaries. Practiced saying *no*. Scaled back on over-committing. Scaled back on your social life. Detoxed from social media. Applied your conflict resolution skills. But you keep attracting drama. It follows you around like a fly to light. And that's exactly how it works. You are a light. And the drama loves to dim the light. It can't find its own, so it wants yours. And it's relentless.

But if you're doing all the work, then why the heck can't the drama just leave you alone? Maybe you feel like you're lost in a sea of regurgitated information. There are many amazing mentors with valuable guidance. But as I stated earlier, there are also plenty of self-proclaimed gurus who package the "perfect solution" in a one-size-fits-all box. And that simply doesn't work for everyone.

No two handprints are alike. We all wear different shoe sizes, have different preferences in food, and like different movie genres.

Some people are more visual, some more auditory. Some more sensory, some more practical. Some are more emotional, and some more logical. Some believe in the mystical, while others require scientific proof. Some learn information linearly, and others need a more creative way to absorb and process the data. Some are vegans, some are carnivores, and others are speckled along the spectrum. Some are timid while others are bold. Some are ambitious and others need a push. Some are introverts, some are extroverts, and if you're like me, you're an extroverted introvert. So, it's no wonder that we all don't fit into the same mold. *We were never meant to*.

And with all the noise in the world, how do you know whom to follow, whom to listen to, whom to believe? The answer is simple. The person to listen to is … *you*. Your inner being. Your higher self. Your intuitive voice. You know inherently where you need to go.

You just need some guidance on how to use your internal GPS to navigate your journey. Some assistance to help you with your tech issues when your audio to your inner voice is glitchy. Someone to hand you the microphone so you can use your voice to speak your truth.

That's where I step in. Or rather, this book. I'm handing you the keys to **The Drama Diet**. Trusting you to navigate your life in your own customized vehicle. You can repaint the outside, decorate the

The Drama Diet

inside, whatever you want your life to look like. It's ever changing, malleable, and evolving. And the process is too.

So what makes **The Drama Diet** different? What makes *this* formula work? Well, for starters, despite our differences, we know that what's personal is universal. That there is a common thread among us that craves freedom. And we also know that, inherently, we're all looking for love and to be loved. We want to feel seen, get heard, and be accepted for who we are. We know that no matter where we are scattered in the world, there is a hidden similarity among us that is deterred by fear, and that we all have a dark side we try to suppress. And we also know that we all have a shining light within us burning to glow. *And who doesn't want more peace in their life?* Even those who thrive on drama need a break once in a while from their addiction.

> In a world built on duality,
> we really are all one.
> We are divisively united.

And so, when you **adopt** the formula and **adapt** it to your life, you will find the right recipes and exercises that fit your way of life. In **Chapters 5-11**, I provide tools for actionable steps. *Recipes. Exercises. Journal prompts.*

This book provides *exercises* to *work out* your thoughts, so your thoughts work out.

It gives you not just the *ingredients* to your transformation, but the whole *recipe*.

The Drama Diet is not about starvation. It's about the *elimination* of what doesn't serve you while adding the right ingredients you've been missing in your life. You will not feel deprived or malnourished on this diet. In fact, quite the opposite. It's all about *nourishing and flourishing* your mind, body, & soul. You will be filled with servings of love and goodness that will replenish you.

And for all you meat lovers out there who don't like to eat their vegetables, you know what I'm gonna say next. You gotta make sure you're getting your daily nutritional quota for all components of your life. No skipping corners. No cheat days. Well, actually, the diet allows for a few cheat days. *Guilt-free.* I'm all about the 80-20 plan. This keeps it fluid. *Forgiving the days we regress.*

It's a blueprint to freedom. A roadmap to peace. A process to gain clarity from chaos. **Permission to choose love over fear.** It's about dancing with your emotions, even the dark ones. It's about being able to stand in the fire of truth, especially when it's uncomfortable. It's about finding peace with what is. *It's about flipping the drama magnet and repelling the drama of others.* It's about attracting your deepest desires unapologetically. It's about shedding the weight of what doesn't serve you so that you can lead a life of service by shining your light. It's about freeing the burdens from your soul by living your truth rather than someone else's expectations. It's about preserving your self-worth to its fullest and setting loving boundaries.

This book is about taking back the pen and writing the story of your own life—your authentic story, not the one scripted by others. Remember, you are the director, producer, actor, and final writer of the movie you will call your life. **The Drama Diet** is about living in your truth, unapologetically. It's about owning the rights to your story, instead of letting others write it for you. And the pages before you are blank ready to get filled in. Your story is still unwritten.

It's about becoming a **Drama Ninja**, able to master the dark forces with ease and navigate the roads of life with confidence. Move over, *Darth Vader*. There's a new force in town. *It's about navigating with fear but leading with love.*

And it's in your hands. *Literally.* Either you're reading this book or listening to it on audio. But I'm not just talking about the book. Your happiness, peace, clarity, joy, freedom … it's all in *your* hands. And as I said earlier, *we know that no two handprints are the same.*

Transformation Station

Let me take you on a journey.

Imagine you're sitting at a train station waiting to board your dream train to your desired destination. But you're scared to board, or just hesitant enough to back out, because you don't know where exactly it will take you. Or, you don't really know *if it even knows how to get to your destination.* Nor do you know how long the ride will be, or how many stops along the road you would have to take to get to where you're not even sure you're gonna end up. You don't know how many transfers you'll need to take, how many layovers you'll need to patiently wait at, or even if the train's gonna run out of fuel before it gets to your desired destination.

You're worried that the train will derail your plans. You're stressing over whether the trip will be too hard, long, exhausting, lonely, and filled with sleepless nights and anxious days. You're not sure how much the ticket will cost you, nor the price of any unexpected complications. Or that the ride will have too many delays, and you may be running late, missing your moment. Or even get you there early when you're not feeling ready enough.

You don't know who is going to be joining you on the ride, who you will be leaving behind at each stop, and who you are going to meet along the way.

You're not sure what you will risk giving up to risk getting everything.

Sounds awful, right? So why are you still sitting there instead of hightailing it home?

Because you believe in your heart, your gut, *your core* that if you don't get on that train, you will always regret it. *And you feel that the regret of not boarding far outweighs any risk ahead of you.* You have a burning sensation to get on that train, ride into the unknown, and pursue your passion and purpose. You just can't get your stuck body to get up off that bench and move in the direction of the train.

Suddenly, the doors to the train of your desired dreams open.

It's eerily quiet. You can hear yourself thinking out loud without a sound. *Grab the opportunity. Grab a seat on the train.* **Buy the damn ticket**. But you don't know how. You need backup.

If you want to bring someone along to hold your hand and cheer you on … call your bestie. That's not me. I'm not here to hold up a *Bon Voyage* sign before you depart on your path. I'm not interested in all the sightseeing places that will *distract* you from your vision. I don't need a postcard or any kitschy souvenirs that *delay* your progress.

But, if you want someone to guide you in dealing with your inner conflicts that are getting in the way of you and your dreams, I'm that person. I'll meet you at the train station and sit with you on the platform. I'll help you figure out which train to get on. *Hell, I'll even hop on your transformation train and ride the journey with you for as long or as short as you need.*

I will help you find direction. I'll provide a blueprint to help you reach your destination.

- Tips on how to make the ride smoother when the road gets bumpy.
- Hacks on how to pack light so you don't bring unnecessary *past luggage*.
- Tools on how to settle your mind when you start to *future trip*.

The only trip I want you to go on is a vacation from your limiting beliefs.

I will take you from point A to point B, whatever that destination may be, and provide you with your own roadmap on how to get there so you won't get lost the next time around. And once you're there, I'll bid you adieu. Until the next time you want to level up and don't know how. Or you need someone to guide you from getting that ticket to figuring out which train to board. Or to help you with your train transfers. I will be by your side again, *judgment-free*. Again, and again. I'll even bring French macarons. Guilt-free and gluten-free.

You see, I don't believe that there's one destination in life.

> Life is not a destination
> with many journeys.
> Life is a journey with many destinations.

And there are many adventures that await you. But it really all boils down to you. *You* need to take the first step and buy the ticket. Which you did. By buying this book, you have taken that first step, and through the processes of **The Drama Diet**, I will make sure that you continue to take the subsequent steps.

If you need accountability, consider this. I will be your accountability advocate. *No legal advice, just counsel*, throughout this book, and beyond. So let me show you how I did it.

How I lost the weight

- The weight of other people's opinions.
- The weight of my outdated stories I was dragging around.
- The weight off my shoulders of all my guilt, imperfections, and limiting beliefs.

My advice ... Take the *L line* on your transformation train.

Lisa's L Line

Leave the emotional baggage of toxic behavior you've been carrying.
Lean into the lightness of your being and protect your energy.
Learn from comparison-itis.
Lose the weight of judgment.

Let go of the limiting beliefs and outdated stories.
Lighten the pounds of mental weight you've packed on over the years.
Lesson the trauma from the drama.
Listen to the tug in your gut.
Light the fire within you.
Love yourself first and fiercely.
Live a life true to yourself.
Laugh. A lot. Even at your own shortcomings. Laughter is truly the greatest gift we can share.

Results: You will *Own Your Worth*.

And more so, you will ...

Scale your life without the need to measure your weight in worth on a scale.

- You will shed pounds of excessive overthinking.
- You will feel lighter and more agile in your approach to life.
- You will cleanse your spiritual system.
- You will emerge a more vibrant version of yourself.
- You will detox the drama.
- You will radiate peace.
- You will clear the junk from your mind.
- You will choose your thoughts wisely.
- You will feed your brain kindness instead of abusive thoughts.
- You will only binge on things that bring you joy.
- You will eliminate the emotional toxins.
- You will lose the weight of other people's opinions.
- You will shed the heaviness of judgment.
- You will set boundaries, so you don't have the urge to splurge your energy on things that deplete you.
- You will trim the distractions.
- You will fill up on what feeds your purpose and passion.

- You will carve time into your day for what lights you up.
- You will breathe in freedom and space rather than squeeze in time like you're squeezing into a pair of jeans two-sizes-too-small.
- You will chisel away the built-up residue to reveal your authentic self.
- You will sculpt your thoughts to propel you to your goals.
- You will quench your soul when it thirsts for more.
- You will learn to be your own trainer and train your brain.
- You will work out your thoughts, so your thoughts work out.

And you will feel lighter, have more clarity, and enjoy freedom.

So how does The Drama Diet work?

The Drama Diet is a lifestyle to move effortlessly through and eliminate internal chaos and external drama. It's a daily practice integrating the mind, body, emotions, and soul. It's designed to fit whatever current situation you're in. Whichever train stop you're stuck on at the transformation station.

The Drama Diet works. But it takes work.

- It's sustainable. But you must sustain consistent practice.
- It's not all-consuming. But it does matter what you consume – mentally, emotionally, energetically.
- It's not a one-and-done. It's a marathon, not a sprint. Equipped with water breaks and all. To hydrate your essence.

And it's guilt-free, judgment-free, and shame-free.

I mean, aren't you tired of FAD diets that attempt to detox the drama from your life, but never stick? You know, the ones filled with ingredients such as

**F-ear
A-nxiety
D-oubt**

The only F.A.D. diet recipe I want you to follow is comprised of these nourishing ingredients.

**F-aith
A-ction
D-edication**

This is not a yo-yo diet. It's a *you-you* diet. *You do you.* Keep the focus on how you want to feel, *not* on how others are making you feel.

You may have heard the concept that people need to audit their lives. With the help of the IRS. You know, take Inventory, Reassessment, and Stock of where you are – **the I.R.S.**

Inventory. Reassessment. Stock.

While you can certainly **audit** your life, I believe you need to **edit** your life. Edit things in your life that are cluttering your space – your mental space (*mind chatter and brain drain*), emotional space (*guilt and worry*), and physical space (*energy vampires and drama daggers*).

And I love a good play on words. And guess what.

Rearrange the word EDIT and you get DIET ... and TIDE.

When you go on a *diet,* you are rearranging your life. You are essentially claiming that you need to *edit* your life. Remember, change the way you look at things (*words, letters*), and the things you look at change (*solutions appear*). Then you can ride the *tide* and effortlessly *edit* your life.

Maybe you've tried a juice cleanse or some other physical cleanse in your life. We go on cleanses for our bodies. Why not do a cleanse for the soul? *A* **Drama Detox**. Flush out the toxicity and make space for peace and joy. Go on an emotional, mental, and energetic cleanse.

Although you detox, **The Drama Diet** doesn't deprive you.

It indulges your cravings to live a life you dream about and deserve.

It feeds your hunger to move through your fears and achieve your goals.

It nourishes your desires to follow your gut and cut out the noise.

You can break free from all the chains that have been holding you back. You can throw away the shackles to preconceived expectations.

You can detach from toxic relationships that have been a total time suck.

It all comes down to *decision, diligence, and determination*.

And speaking of D's, we are going to dive deep into the **3D Formula** - *Disrupt, Deflate, Detox*.

So let's break down the formula into even more subparts starting with ... you guessed it ... the letter D. I sound like a sponsor for *Sesame Street ... The Drama Diet program is brought to you today by the letter D and the number 3.*

So each "D" of the **Drama Diet 3D Formula** is further divided into two components:

> *What you need to release* - **Delete**
> *What you need to add* - **Designate**

Remember, the law of duality. *What divides us can unite us.*

Everything is balanced in this world. And later in this book, I explain how we don't need to have balance in our lives to maintain balance within. While we may not have a balanced external world, as long as we maintain balance within it, well, it balances out. The yin and the yang. Contrast keeps balance. *Who knew?*

The Drama Diet Cheat Sheet

And so along the same lines, **The Drama Diet** formula has its own yin and yang. Something to **detract** and something to **add**. And each subpart deals with both the **internal** and **external** drama.

I wish I could put up my flowchart on an Elmo right now. And no, I'm not referring to the character on *Sesame Street*. For those of you who aren't familiar with an Elmo, think of it as the visual version of a cassette tape. Antiquated yet effective.

So, for each subpart think of …

Internal Deletion / External Deletion
Internal Addition / External Addition

It's like a deletion and addition both within and without. It's an all-encompassing formula moving in all directions. I can totally see the system operating in my mind. I know …the labyrinth of my brain.

The Drama Diet could be construed as a **9D formula**. The trine of nine!

Fun fact: I once had my astrology chart read many moons ago. Yes, I've been dabbling with horoscopes and astrology since I was a little girl. It always intrigued the mystic in me. In case you're interested, I'm an Aquarius with Scorpio rising. And although I don't remember much of what I was told, I do remember that I was told I have nine trines. Which meant nothing to me. But which apparently is good. And apparently it means that I'm aligned. I didn't even know what that meant at the time. But I guess since there are no coincidences, I was always meant to create a nine-trine drama-free diet program.

And here's the breakdown.

DISRUPT. DEFLATE. DETOX.

#1—DISRUPT

The first D to becoming a **Drama Ninja** is by *disrupting* the drama. But this has to be an *intentional disruption*, not like the squirrel syndrome. It has to be a conscious interruption of your go to reflexes when you're faced with an uncomfortable situation. And the way you disrupt is by the following:

Delete the thought pattern.
Direct your desired vision.

Delete the things that are holding you back. Literally, figuratively, energetically. Take stock of your thoughts. Ask yourself, are your thoughts true or just your inner critic voicing their opinion based on years of conditioning and solidified beliefs? Delete the auto-responses to external situations. Stop the knee-jerk reactions. Don't react. Instead, take a moment to pause. Reflect. Respond.

Direct your desired vision. Now that you've ripped up that outdated Checklist, write a new one. Add your desired vision. Decide what you *deserve*, not what you want. *Want* and *Deserve* are 2 different energies. *Want* is a longing, a feeling of lack. *Deserve* is a feeling of completeness. *Desire* is directly correlated with your worth. What you believe you deserve. *Direct* your attention on your dreams. Imagine it. Visualize it. Encapsulate it. Be the director of your movie.

So first *delete* then *direct*. Use your hand motions. Stop the drama. Let it bounce off. Redirect it. With intention.

This shows you how to **Navigate with Fear**.

#2—DEFLATE

But stopping the drama is not a one-and-done. It will keep coming back like pesky ants that won't leave you alone at a picnic. You need to pierce the drama balloon. Deflate its energy source. And in order to know what needs to be deflated, you've got to find the source of the problem.

Determine the source.
Dissolve at the root.

Determine the problem source to be deflated. This is the opportunity to solve the problem and be free. Remember ... the goal is freedom. Freedom from the shackles that fear places on us. When you focus on the solution rather than the problem, solutions appear. This causes the problem to shrink rather than grow.

Determine the root of what's been holding you back then pull out the weeds that keep your thought patterns running in circles. Determine what inner and outer dialogue control your actions. Determine which thoughts in your mind consume your belief system. Determine which opinions, judgments, and beliefs imposed by people in your life affect your decisions.

Dissolve the problem source. Dilute it. Water it down. Diminish it. Diffuse it. Do the work and deflate the problems. Remove the judgment, the victim mentality, the darkness that eggs you on. This allows you to lead with love in the **drama dance**. Because if you know the source of pesky ants, you can spray ant killer on them and/or directly on their incoming path. But, if you don't know the source of where those ants are emanating, they will keep on marching, one by one, as the song goes.

By deflating the drama, you shrink the effect, the reaction, the magnitude, the heightened stories, the irrational fears. You take away its power. You've taken the reins back.

Now you can **Lead with Love**.

You are one step ahead in the drama dance. So let's stay connected to this rhythm of leading with love and don't fall a step behind. In order to do so, you need to learn the last step of the dance.

#3—DETOX

Detach your personal perspective and become a habitual observer. This segment of the **3D Formula** deals with identifying what is subjective vs objective. Personal vs observation. Let go of the B.S. and surrender. When you *detach* with love, you *attach* with purpose.

Detach with love. *Dance* with purpose

Detach with love so you don't let things cling to you like lint. So that things don't attach to you. **Detox the drama**. On repeat. Surround yourself with a shield before the residue builds up. We can't control other people's words, thoughts, emotions, reactions, or lack thereof. Silence speaks volumes. Detach and *flick*. Remember the hand movements? Flick away what you don't desire, what you don't deserve. I used to defer pain in emotionally painful situations by digging my nails into my hand. True story. Now I flick energy away when it bombards me.

Dance with your darkness but lead with love. Once you do this, you can attach with purpose, so you know exactly what it is you are looking to receive and benefit. *Decide* what you *deserve* and *dance* on the border of your boundaries. Bring the light so you see the definition of the boundaries you set. No point dancing erratically out of sync. Be intentional but not judgmental. Be graceful but not forceful. Be fluid but not fearful. Dance with precision but not perfection. Perfection is a goal; precision is what you aim for. Focus the arrow on the target and then do your best. Remember, it's an 80-20 rule. Judgment free.

Dance with purpose. It's a journey, not a destination. It's an ebb and flow. A release and surrender. When you learn the graceful skills of how to navigate with fear but lead with love, you dance with ease. You move through the eye of the storm with clarity and calmness.

- You **disrupt** the drama, so the drama doesn't disrupt your flow.
- You **deflate** the drama, so the drama doesn't escalate and overshadow.
- You **detox** the drama, so that love always wins.

Remember, the most supreme L.A.W. is...Love. Always. Wins.

And once you master this, you become a **Drama Ninja**.

RECAP

Navigate with fear but lead with love
That is the goal.

When you **Disrupt Drama**, you learn to *navigate with fear*.
When you **Deflate Drama**, you learn to *lead with love*.
When you **Detox Drama**, you become a *Drama Ninja*.

Any questions? I thought so. That's why the remainder of this book is broken down to each of the above sections. In detail.

I will demonstrate how this formula applies to your everyday life. How it is designed for both *internal* and *external* drama.

I'm excited for you to embark on your transformation journey. The possibilities are limitless. The destinations ... endless. Ready to buy the ticket?

All aboard.

5

DISRUPT PART 1

Drama Magnet

> ### Case Law: *Responding vs. Reacting*
>
> Life is going to throw all types of situations at you, many of which you may not be able to control. But what you *can* control is how you *respond* to each set of circumstances. It's how you *respond*, instead of *react*, to these situations. Responding keeps you in control of how you *react*, versus reacting, which is a knee-jerk defense mechanism. The key difference between *responding* vs. *reacting* is being *aware* of the drama. Conscious awareness is key. When you *respond* to drama, you are consciously aware of its existence and the control you have over it. When you *react* to drama, you are subconsciously aware of the drama and its control over you. So … how will you respond to the incoming and oncoming drama when it's coming at you at 100 mph? The first step is to **disrupt the drama.**

DISRUPT

The first prong of the **3D Drama Free Formula** is to *delete* what is holding you back so that you can add your *desired* vision. And everything starts with a thought.

But. Does the hamster wheel of your mind chatter, clutter your thoughts? Keep you from moving forward? Make you feel overwhelmed with emotions, fatigue, and analysis paralysis? All of the above?

Thoughts create emotions. But emotions can create thoughts too. Like a carousel going round your mind, thoughts stir emotions awake through the words that swirl around your head. But in the chaotic frenzy of the carousel, maybe it's the emotions that are stirring the thoughts awake? Let's explore.

Thoughts stir up emotions, determine habits, and decide actions.

So how do you delete the thought patterns that are holding you back? Let's break it down and start with the deletion of outdated and toxic thought patterns.

You are what you think.

According to research at Stanford University, studies show that people have an average of 60,000 thoughts per day - 90% of which are repetitive thoughts from the day before. So essentially if you are what you think, then you are living on repeat each day, only allowing roughly 10% of new thoughts daily.

Now let me throw another wrench into the mix. If we know that 80% of our thoughts are negative, then 4/5ths of the 90% of repetitive thoughts are negative!

Can you feel how burdensome it is to lug around such a heavy load of negative thought patterns each day?! Imagine how much extra weight that is!

Don't worry. I'm not asking you to do the math. But I *am* asking you to lighten the load. *Go on a* **Drama Diet**.

When your thoughts are on repeat, it's like Groundhog's Day in your brain - literally and figuratively. Those thoughts act like little groundhogs, always looking for the shadows (*negative thought reactions*), thinking it'll shield you from getting burned by the sun (*situations out of your comfort zone*). But the sun is always shining. Yet it's the negative thoughts that are burning into our brains. It's ok to step into the sun and let the repetitive– *roughly 43,000*– daily negative thoughts melt away. Yes, I did the math.

> Negative thoughts are disruptive to our lives. The first step is to disrupt the disruptive thought pattern of negative thoughts.

Thoughts are the words to the emotions we feel, yet thoughts trigger emotional reactions. Thoughts try to *think* the emotions away, but instead, they alchemize emotions into physical symptoms. Thoughts are just a reflection of where we've been, and thoughts try to make sense of where we are going. Thoughts think they are protecting us by interrupting our momentum when we enter a new or uncomfortable situation. But in trying to *protect* us, our thoughts tend to *disrupt* us.

So we need to be proactive and *disrupt the thoughts*. Law of duality.

How? When we **react** to a situation, it creates *disruptive thoughts* in our minds that hold us back. When we **respond** to a situation, we can *disrupt the disruptive thoughts* and move forward. Once you become aware of the disruptive thoughts disrupting your day, you can respond from a place of observation rather than defensiveness. Awareness is key.

Disruptive thoughts could be self-sabotaging mind chatter about our own limiting beliefs, or thoughts imprinted from others based on their opinions and judgments. It could be the mean girl stirring the pot in our minds or the mean girl in our lives throwing *drama daggers* at us. Perhaps it's the guilt that consumes us from our own insecurities or the guilt that's thrown at us from other people's unattainable expectations of us.

The Drama Diet

Whatever the case may be, you need to put a cog in the hamster wheel of thoughts. Disrupt the momentum before you can take the next step. Stop the thought in its tracks before it stops you from moving forward. And I imagine it like this.

The Carousel Loop of Thoughts and Emotions

Imagine a carousel of thoughts rotating around your mind, going nowhere but in an endless loop on repeat. Now visualize that your emotions are the horses on the carousel going up and down. A happy or peaceful thought causes your horse to rise high. A worrisome or fearful thought causes your horse to dip low. *So while your thought loop is going round and round, circling your mind, they're causing your emotions to go up and down depending on the type of thought.* Now your horse is all over the place, flying high or falling low, all the while your thoughts are rotating on warp speed, going nowhere but in circles.

Can you feel how frenetic this energy is?

Scan the QR codes and watch my video.

https://lisastuart.com/qr-codes/3

What typically ends up happening is that a drama-induced situation leads to thoughts which then *stir* certain emotions awake. Like sleeping zombies. And now those emotions are permeating throughout your body like the walking dead. They're deeply ingrained in your vessels, bumping into each other, trying to find some semblance of reprieve.

Remember our good friend "Energy in motion" going under the alias of E-motion?

The E-motions, energies in motion, find a resting spot. Perhaps in your neck. *Hello, stiff neck.* Or your head. *Welcome migraine.* Or your gut where most emotions dwell. *Familiar gut-wrenching pit in your stomach.* See a pattern? Thoughts provoke emotions. Emotions lead to physical manifestations of pain. *Pain magnet.*

Or, on the flip side, a familiar situation triggers a subconscious emotion stored in your body that has been in *resting mode* ... until now. That awakened emotion causes all sorts of thoughts to circle your mind hoping to make sense of why you're feeling the way you do. Trying to make sense of stored E-motions *stored energy in motion* is exhausting.

This can cause what I refer to as an **emotional hangover**. Exhausted, depleted, and fatigued simply by energy drained and wasted on sh*t that really doesn't matter and certainly doesn't enhance your life. But we do it anyway when we are in **drama dweller** mode. (See the Recipe for Emotional Hangover Elixir at the end of the chapter.)

The **Brain Drain** is real!

In **Chapter 3**, we talked about how our thoughts affect our emotions. And how our subconscious tries to protect us from going to the most *thought of thoughts,* eliciting a predictable emotion. We talked about how our mind thinks it's protecting us because it doesn't know any other way to respond in a similar situation. And we talked about transmuting that energy. We can choose another thought at any time to provoke a different feeling. We can put our hand up like a stop sign and disrupt the cycle of the carousel.

We can disrupt the drama.

And here's how I did it. I decided to hire a bouncer. I know what you're thinking.

Your husband owns a security company.
True story.
And maybe you wanted some protection.
Well … I do. But not that type of protection.

I decided to hire a bouncer at my mind's door. I wanted protection from negative energy and draining thoughts, so they don't clutter my mind and take up unnecessary space.

You see, I had been allowing way too many self-limiting beliefs and drama-filled reactive thoughts to enter and reside rent-free in my mind. Imagine all the money I could have collected, interest and all. Well, money is just energetic currency. And the preservation of my mental and emotional energetic currency is just as important to collect, store, and save. My mind is my emotional real estate where I am the one and only landlord. Any freeloaders are on my watch, and it is my responsibility to kick them off my property. Therefore, hiring a *bouncer* to block those thoughts from penetrating my mind seemed like a good idea, to prevent them from entering in the first place so I don't have to go through the trouble of kicking them out and sanitizing my mind.

Prevention is key. And no freeloading ideas should have the *key* to the door of my peace haven.

So I thought, *hey, my mind's bouncer will do the work for me and bounce those negative thoughts right out of my head and into* …. well … it doesn't really matter where they go as long as they don't enter my precious real estate! Remember, the first law of property is *location, location, location*. And my brain is prime real estate. It attracts a lot of looky-loos, and I like my privacy.

These free-loading thoughts love to gravitate to **drama magnets**. Fear attractors. They know where they can multiply. Drawn like a moth to the flame. Mesmerized by the prospect of breeding more juicy thoughts. To stop this, you need to figure out a way to be a bug zapper. So that even when you attract these toxic thoughts that stick in your mind, they instantly get trapped and zapped.

Chapter 9 will go into how to be a *drama zapper* and disintegrate these thoughts at the source.

But now that you are becoming *aware* of these thoughts, you have the power to *stop* the thoughts before they have a chance to wipe their feet on the doormat. And yes, *you are* the proverbial doormat that these thoughts are willing to step on and walk all over. Let that soak in.

Don't be a doormat. *Hire a bouncer.*

And here's the **recipe:**

B.O.U.N.C.E.R.

B-lock drama daggers
O-wn your worth
U-nderstand your power
N-egate negative thoughts
C-ultivate clear boundaries
E-liminate rumination
R-epeat often and as needed.

When you know your worth and *own* your worth, you will have too much self-respect to allow intrusive thoughts to linger past the front door. You are stronger than you think. *And you are stronger than your thoughts.*

Limiting beliefs are a form of drama. Once they've entered your peaceful mind, sneaking past the *bouncers* or slipping them a $100 bill to enter through the back door, they start to settle in comfortably in your mind. *Comfortable for them, not for you*, as they stir the pot causing all sorts of chaos in your head. But if you can become **aware** of the thought before it enters your mind for an extended stay, you can bounce those thoughts out of your head.

Consciously Responding vs. Subconsciously Reacting.

Now let's have some fun.

Let's play a good old-fashioned game of darts. **Drama Darts**.

Let's throw some limiting belief darts at the dartboard of drama. Whatever sticks is what needs to be addressed. Especially those that hit the bullseye.

Which ones do you resonate with the most?

- *I'm not good enough.*
- *Who am I to do this?*
- *It's too late to change.*
- *What will they think?*
- *I'm too old, I missed my moment.*
- *I'm too young, who will listen to me?*
- *It's already been done.*
- *What if I fail?*
- *They'll judge me.*
- *How do I start?*
- *Change is hard.*
- *How can I follow through?*
- *I can't handle rejection.*

How many of these do you relate to? How many more limiting beliefs did I *not* write that you identify with? Take a moment and jot down a list of your top five limiting beliefs.

Now let's kick these limiting beliefs to the curb.

If you just stare at these words on a sheet of paper in a book or listen to them on audio, they're just that. *Words.* Made up of letters. Strung together by the thought processes of your brain. *That's it.* But we are the ones attaching meaning to these words. We are the ones breathing life into them. We are the ones attaching truth to them. But are these beliefs true? Are what you are thinking or people telling you actually the truth? Take a moment and reflect.

No one is tattooing these words on your head and forcing you to live by them. No one is shoving these words down your throat forcing you to voice them. No one is attaching these words to your essence forcing you to claim them. No one is branding these words to you making these words part of ... your brand. Your composition. Your constitutional makeup. No one is making you believe them to be true... except for you.

I don't care if 100 people threw shade at you and told you that you weren't good enough. Or that it couldn't be done. Or that you'll never succeed. Or any other mega hurtful limiting belief. Yes, I know it's painful to feel those words, like you just got stabbed by a **drama dart**. You're feeling the sting because you are attaching an emotion behind the words and absorbing that into your body. But know this.

> Those people are coming at you from their limited perspective with *their own* limiting beliefs.

They are not living in your shoes, *just your shadow*. They don't determine where you're going. *They can only validate where you've been.* So, you're always one step ahead. And one step away from a new path, and a new thought process.

It's truly amazing how 99 people can tell you that you're brilliant, but if one person told you that you were a fraud, you would most probably dwell on that one person, feeling the sting of the 1% criticism like a thorn in your side. *Fueling your imposter syndrome.* On the flipside, if 99 people told you that you were a fraud and one person told you that you're brilliant, who do you think you're gonna believe? Chances are good that you'd side with the majority.

We are so trained to focus on the naysayers, the negative, the non-supporters. Any little thorn could devalue the beauty of 99 roses.

We are taught to please others so that they can validate our worth.

When we know our worth and *own our worth* then we can save validation for parking tickets. We can acknowledge the noise from the peanut gallery but realize that their view of our lives is perceived from the cheap seats, not the arena. Still, it's hard to stand in the middle of the arena when hecklers are throwing tomatoes, rather than roses, at you.

Oftentimes we get heavily affected by words people throw at us, and we tend to stew over them. Or make them into a stew of some messed up version of alphabet soup, arranging the letters into words that define our emotions. We allow the words to penetrate us, gnawing at our minds, gnawing at our insides, perpetuating the cycle. But we can stop the momentum of that cycle. We can put a cog in the carousel of thoughts.

My beloved grandmother who was the queen of our family until she reached 101 years young, always had the best pearls of wisdom. She taught me this:

...Never take people's words to heart.

They're just words after all. And although it's the intention or meaning behind the words that sting us, we don't have to let them pierce our heart. We don't have to accept it. We don't have to accept other people's negative energy.

Don't accept the drama. Period.

Yep. Just because someone throws shade at you doesn't mean you have to be a receiver and catch their ball of judgment, shame, or guilt. Don't accept it. Decline it like an RSVP to a toxic party you have no interest in attending. Put your hand up and block that energy. Deflect it away from you. Reject the incoming drama.

Disrupt it.

Ok, this sounds simpler than actually doing it. Trust me, I've been there. In fact, the first time someone suggested to me that I don't have to accept the drama I looked at them like they had three heads. I didn't understand.

Don't accept their guilt, anger, judgment, shade ...

I responded with a head tilt, *Ya ... not getting it.*

When it comes hurling at you, you don't have to take it. Don't accept it.

I nodded, as if it was dawning on me, but silently I was screaming "What the hell do you mean? Don't accept it? How?"

I am proud to say that years later (*hey, no judgment*) I finally figured out what that meant. It meant that just because someone is ...

- ... irrationally upset with you
- ... trying to make you feel guilty
- ... telling you everything that you did to them (or didn't do)
- ... judging you
- ... projecting their insecurities on you
- ... tearing you down
- ... depleting your time and energy

You don't have to accept it. You can acknowledge it. Understand where they are coming from - their limited lens of how they perceive you. Maybe you've heard the phrase *what people think of you is none of your business.* It's nothing personal. People's actions usually have nothing to do with you. Everyone is dealing with things you know nothing about.

You can have a productive conversation surrounding their story as long as you don't allow yourself to get sucked into their story.

Stay grounded. Stay focused. And when you become aware that they are pushing your button ...

Move The Button

EXERCISE

If someone knows how to push your button, take your power back and *Move The Button* by:

1. Having *awareness* of the situation you are in.
2. Put your hand up to disrupt their words before they reach your button and *visualize* them disintegrating against your hand, letting the letters fall away.
3. *Respond* from a place of observation, not attachment.

It's how we *receive* those words and *believe* those words that cause us pain. But if we truly receive those words for what they are ... letters of the alphabet arranged in various ways ... we would not be as affected by them.

And you know how much I love a good word play. So let's play with words for a bit.

When you rearrange the letters in the word **life** you get **file**.

Remember when I talked about the file in our brain that stores all previous events in life? The one that our subconscious automatically reverts to so it can make sense of a situation? That file contains our belief system. Your *life* is contingent on the *file* in your mind. And you have control of that file. We know that thoughts come from our previous experiences. Remember, 90% of our thoughts are repetitive from the day before. And a belief is just a thought that you think over ... and over ... and over .... Change your thoughts, change your beliefs.

Although I haven't read it yet (she says with her head hung low), Wayne Dyer wrote a book called *"Change your thoughts, Change your life."* The premise is that *if we can change our beliefs surrounding our stories, we can change our life.* And it starts with the words you file away in your mind. Just as you can rearrange the letters of a word, you can rearrange the thoughts of your mind to create a whole new set of beliefs.

When we work out our muscles, lifting weights or using resistance bands like in Pilates, we are ingraining *muscle memory* so that the next time we work out our muscles are more receptive to the exercise. Maybe I butchered the science behind this, but you get the gist. The more you do something, the faster it becomes an automatic. Like driving. Remember the first time you drove to a new place? You probably needed to Waze it, or if you're old school like me, you had to *Map Quest* it back in the day. But if that route became a daily routine, over time, you would drive there on autopilot, often not remembering how you got there because you were on the phone (speaker phone of course), talking to someone in the car, or singing along to the radio. The point is the route became ingrained in your subconscious that you didn't have to think about it. Your subconscious took over. *Muscle memory.*

Work out your thoughts and your thoughts will work out.

The same goes for our thoughts. According to the teachings of Abraham Hicks, you only have to hold a thought for 17 seconds in order to activate the energy for manifesting that thought. Then if you can sustain the thought three consecutive times for another 51 seconds, it is said to start the manifestation process, for better or for worse, depending on the thought.

This may sound too spiritually out there for some of you, but there is science behind the infamous law of attraction. The more you think a thought, the more that thought becomes automatic. Habitual. And so over time, when you become consciously aware of the thoughts you think, *you can become a disruptor of the roughly 43,000 daily repetitive negative thoughts.* Then you can actively and *consciously* replace them with positive thoughts. Get accustomed to creating a brand-new thought pattern. Ingraining a new belief system with muscle memory.

This is your new response system. When we react to drama stimuli with our most thought of thought, we stay stuck in the victim drama zone. When we acknowledge it but don't let it penetrate us or suck us into our knee-jerk reaction, we respond to it calmly.

> We *see* the drama, but we don't *become* the drama

And while 17 seconds of sustained positive thought does not sound like a hard thing to do, try it. Next time you're spiraling down a negative thought loop, set up your timer and consciously sustain a pure positive thought for 17 seconds. Then do it again. And again. And again. How did it feel? Was it annoyingly uncomfortable? Did your body cringe? Were you able to hold it for 68 seconds? If not, you will. With practice. Once you train your brain.

Train Your Brain

If we can change our thoughts, we can change our *beliefs*.
If we can change our beliefs, we can change our *stories*.
If we can change our stories, we can change our *lives*.

It's about changing your life one thought at a time. So get in the habit of becoming aware of your thoughts. A habit is something you train yourself to do. A belief is a thought you train your mind to think.

And it all starts with a simple thought. But if we can harness that simple thought, then the smallest act of changing a thought could have the most profound ripple effect on the trajectory of your life. Just changing the trajectory on an airplane course by two percent could land you in another country. Imagine where you can land in life just by changing the trajectory of your thoughts.

And if a dark thought floats in, acknowledge it. Say *hey, I see you, I feel you, and now I'm gonna let you float through me like an evaporating cloud.* You see, you don't need to *feel good* for 51 seconds if you just can't flip the switch to turn on the light thoughts when you're in a dark place. You just need to *not feel bad*. Don't ignore what's going on. But be *neutral*. Any neutral thought is better than a negative one. Focus on the weather, or what you're going to eat for your next meal. Or just listen to the buzzing of traffic or symphony of birds chirping, depending on where you are situated.

Even just reorganizing books on a shelf could help you reorganize thoughts in your head. Rewiring our minds is not just a concept. It's scientifically backed by **neuroplasticity.** The theory of *neuroplasticity* regarding the rewiring of our minds with different thought patterns revolves around the brain's ability to reorganize itself by forming new neural connections throughout life.

Our minds are wired based on our previous thought patterns. When we learn a new language or musical instrument at any age in life this involves the brain rewiring itself. Rewiring our thoughts reorganizes our minds to dissolve old neural pathways and form new ones. The more we utilize the new pathways versus the old ones, the more we strengthen the new neural connections so that our brains become *hard-wired* to respond to situations in a newly learned way. The old ways–outdated thoughts, stories, negative patterns–weaken in a process called *neural pruning*. How cool is that!

Repetition is key to reprogramming the brain. You've heard of the phrase *neurons that fire together wire together.* Now you know why. Neuroplasticity.

Now that you are aware of this, you can flip the narrative without judgment or guilt–two wasted emotions that clutter your mind.

But what if your thoughts are a result of external judgment or guilt? Remember, you don't have to *accept* their judgment or guilt. You can acknowledge their words without attaching their meaning to you.

Here's an example to show that the *power of thought* is not truly the words spoken, but the meaning we attach to them. If I were to speak to you in a language you didn't understand, you would only be able to determine the intention behind my words by my tone. For instance, if I said the sweetest things to you but in an angry tone, you would feel attacked without even realizing the sweet words coming out of my mouth. On the contrary, if I said despicable things to you in the sweetest tone, you would feel all warm and fuzzy, not realizing all the judgment and criticism I just spewed at you.

They're just words, subject to interpretation, and accepted or rejected by our mind's Bouncer.

Because you could not understand the negative words, I was saying to you in a language you don't understand, you would simply ignore me, the way you would receive a letter from someone that you cannot interpret. It would not affect you. You would let those words *bounce,* or *slide,* right off you.

And speaking of sliding, here's another one of my grandmother's favorite mantras: "When people shower you with hurtful words, wear a thick raincoat and let the words slide off you." Meaning, don't let the words penetrate you. Again, in congruence with her mantra of *never taking people's words to heart*.

I've learned that when people throw **drama daggers** at me, *I wear a thick raincoat* and let the words *slide* off. The daggers might leave scratches on my raincoat but at least I can take the coat off, shake off the drama residue, and walk away relatively unscathed.

But I also use that coat as a shield to protect my energy. I consciously choose not to be a victim of other people's words. As my wise and beautiful mom always says – "There are no victims, only volunteers."

Take celebrities. I give them a lot of credit in the sense that they are constantly in the spotlight. Nothing highlights their life more than the media. Especially social media. With the onset of Web2, it invited an interaction with celebrities like never before.

And they have had to handle an onslaught of praise in conjunction with a ton of shade being thrown at them. Verbalized in comments. Exposed to the public eye.

This can affect a person in two ways. You can focus on the positive responses you receive. Or you let the bitter comments sting you and invade your peace of mind. Sometimes it's a hybrid of the two, depending on the mood you're in.

The evolved celebrities learn to shake off the comments, good and bad, knowing that their worth is not contingent on the amount of praise they get. And knowing that a dip in their "likes" does not devalue their worth. Also knowing that a spike in their follower engagement does not elevate their value because it may be fleeting.

Which leads me to **future tripping.** Have you ever had a full-on conversation, *or even fight,* with a friend or relative ... but it was *all in your head?!* Raise your hand if you know what I'm talking about! *Me, cringing in the corner with my hand barely raised.* Ya, you know the conversation. The one we make up in our mind that we anticipate will happen. Maybe a friend did you wrong and you imagine how that confrontation will go. Maybe a family member ghosted you and you start to believe that there's a whole party being planned that you're not invited to. Whatever the imaginary drama may be, it's just that. **Imaginary.**

And typically, at least for me, those conversations in my head *never turn out that way.* Maybe I got it out of my system and manifested a better result? Maybe I just created a whole drama-infused situation out of nothing at all? But I'll tell you something: On more than one occasion I have been guilty of seeing a friend after my *imaginary fight* with them in my head and literally thought to myself, "Wait...are we in a fight?"

Try not to future trip. Try not to create scenarios in your head that actually haven't happened. Try to cease *making up fights with friends.* Put your hand up and disrupt the thought pattern.

And likewise, stop rehashing the past. What's the importance of putting a cog in the carousel of *past regret*? *A lot*. When we live in the past, we are doing more than just drudging up old memories. The crazy thing is that when we rehash a situation, our bodies don't know whether we are living it out in real-time or on replay.

And so while our minds are literally living in the past, our body is actually experiencing it in real time!

Talk about a toxic time warp!

Dr. Russell Kennedy, a.k.a. the Anxiety MD, refers to this as *emotional time travel*. When we relive an event *in our minds* it elicits the same emotional response as if we were experiencing it for the first time. It's like our minds are living in an augmented reality that is not happening in the present time, but our thoughts of the past trick our minds into thinking that we are. This then manifests into an emotional roller coaster, causing physical reactions that knock our equilibrium out of balance. I'm sure you've heard the notion that disease is *dis-ease*. When the body is not in ease, chaos breeds.

Stop pressing re-play on your thoughts. Hit the stop button, or at the very least, the pause button. Disrupt the thought. That's enough to snap you out of the emotional loop of your thought trance.

So now that you're aware of this, *hire that Bouncer*, not just to stop new self-sabotaging thoughts from entering your brain, but also to kick out those that have been squatting inside rent-free— the ones you play on repeat because you are either projecting anxiety about a future event or you are agonizing over what transpired in the past. Either way, those thoughts looping around need to be escorted out ASAP.

Stop the cycle. Drop the thought.

S.T.O.P. and D.R.O.P.

S-tart
T-hinking
O-nly
P-ositive

and

D-isrupt
R-eally
O-ld
P-atterns

When you start thinking only positive thoughts, you disrupt really old patterns. Stop and Drop.

When you learn to filter the soul sucking thoughts from your brain, you really are maintaining your mental and emotional hygiene. It is the first step in retraining your brain to think new thoughts. It is the first step in rewiring your mind to *not* instinctively go to your *go-to thoughts*.

Disrupting drama means courageously putting your hand up to abruptly stop the drama in its tracks. Push it off kilter. And when that drama, or set of thoughts, comes charging at you at 100 mph and slams into your hand, guess what? It will also throw *you* off kilter.

Sticking a cog in the wheel of your spinning thoughts is a jolt to the system. Your mind is spinning so fast, like a pinwheel on steroids, that when you abruptly *disrupt* the momentum, it can throw you off balance. And that jolt may feel super uncomfortable in your body because it leaves you in a space of the unknown.

You may not be used to going cold turkey. It's as if you were running on a treadmill at full speed, when suddenly the machine's safety button unplugs, abruptly stopping the machine, yet you are still moving with the momentum. Where would you end up? Flying off the machine? Face smacked down against the screen? This can be painful or uncomfortable, as it's a jolt to the system, which is why it's difficult for people to do it.

And this is why some people would prefer to stay in the comfortable chaos of the familiar thought loop.

But the more cogs you put in the carousel of toxic thought loops, the slower the thoughts start to spin around your mind. *And with practice, you can disrupt the disruptive thoughts with minimal collateral damage.* So, the next time your mind spins like a computer buffering, hit the refresh button. The more you do it, the faster it'll reset. Soon that spinning rainbow wheel will buffer slower and slower until you can literally stop the 100 mph trainwreck of thoughts in a matter of seconds.

Repetitive thoughts are just like a broken record.

Spinning round and round like a broken record stuck on replay. But if you scratch that record then it interrupts and disrupts the song. (Where are all my Gen Xers?) The same thing can be done to disrupt the flow of thoughts as they circulate in your mind like a broken record. And the fastest way to disrupt a negative thought-emotion loop is to put on your favorite record *or stream your favorite song*, and dance. *Dance with your drama.* Move that energy in motion to improve your emotional wellbeing. Break the pattern.

Let's explore *how* stopping the thought in its tracks - *disrupting the drama* - is key to your emotional wellbeing.

First identify the external drama in your life by taking inventory of the chaos, disorder, and clutter dripping into your day and draining your time and energy. This includes any relationship drama, chaotic conversations, and unattainable expectations of others causing guilt and shame.

It could be that you're faced with an uncomfortable situation throwing you off kilter. Maybe you got into a fight with a loved one, or maybe you're anxious about that upcoming presentation at work. Maybe you are over-obsessing about that conversation you had with a friend. Or the one you're avoiding with your partner. Or the one you're anxiously waiting to have with a prospective business associate.

Your **mind chatter** is probably draining your own battery. Depleting your energy. Which directly impacts your Emotions - Energies in motion.

You need to "Stop! In the name of love" ... The Supremes had a point.

Remember when I said that, as a lawyer, the most *supreme* L.A.W. is that Love. Always. Wins.

Always lead with love. Dance with the drama, but let love take the lead. Drama drains. Love revitalizes. Acknowledge the repetitive thoughts and then lovingly lead them out the door. And when those negative thoughts start sneaking in the back door, face them head-on, put up your hand, and in the words of *Arya Stark* say, "Not Today!"

When these thoughts enter our mind, we actually have only two choices. *React or respond.* Like a knee-jerk reaction, words or actions from others float into our awareness by way of our brain. Our brains then translate those words or actions from others to something we can inherently understand. This happens so fast that our gut usually feels a pain before we register that our brains have processed it. That's how micro-fast it happens.

But if you can get ahead of the thoughts, and become aware of the thoughts, you can disrupt the emotional havoc that can occur because of the thoughts. Acknowledge the thoughts, but don't give drama your attention. Acknowledgment is different from attention. When you give negative thoughts your attention, you feed it power, and it amplifies. You fall victim to your thoughts. When you acknowledge negative thoughts, you bring them out from the dark so they can't linger undetected, which deprives them of their power. You're basically saying "Hi thoughts, I see you, I acknowledge you, and now I release you. Thank you for coming to visit but you have outstayed your welcome in my mind and I'm not inviting you back."

Disrupt your day in a good way.

To disrupt the flow of thoughts, you must interrupt the pattern of habits.

When the *disrupt* is *abrupt*, you put your system into a sort of shock to snap it out of its *trance of thoughts* that have been operating on autopilot. Quick tip to get out of a *thought trance* - just *dance*. Movement is one of the quickest ways to move that *energy in motion*.

Exercise. Do a Disruptor Dance.

Then you can get off the spinning carousel and realign your mind to where you want to direct its attention. You may feel dizzy from all the spinning but once you realign, you can take action to where you want to go instead of focusing on what is holding you back. What action steps can you take to propel you in the forward motion of your goals and dreams? This chapter started the conversation on how to respond to your thoughts (*disrupt them*) rather than react to them (*succumb to them*). Once you become aware of the thought and acknowledge it, then you can redirect it and focus your attention on what serves you rather than what distracts you. *From distraction to action*. This is a perfect segue into the topic of the next chapter - *Act, don't react.*

Turn to **Chapter 6** for tips on Act 1: The Movie of Your Life. Popcorn optional.

Recipe

Emotional Hangover Elixir

Here's my quick fix elixir for an **emotional hangover**:

Ingredients

- Add a dash of positive thinking [*train your brain to reach for high vibe thoughts*]
- Add a splash of mindfulness [*pivot your mind to focus on anything that does not drain your brain*]
- Then add movement - mix it up, shake it up, get moving [*move your body to set the emotion free*]
- Squeeze out the juice [*let it go*]

Instructions

When ruminating thoughts about the past disturb your peace, or anxious thoughts about the future consume you, learn to blend it to your favor.

Drink up the peace. Cheers!

*****

EXERCISE — ELIMINATE NEGATIVE THOUGHTS

The three main tools to a successful law practice are.... practice, practice, practice. Here are three practice tools to help eliminate negative thoughts:

- *Practice* redirecting your thoughts every time your mind

wanders to the dark side of drama. Don't obsess over what happened. You can't change the past, but you can control the present. Shift your thought, shift your mood.
- *Practice* your breathwork while you are in the midst of a situation. [Breathe in for 3 - hold for 3 - exhale for 3 - hold for 3 - repeat 3 times.] It will help you deflate any escalated feelings emanating from the drama. It moves the frenetic energy through and out your body.
- *Practice* getting off the drama carousel. Move your body so your mind doesn't wander in circles. Movement disrupts the thought loop. Once you stop the recycling loop of thoughts, you take away the power it has over you.

*****

DRAMA DIARY JOURNAL PROMPT

Bouncer to Your Brain: Journal Prompt

Your mind is the VIP section — and it's time to bounce out the limiting beliefs that don't belong.

1. **List 3-5 limiting beliefs that have been hanging around in your head like party crashers.**
   (Examples: "I'm not good enough," "No one will buy this," "I don't have enough time")
2. **For each one, ask:**
   What is this belief blocking me from doing, creating, or experiencing?
3. **Now call in your Inner Bouncer. Reframe each belief with a new empowering truth.**
   (Example: "I don't have enough time" "I make time for what matters, and this matters to me.")
4. **Final reflection:**
   What's one bold or tiny action I can take this week that proves I've kicked that belief to the curb?

Bounce out the drama. Make space for your power.

You're the one in charge of who gets to stay in your mind.

The Drama Diet

6

DISRUPT PART 2

Creative Director

> **Case Law: *Acting vs. Reacting***
>
> Maybe you *should* grab your popcorn. This is gonna be a longer chapter but well worth the ticket price. In **Chapter 5**, we learned that disrupting drama requires a re-sponse, *rather than* a knee-jerk *reaction* because it brings awareness to the drama-induced thought or situation. Acknowledging the drama allows us to now act. This chapter will dive into the *art of acting* and why this takes precedence over reacting. Acting is taking control of your power. Reacting is giving your power away. *When you react, you reinforce*. When you act you create. And guess what? **Reaction** and **Creation** each have the same letters just rearranged! Same letters ... different energy. Creation through action propels you to your destination. Reaction reinforced keeps you stuck in a time warp. Any questions? Read on.

When you put up your hand and let the drama bounce off you were probably left with bruises and bumps from the force of the impact. Receiving these blows can also knock you off balance. Nonetheless, you stayed the course. I'm proud of you.

Disrupting the Drama is a two-fold act. When you put your hand up to disrupt the incoming and oncoming drama, you create

The Drama Diet

a barrier between the drama trying to ingrain itself **on you and in you** and your peace and protection. The drama you've disrupted is not permanently gone. Just a momentary reprieve to grab an opportunity of peace while the drama is dazed and confused by your disruption of it. This is your time to change things up.

But now you're asking, "So I stopped, or at least slowed down the oncoming and incoming drama. Now what?"

The second prong of **Disrupt** allows the drama to rebound off your hand so you can focus on what you desire without distraction. Attraction of drama creates a distraction.

When you are attracting drama like a **drama magnet**– flip the magnet.

This is your opportunity to **flip the script.** If you've always wanted to know how it feels to be a director, this is your chance. You get to be the **Creative Director** of your life. This means **you** get to **direct** the drama to where you want it to go (away from you) and **redirect** your energy, your choices, your actions, your destination, **your life.**

Remember the **Transformation Station** from **Chapter 4** which is designed to move you from where you are to where you want to go? This is the chapter to jump on your desired train to get you back on track. This may be a burning passion or goal you've had within you for quite some time. Or you may have no inkling of what your desired dreams look like. It doesn't matter, you will sort it out through this book.

"Wait a second," you think, "I thought this book was about elimination of drama, not figuring out the direction of my life?"

"Well," I reply, "Can you do one without the other?"

(Stops to pause and think.) "Go on. Explain."

Are fears from drama and judgment holding you back from living your life full out? Once you identify and disrupt the drama, you get to choose the direction you envision your life to go. How? **The drama defines the destination.**

Disrupt Part 2

Contrast illuminates the way to clarity.

Where you are today is simply a reflection of where your energy has been.

You need to change your energy because you can't get to where you want to go with the energy of where you are. Make sense?

We can be **master manifestors** by flipping our current energy to embodying what it feels like to have what we crave, to manifest what we deeply desire, even before it's created. And then like any online shopping order, we need to wait for delivery. Sometimes it's more immediate with same-day delivery. Other times it's courier pigeon slow. But if we linger too long in the energy of lack rather than abundance, this can backfire and what should have come by Amazon Prime will now make its way by snail mail … or worse … get sent to the wrong address. This is a cause for a pause–and makes me think twice - when I am upset in the moment of how this energy will unfold. With my luck, it will probably reveal itself when I'm having an amazing day, and my luck randomly turns sour, and I can't remember why. **Subconscious drama magnet.**

To emphasize, sometimes our manifestations are instant. And sometimes they linger, waiting to present themselves long after we've forgotten we placed them there. I always say, when you manifest, set your intentions then forget them: **Set it and forget it.** Like an online order you place in the middle of the night, when you're half asleep, and forget about, until the box shows up at your front door. **Don't tell me I'm the only one that does this!**

And it is great when we manifest the good stuff. But we forget this universal law when we are swimming in toxic waters of our past manifestation energies. That's where awareness and acknowledgment are key on your transformation journey.

Your current situation is a mirror reflecting all your previous choices.

If you want to course correct, you can't use your current energy as the foundation or you will simply get more of what you don't want. You must **flip that energy.** This applies not only to your current situation but also trickles into all aspects of your current life–– relationships, profession, finances, health. Even **emotional health.** If you're not happy with where you are, change course. And serve yourself the **main course** of **The Drama Diet.** Choose you. Everything is either a gift or a lesson – and lessons are in and of themselves gifts. So, treat where you are as a reflection of your past and get to where you want to go with renewed enthusiasm.

Remember way back in **Chapter 1** where I touched upon **The Checklist**? As a refresher, **The Checklist** is the proverbial list you **think** you need to fulfill, but which was most likely created by others. Even those who have come before you. It's some mass-produced list that people seem to be handing out to make you feel like **if you don't check off all those boxes then you aren't enough, accepted, successful, worthy, etc.** How exhausting. Ugh. Good thing you're going to R.I.P. up that outdated checklist and bury it behind you.

R.I.P. outdated stories, beliefs, thoughts, and even habits.

So how do we do this? I know some of you may have started to toss out **The Checklist**, crossing off what doesn't serve you. Some of you are already making mental or physical lists of everything you desire on **your Checklist**. But let's break this down.

If you haven't done so already from **Chapter 1**, and no judgment here, then I want you to take inventory of **The Checklist** you have been working off.

THE CHECKLIST PROMPTS

What you do daily: Make bed. Get kids ready for school. Work. Workout. Pay bills. Watch reality shows. Whatever your guilt-free guilty pleasure is.

What you think you need to be doing to validate your worth: Volunteer for charities. Accept invitations to parties and events. Keep your house in pristine order. Create home-cooked meals every day. Please others. Do everything yourself. You know ... be perfect.

What others expect from you: Get married by a certain age. Go into a certain profession. Act a certain way. Make them happy. Follow **their** checklist!

And while you're free to use the examples given above, make sure to tailor the answers specifically to your individual circumstances.

Now look at **The Checklist** and decide what's really a priority in your life; what truly needs to get done to further the life **you** want, what lights **you** up. Remember, it's like an Amazon order you're concocting to create your dream life. If something doesn't add to that desire, don't add it to your cart. Or at the very least, put it in the "**saved for later**" section.

Next, I want you to get laser focused. I don't want you to imagine what your dream life looks like. I want you to **embody** how that dream life **feels**. Does it bring you joy? Freedom? Peace? Once you feel it, you can envision it in your mind. Close your eyes and let those feelings wash over your body as images of your dream life float through you.

Once you've created a vision of your life based on the projected feelings emanating from you ... congratulations. You have just dabbled with the concept of **visualization.** A spiritual concoction of manifesting your desired life by feeling what it's like to have before it materializes in your life. **Being it before seeing it**

IRL. Sure, you **see** it in your mind's eye, but it's the notion that it's already in existence before it's a tangible reality. A little flip the magnet, flip the script trick.

Ok, now you're ready to write **Your Checklist.** Authentically. Without the fear of judgment or criticism from others. In other words, **what would you be doing if validation and support from others was guaranteed no matter what!**

Imagine how it would **feel** to change your profession. Go out with that person. Follow your passion. Speak your truth.

> Imagine how it feels to say "no" to others without guilt and say "yes" to yourself without fear.

Be truthful with yourself. What deep desires have you repressed because no one gave you permission to pursue your passion? Or you started to, and then shrunk when other people ridiculed you or criticized you for going after a distant dream only you can visualize? Isn't it amazing how many unhappy, unfulfilled people are out there telling you how ridiculous your dream sounds to them?

You know what I say?

Who Made Up the Rules Anyway?!

Who put others in charge of your emotions? Your happiness? Your worth? Your value? Your life?

Who decided that you can or cannot do something? Was it someone who was trying to **protect** you because they could not fathom the possibility was real? Or someone that wanted you to get a **"secure"** job instead of **your** dream job that seemed so out of touch with **their** version of reality? Or is it something about your upbringing that made you believe you couldn't be who you want to be? That you aren't worthy? Or maybe it is part of societal expectations that **this isn't something you should be doing?**

Remember—You are the star of your movie. So make it authentic. Stay true to you.

Pay attention to whether you feel **internal** or **external** pressure not to pursue your dreams. Pressure reveals what you truly want and **how badly you want it.** It's an indicator of the strength of your desires. Your dreams are your diamonds in the rough. And pressure squeezes the truth out of you. Like a diamond revealing itself from coal. The gem— **the truth**— always gets squeezed out.

If you didn't feel pressure, it's because you really didn't want it. Pressure is good. It's resistance. Resistance from others is a road map to where we truly want to go. It defines the path. It creates an action plan. It reinforces our desire. Law of duality.

You are meant to be the star of your life. **Be a *Star* ... Not a *Starfish*.**

I used to feel like I was pulled in so many directions. My body literally felt as if it was outstretched like a starfish! Then one day, I found myself explaining to someone why I couldn't go after something I desired because I had too many obligations, too many things to do on **The Checklist**.

And I said with a heavy sigh, and a light dose of martyrdom, "I'm just pulled in so many directions."

To my astonishment, that person looked me squarely in the eyes and asked:

"Which direction do you want to be pulled in?!"

I just stared at him and didn't answer. I didn't know. **No one had ever asked me that before and I never knew I had a choice. A voice.**

But now I know. **When you're not a *reactor*, you're an *actor*.** I know which direction I want to be pulled: **The direction of my dreams.**

Don't put pressure on yourself for trying to win a race you never signed up for.

Follow **Your Checklist**, no one else's. Figure out what direction **you** want to get pulled in and act. And don't compete with other people's timelines. Don't get sidetracked by checking out how far others are ahead of you. When you see someone else doing what you want to do, your green-eyed monster may surface and say in a competitive, bitter voice, "I can do that," folding its green monster arms in the process.

But let's take that scenario and change the recipe. Infuse a bit of enthusiasm into the formula, flip the energy, and exclaim with excitement, "I **can** do that!" Do you feel the shift in energy? Same words, different energy. It's all about seeing things from a different angle, changing the lens of perspective.

COMPARISON-ITIS

Don't compare where you are in life to anyone else. Not everyone has the same timetable. The only person you need to compare yourself with is who **you** were the day before. **Ditch the drama.** Stay in your lane. You do you.

The only clock you're racing against is the one in which you set the timer.

Did you know that when racecar drivers speeding at 200 mph turn around a curve, they don't look at the wall they're trying to avoid? Instead, they look in the direction they **want** to go, and their hands subconsciously follow, turning the steering wheel in that direction. Otherwise, they would most likely smack into that wall! So even if they **intend** to go in one direction, if they get distracted and don't stay laser-focused, they will drift into danger.

This is a great analogy for executing your life. The racecar driver stays in their own lane and doesn't fall prey to **comparison-itis: trying to win a race they didn't sign up for**. The racecar driver signed up for this race! They're in it to win it. Be like a racecar driver. Pick your race. Then be intentional. Driven. Motivated. Refueling and recharging for (tire) breaks. And yes … be fast. Fast to fail. Fast to rise. Fast to disrupt negative thoughts. Fast to take action. Fast to course correct on the track of life. Fast to forgive yourself. **Fast to believe in yourself.**

And don't get complacent. In a world full of fear and judgment, it's so easy to get caught up in **comparison-itis** and let it deter you. But not doing something because **[insert whatever lame excuse you can come up with]** is just an excuse. When we allow our excuses to dictate the course of our lives, we are flowing with the current that we think we are **supposed to** float in. Because it's safe, familiar, laid out in front of us. Instead, think of your life like a racecar track that changes course depending on the destination you set. Doesn't that feel exhilarating to navigate into the unknown of limitless possibilities?

Confessions of a Drama Magnet

I have a theory.

I believe that the reason why we each have our own unique dreams is because they are meant for us. They are our purpose. And we can have many different purposes depending on where we are in our journey. And if you don't know your purpose, this can help explain what it is.

Why is it that we can look at other people's fulfilled lives and be so happy for them? Yet, other times the green-eyed monster appears, and we desire what they have? It's because it highlights what we desire. And feelings of envy are breadcrumbs.

Feelings of envy are positive! **Wait, what?** Yes … you heard

The Drama Diet

me right. Feelings of envy, jealousy, and comparison light up the path to what we are missing in our lives, highlighting what we desire. Feelings of envy are simply **magnets of desire** –pulling our desires to us as we're being pulled to our desires. Instead of letting **comparison-itis** divide us and **repel** our desires away, we can flip the **drama magnet** to attract what we desire.

When we root for others, we are essentially telling the universe that we want more of that in our lives. And the universe doesn't understand words, only energy. So an envious feeling repels what we want because the universe thinks we don't want more of that, while an excited feeling attracts more of what we want, and so the universe supplies.

That's why we need contrast.

When we see someone have something we want, and it sparks envy in us, it's because the spark highlights our deficiencies (the contrast of what we don't have) and illuminates what we desire. The contrast defines where we are vs. where we want to be. *Use that envy emotion as a spark.* Turn **envy** into **eagerness** and go after your dreams.

From **jealous to zealous**– alchemize that energy and synthesize your envy to excitement.

It's not necessarily that you're jealous of others because they accomplished what you have not. You're feeling jealous because **you haven't made it yet … and you know you can.** You're feeling behind and looking at how far ahead **they** are from **you**, sometimes requiring binoculars or a telescope because the distance feels so vast. And that can make you feel less than worthy. Is this hitting a nerve?

It's okay to acknowledge that you feel this way. What's **not** okay is to stay in this space. So, let's work on transmuting that energy. Let's change the energy from **jealous to zealous**. Because, in my opinion, the reason why the universe is shoving other people's wins in your face is not to rub it in to make you feel bad. **It's to show** you how badly you want it and how close you are to having it.

The universe is saying
"It's possible. You're that much closer.
You're on the right path."

I have an acronym (obviously). **EAGER is the new ENVY.** When the green-eyed monster rears its ugly head, flip the emotion - energy in motion. Stop feeling **envy**. Start feeling **eager.**

E.A.G.E.R.

E - Excited about your goal
A - Anticipate your achievements
G - Grateful for the process
E - Expect success
R - Receptive to success

Get eager that what you desire is already yours.

When you know what you don't want, you know what you desire.

When you know what triggers you, you know what you desire.

When you feel envy, you know what you desire.

Don't judge these emotions. They're just roadmaps highlighted on your inner GPS system. Instead of feeling shame and guilt around your dark emotions, let them light the direction you need to go in. Remember, **darkness isn't bad**. It allows you to see the spark lighting you up. **See the positive in it and dance with it.**

And never wish for something you want when you're feeling down or falling down a negative spiral, and you're coming from that low vibrational energy.

That's a guarantee to repel what you desire. It's at the low points that we want more, but it comes from a place of lack and desperation– **two emotions guaranteed to block your dreams.**

When you come from a place of inspiration, and let others inspire you to continue on your path– **even if it brings up feelings of envy–** that's a recipe for success.

> Flip the dialogue. Thank the universe for the breadcrumbs that what you desire is desiring you. Then go and get it.

I truly believe the universe sends people and situations along your journey that are doing or have what you desire …

…to show you what is **possible** for you.
…to test you on how **badly** you desire it.
…to confirm how **close** you are to reaching your goals.

And why is it that we desire certain things over others? I believe that we desire the things that are meant for us. It's somehow ingrained in our essence, even subconsciously. I've thought about this a lot. Why do I have a burning desire to write this book, work on my music, finish my novel, create a musical, and speak on stage if I have a full life with an amazing husband, three amazing children, and a law profession? My time is limited, my energy gets drained, and I'm up late writing this book as we speak.

The answer is, I don't have a choice. I am **compelled** to fulfill my passions, no matter how long it takes, and this book has been a labor of love, usurping much more of my time than I anticipated! But my passions have been burning inside me for years, until I couldn't take the intensity within, feeling as if my insides would burst open if I didn't share my thoughts with the world, living my purpose. And where purpose meets passion, miracles happen. That's the sweet spot. That's where fulfillment lies.

And that's what we all strive to feel, that we are here on this spinning rock called Earth for a finite amount of time to fulfill whatever purpose we were meant to have. **And who says we only get to have one purpose in life?**

> You can recreate yourself at any age, at any stage, at any season, and for any reason.

You know you're meant for more. You can't explain it, but you can feel it. Now you have a choice. You can **ignore** this feeling. Or you can **ignite** this feeling. But when you don't choose, and both options consume you, overlapping with each other, you end up with chaos.

An **internal** riot.

Don't believe me? Just look at the play on words. **Ignore** and **Ignite** share the same letters except for the following four: **R.I.O.T.**

And I don't believe in coincidences. Just synchronicities.

*A **RIOT** typically stems from two opposing sides, two distinct views, that can't come to a peaceful resolution. When we know we are meant for more yet can't make the decision to act on our gut, we wreak havoc within. Gut pain. Rearrange the letters in gut and you get tug.*

TUG in GUT

Believe it or not, we each inherently know what our true purpose is. Yes, I'm talking to you there struggling to figure it out - you heard me right. It's within us. Sometimes buried deep, deep, DEEP within us. Even if we are not sure, it comes to us in glimpses when we feel joy, when we're having fun, when there's no resistance. That's when we know that we are operating from our inner soul, from the whispers that nudge us from within. When we are aligned with our true self, we feel peace.

There's no internal tug of war.

So what stops us from pursuing our burning desires? From speaking our truth? From living authentically and freely? Drama. Our inner voice. Judgment. Mind chatter. Other's opinions. Mean girl talk. Shame. Guilt. **All the limiting beliefs we are disrupting and redirecting.**

When we follow the **tug** in our **gut** and pursue our passion in line with our purpose it can be incredibly scary. In fact, it can be downright terrifying and leave us feeling frozen in analysis paralysis. When we know where we want to go, **but don't know how to get there**, what to do, or where to start, we open the door for imposter syndrome to walk right in and step all over us.

In fact, we practically invite imposter syndrome to dwell rent free in our minds, eat us out of house and home by letting it feed off our fear, and sleep in our thoughts at night as it keeps us up, while it tosses and turns in our minds. Why not just give it a key to our house and access to the Wi-Fi so it can really take us down the rabbit hole!

It all starts, **and ends**, with our egos. It's only when we think with our ego mind that our insides go haywire. But ask yourself, "Is that story you've been telling yourself accurate? Or have you been a character in someone else's story of your life?"

Everyone has a story. It's either the one we **create** or the one we **debate**.

Law of duality. When we resist our true self, our true calling, we fight for all our limitations. We desperately try to explain to others why we are doing what only we can visualize. Explaining gives our power away. Let's take our power back. Change the narrative.

> When we decide to change the story of our life, we realize that we have always held the pen ... but we had temporarily given it to another writer.

Clarity creates our reality.

With clarity, we can create our reality. And we can rewrite the script to our own movie.

Yes, you are the story writer of your life. But you are also the director and main actor of your movie. Don't hand those roles out. Don't be a supporting actor in the script of your life. That only supports how **others** want you to act. How you **act** in your life determines the results. Determine the direction you desire your life to go. Feel it. Embody it. Visualize it as if you were filming a scene that you are directing. Then go and take action. Intentional, mindful, inspired, **messy** action.

A Goal without Action is just a Dream.

You can create a **blockbuster** movie of your life. And as you know, with the **law of duality** you will encounter many blocks on the journey to your dreams. Blocks that take you out of your comfort zone. But use those blocks to your advantage. Be a Block Buster and **bust through your blocks.**

Use obstacles as steppingstones. **Don't stand *in* your story.** You'll get stuck in your story. **Stand *on* your story.** Use your past as fuel for your future.

The great and late Kobe Bryant said (and I paraphrase) "Failure is an illusion ... it's just a word we made up ... it doesn't exist." The story always continues, so don't get stuck on a certain chapter, or page, or phrase, or word. For example, turn the word "no" to mean "not today." (Thanks, Arya Stark, for the gift that keeps on giving.) "No" can mean "not yet" or "not now." Don't get stuck in your failures. Flip the script. Let failure fuel you. The path to success is paved with failures. The more you fail ... the faster you'll succeed.

Step on those failures.
Don't let failures step on you.

Pave your path with purpose and riddle with failures. Declare it with determination, not doubt. Confidence is in **how** you convey your mindset, not the words you use. Release your interpretation of success so you can release your blockbuster of a movie.

Build your story with a solid foundation, one block at a time.

The ABC Building Blocks to a Blockbuster Life: Action. Belief. Courage.

A–Action. As I said earlier, a goal without action is just a dream. Small steps lead to big results. Taking inspired action is the key. Don't try to eat the whole apple at once. Try one bite at a time. You may not know how to start. But if you just begin, the path appears, paved with apple trees. See, once you plant the seed of what you want, roots start to form, and it sprouts into an abundant tree. I'm not sure how it works exactly, other than to say it's an energy thing.

Taking small steps in the direction of your inner compass sends a signal to the universe that you are ready to receive. Have you ever noticed that when you start to focus on something, all of a sudden you start meeting the right people, opportunities pop up, and pivotal connections are made? This gets the ball rolling, and the momentum just builds. That doesn't mean that you won't mess up. Inspired action is messy, riddled with failures. But failures are just detours to pivot you in the right direction. Remember, the more you fail the faster you're uncovering your road to success. So don't give up on your dreams. As Rumi says, "As you start to walk on the way, the way appears."

B–Belief. Believe it to achieve. Belief is the secret sauce to manifestation. If you can visualize a dream in your **mind's eye** it's meant for you. But some people need to wait and **see it realized**

before they believe it. They need proof, **validation**, before they are ready to take a leap of faith. But in fact, it's the very opposite. You need to **believe it before you see it.** Or as Wayne Dyer stated, "You'll see it when you believe it."

To do this you must see it in your mind before you become it. If you don't believe you can receive it, you are blocking yourself from achieving it. Figure out if this is stemming from outdated stories or feelings of unworthiness. Then clear those blocks that are coming in between you and your desires. This removes the mental, emotional, and spiritual clutter and makes space for your dreams to manifest. You need **belief** before you can visualize that dream transforming into a reality.

C–Courage. Courage is not the absence of fear. Courage is facing your fear and doing it anyway. Commit to your courage. Transmute the energy of fear into excitement. Did you know that both energies are the same vibration except one means you're holding your breath? Can you guess which one? What does that tell you? When you breathe deeply you breathe life into your work. You physically transmute the emotions permeating through your body from one of paralyzing fear to one of courageous excitement. Are the butterflies still there? Hell yes! But butterflies in your belly are simply indicators that you are metamorphosizing these energies. Literally transforming them within you. How cool is that?

In sum, here are the ABCs:

- Without **action**, we stay in analysis paralysis and don't move ahead. We stay in 'dreamland.'
- Without **belief** we hesitate, doubt ourselves, self-sabotage. We wager our worth.
- Without **courage** we don't follow through, we revert, we stay comfortably complacent. We make excuses as to why we are stuck.

Scan the QR code and watch my video.

https://lisastuart.com/qr-codes/4

Don't get stuck on drama. Change the channel.

The Genre of Drama

She's being such a drama queen.
He's the king of drama.
They have a flair for the dramatic.
It all sounds so ominous. So intense. So ... **dramatic** I dare say.
Think of a time when you watched a suspenseful movie. Or a tearjerker. Or a comedy. Did they elicit certain emotions from you? Chances are you immersed yourself in the storyline. Now it's time to immerse yourself in the most important storyline - **your life!**

Drama is just one genre to the movie of your life. Grab the popcorn, change the channel, and channel your dream role. Choose the movie you want to star in. Fire the previous director. Break out of your role as supporting actor. And declare:

I.T.'S. M.Y. M.O.V.I.E.

I'm
The
Star

Materializing
Yesterday's

Manifestations
Opportunities
Visualizations
Into
Existence

Visualize what opportunities you want in the future, and experience in present time what it feels like to materialize them into existence. **When you do this, you are essentially time traveling.** You create an experience in the present time, what it feels like to have something before you actually have it. It tricks your emotions into **believing** that you are **already** living that life. Which then sets the ball in motion to take inspired action. **How trippy is that?**

You see, our brains can be outsmarted. As I touched upon in **Chapter 5**, when we think of something it's like flipping a TV channel to stream a certain program. **And the way our minds are wired is such that it does not differentiate between something happening in real time or simply playing out in our minds.** The emotions emanating from our thoughts of the past or worries about the future are very real in the present time.

> Our minds don't know whether we are living these scenarios in the present, reliving the past, or envisioning the future.

This is a life hack for manifestation. But it can backfire. We can rehash the past by recreating scenarios in our minds like they are on **syndication**. We can also **future trip** about events that haven't occurred yet by concocting scenes of what can possibly go wrong. Our minds are simply auto wired to play out familiar scenarios that we are accustomed to whether or not they're happening in real time. Your mind is a **projection** – don't **project** a self-fulfilling prophecy, or a scenario only concocted in your mind.

The past is over. It only lingers in your thoughts to keep those situations alive. If you need to be a historian, write a memoir or a documentary.

The future hasn't come yet. Stop creating self-limiting stories around what will be. If you need to be a storyteller, write a book.

Be in the now. It's the only thing that exists at any given moment. You can feel **grateful** or **regretful** for where you are now.

Fun fact: if you cross off the same letters that both words share– **Grateful** and **Regretful** - you end up with 3 letters that do not overlap. **A.R.E.**

Which just confirms that where you currently **ARE** is directly related to your attitude. Is it an **attitude of gratitude**? Or are you **met with regret**? It's your choice.

Now take back control. Take back the **remote control** to your mind.

You can change the channel of your mind. You can flip the switch and stream a different life story. You can take back the remote control to your thoughts.

And here's how, **and why,** I did just that.

I'm never alone. I always have an incessant chatterbox within me. And no, I'm not talking about my six-year-old. I'm talking about the voice in my head that shows up without an invitation. The voice that clutters my thoughts and keeps me company even when I don't ask.

And my "little friend" usually shows up at the most inconvenient times, usually when I have a really good idea and set out to implement it. She is so kind that she independently runs an analysis for me as to why I shouldn't go for it. She even outlines every possible scenario of what could go wrong. My "little friend" loves to fuel my imposter syndrome.

Enter my "other voice" to chime in with gentle whispers from my soul guiding me towards my purpose. When this voice can outweigh the voice of my "little friend," then I am able to flip the narrative in my mind.

Flip "Who am I to do this?" to "Who am I NOT to do this! Imagine all the people I could help who would be deprived if I don't do this."

Flip "Look at everything that can go wrong!" to "Who cares if I mess up! Failure along the way to success is bound to happen. But think of all the great things that will come from this!"

Flip "It's already been done!" to "It's never been done MY way! I have my own uniqueness to share!"

Flip the narrative. Flip the script.
Flip the **drama magnet**.
Attract what you desire.

As I talked about in **Chapter 5**, you need a bouncer at your mind's door to kick that freeloading tenant of negative self-talk out of your abode and into the abyss. Put on your shoe of choice (i.e. stiletto, combat boot), **stomp on the rising fear, squish out the self-doubt, and kick those limiting beliefs to the curb.**

When you control the remote control to the station of your brain, you hold all the power in your hands.

Change the station. Use the Drama Remote.

Disrupting internal drama means controlling your drama so it doesn't control you. Think of your thoughts like a Rolodex of mind chatter to choose from. And if you're too young to know what a Rolodex is, think of your thought selection like it's an Amazon order. There are so many options to choose from. Don't scroll through your brain like you scroll through social media. Don't flip through your thoughts like you flip through the channels on TV.

Control your drama so it doesn't control you.

Grab the remote to your thoughts and tune your mind into the station that best serves you. When you change the programming of your mind, you declutter the cobwebs that have kept you stuck, and you make space to bring in **self-talk** that is self-loving. When your mind goes to the **what-ifs** or **worst-case scenarios,** I want you to flip the station to what you want to see in your mind's eye. Then live in the feeling as if you have it.

This is a universal concept for manifestation— tuning into the frequency or vibration of the very thing you are trying to attract into your life. The most common analogy going around is that if you are trying to listen to something on FM radio, you can't receive that signal if you are stuck on AM radio. Or if you want to binge-watch **White Lotus,** you need to make sure you are connected to the right streaming platform.

You've got to make sure you are tuned into the right station, the right signal, so that what you are seeking can find you.

Remember, where you are today is a product of where your energy was aligned in the past. To change the future, you must change your energy of today if it's low vibration. Whatever is going on in your life, remind yourself that your energy today will project your reality tomorrow.

Like a movie projected from your mind to a screen.

The present is simply a mirror reflecting where you've been so you can determine where you want to go.

Don't think that you are stuck in a certain "pre-programmed" life pattern that was created from someone else's script. At some point you need to ask yourself, **"Who am I living for?** Am I living to please others? Or am I living my authentic life, even if it deviates from what others **expect** from me?"

One of the biggest mistakes we can make in life is to live to please others at our own expense. I have raised my boys to find their passion and follow it, because at the end of the day, this is their life, not mine. I have told them countlessly, "I gave birth to you, but I do not own you. So go out in the world, fly, fall a million times, learn to get back up, try new things so you know what you like and what you don't like. But above all, find your passion and follow it. Because if you do what you love, you will love what you do, you will automatically be good at it and be successful!"

I will be telling my six-year-old daughter a very similar message. I will be teaching her to be true to herself. I will be showing her how to discern authenticity from **snake oil** gimmicks trying to dissuade her.

And such, I created a recipe called the ***Cobra Concoction***.

C.O.B.R.A.

C-onceive
O-pportunities
B-elieve
R-eceive
A-chieve

When you live like a **cobra** you become very clear about following your path, you believe in your goals, and you expect results. You disrupt what isn't working, and you ricochet off that disruption towards your vision, like a pickleball ricocheting off a racket. It doesn't matter how many times you ricochet to get back on course, as long as you keep your eye on the ball's destination and get energized by your desires.

Cobras are resilient. They shake off what doesn't work by shedding their old skin, to reveal a new, more vibrant skin beneath.

The Drama Diet

This is also a good way to figure out **what** your desires are by trying out different roads. When you try something new, just shake off what didn't serve you and move on with new vibrancy.

> Once you figure out what lights your fire ... then be the match. Literally and energetically.

You can achieve this literally by lighting yourself up to go after it. And energetically by aligning your vibration to match the frequency of what it feels like to have what you have yet to have. Tune into the correct station and just start.

But to start, you must **decide to start. Drama is the inability to decide.** Indecision will disrupt your peace. Disrupt the drama so it doesn't disrupt your peace.

Overthinking is a waste of energy. "Will they approve? Will they like it?" Who gives a sh*t. Will **you** approve? Will **you** like it? If you don't do something because overthinking has taken over your brain and you can't get off that train of thought ... you will regret the indecision. That's the key.

When the regret of not doing something outweighs the fear of going after it, that's when the scales of duality tip in your favor to go after your dream once you decide to do it!

There's hustle culture ... and then there's **Russell culture.** My husband, Russell, has a mantra: More Action, Less Talk. Or as I like to refer to it as the M.A.L.T. Recipe.

More. Action. Less. Talk. saves energy. It prevents you from having a meltdown like ice cream melting on a hot day. Stop dripping in drama and melt the drama away. When you preserve your energy and decide to take action, you prevent **brain drain** from overthinking.

And, you know I love my acronyms.

D.E.C.I.D.E.

D-ecision. **Make a decision to start.**
E-nergy. **Align your energy with the frequency of what you desire.**
C-ommit. **Commit to taking action towards your goals.**
I-nvest. **Invest in your beliefs, not your excuses.**
D-o. **Do something every day to propel yourself forward.**
E-xecute. **Without action, your goal is just a dream.**

Decide to be decisive.

Stay laser focused on where you are heading and not where you have been. Stay laser focused on your **why.** Keep those reasons up and front in the driver seat of your life. Put it on a bright neon Post-It Note on your rear-view mirror so every time you're tempted to look back on the life you're leaving, which may include people and situations that didn't serve you, you will be immediately reminded of what's up ahead of you with that bright Post-It glaring in front of your eyes.

So what will you put on your Post-It Notes? Write your goals, affirmations, mantras, dreams, steps, whatever it is that you need in the moment.

Put I.T. on your Post-it Notes.

I.T. — Intentional Thoughts.

Post **intentional thoughts** on your Post-it Notes. Our minds work the same way as computers in that we need to hone into our personal IT, **intentional thoughts,** so that we curate what we create, how we process, and where we store information. Use your IT to guide you on your journey to your destinations.

How fast or slow do you want to go? It's all about how you feel and what moves you where you need to heal.

M.P.H. — Meditation. Patience. Humor.

These are three key ingredients to keep you feeling good and not stressed. If you want to move faster, take more steps. Literally. Move forward in the direction of where you want to go. But always keep your eyes focused in the direction of your dreams. Don't get distracted by other people's lanes, or you'll end up off course.

Dare to desire. Energy flows where attention goes.

My 3D Blueprint
Dream it. Decide it. Do it.

Dream it– First, and foremost, you must get clear on what you **desire**
Decide it– Make a decision to commit, **no excuses**
Do it – Take action and **execute**

Now that you've got your **act together** to **act and not react** ... what's stopping you from moving confidently in the direction of your desires?

Fear.

But don't fear. Remember, if you wanna go fast, go alone. If you wanna go far, go together. You can bring yourself to the other side of fear. And I'll explain why it's okay to bring fear along with you for the journey.

Remember, once you learn how to **disrupt drama** - the first prong of **The Drama Diet Formula** - you become a master at **navigating life with fear**. The path to freedom is through fear.

So flip the page to learn how to flip the **drama magnet of fear.**

RECIPE

THE REALITY REARRANGER

Where does DESIRE RESIDE?
Is it a TUG in your GUT?
When you ADMIRE something in someone ...

You're saying 'I DREAM" of having it.

What do the above words in all caps have in common? They have the same letters. Just Rearranged.

>GUT-TUG
>DESIRE-RESIDE
>ADMIRE-I DREAM

- If we rearrange our thoughts ... we can rearrange our beliefs ... our choices ... our lives.
- Our visions become our reality.
- If you can Imagine it ... you can Create it.
- An Investment in your Imagination is an Investment in Yourself
- Invest in your Desires ... that's how dreams come true

*****

EXERCISE: Dream it. Decide it. Do it.

Do you have a dream buried deep inside of you? Do you feel like that dream has died? Let me tell you something...your dream is not dead. Your dream is still alive! Just the fact that you acknowledge there was a dream once upon a time means that a little seed is still sprouting waiting to be watered and nurtured into fulfillment.

So, what are you waiting for? Permission to go after it? The right timing? The perfect scenario?

THIS is your permission. THIS is the right timing. THIS is the perfect scenario. Because there's never going to be a 'perfect' time or scenario.

Just start. If you don't know how, here's some tools to help bring your dream to life:

Mark your calendar – Actually schedule onto your calendar a daily reminder to do something that propels you towards your goal. This could be an emoji, a phrase, or something as simple as 'take a step' or 'just do it'. Now mark your calendar with this for 30 days!

Take inspired action – Now that it's calendared, take action daily by doing something that brings you closer to your dream. If it's writing a book, just free write. If it's starting a business, do the research, or listen to a podcast. Find what inspires you and lean in that direction. And it could be as short as 10-30 minutes, but take that block of time each day. It doesn't have to be at the same time each day, but it has to be **every** day in order to show up consistently.

Find joy in the process– This should be fun! Whatever you are doing should light you up or be the catalyst for your passion. And your passion is what fuels your purpose. And your purpose is what you are inherently here to do. So don't take things so seriously... find the fun and play with it! Light some candles, play your favorite music, and revel in your environment as you **bring your dream to life!**

*****

DRAMA DIARY JOURNAL PROMPT

1: CLEAR - Name It to Tame It

When a negative thought hits, don't resist it – **write it down.** You can't heal what you won't name.

Prompt:
What is the exact thought that's looping in your mind right now? Examples:

- "I'm falling behind."
- "No one cares what I have to say."
- "I'm not good enough to do this."

Now ask:

- Is this 100% true?

- **Whose voice *is* this really?** (Is it even yours?)
- Just noticing begins to loosen its grip.

2: SHIFT - Flip the Frequency

This is the reframe — but it has to feel **believable**.
Use one of these "soft reframe bridges":

- "Even though I feel ___, I choose to believe ___."
- "I'm learning that ___ is not the truth — the truth is ___."
- "What if the opposite is just as true, or even more true?"

Example:

> "Even though I feel like I'm falling behind,
> I choose to believe I'm right on time for **my** path."

The brain starts creating new grooves instead of running the old track.

3: REWIRE - Anchor the New Truth in Your Body

Now make it **real** with a short embodiment practice. Choose one:

1. **Say it out loud** in the mirror, looking into your eyes.
2. **Write it on a sticky Post-It Note** and put it where you'll see it daily.

Take one tiny, aligned action that proves the new belief.

Example:

If your reframe is: "My voice matters," send a text, post, or note that shares something true. **Action is the cement that locks in belief.**

EXAMPLE IN ACTION:

Negative Thought: "I'll never be successful."
Clear: That's fear talking. It's not a fact.

Shift: "Even though I'm scared, I choose to believe success is unfolding for me one step at a time."
Rewire: I breathe deeply, stand up taller, and send one pitch/email/post with that belief in my heart.

7

FRIENDING FEAR

The biggest blocker to our dreams

> ### Case Law: *Fear vs. Love*
>
> In any given moment, we can tap into the energy of fear or the energy of love. Although both energies are always there competing for attention, *like sibling rivalry*, only one energy prevails at any given time. The law of duality defines the contrast between love and fear. We cannot recognize one without the other. We need the stark contrast to define the competing energy. Which of these energies that you're dancing with will take the lead on the dance floor of life? And the verdict is ... only *you* can decide

Fear: The biggest blocker to dreams, the biggest deterrent to forward movement, the loudest voice in people's heads, the strongest emotion that can manifest symptoms making you feel physically ill. They don't use the expression *fear rears its ugly head* for nothing.

But ... what if we beautify fear, destigmatize its scariness, dress it up in relatable outfits and, yes, *even friend it*. What do you think will happen?

Well, let's play around with fear and find out.

> Without taking courageous steps and facing my biggest fears, I would still be the same stuck person that watched others realize their dreams from the sidelines.

Does this sound like you? How many times have you sat on the bench during the game of your life, watching other people participate? Win? Go after their goals and score? Did you sit on the sidelines paralyzed by fear? Not feeling ready enough to play the game? Not feeling *worthy* enough to jump in? No more. This is your time.

If not now, *when*? If not you, *who*?

In the last chapter, we talked about how you are no longer playing a supporting role in the movie of your life. As the main character, the protagonist of your story, you almost have no choice *but* to play big and bold.

You owe it to your younger self, who is cheering you on by showing you how far you've come.

You owe it to your older self who is waiting for you to transform into the person they know you can become.

Yet sandwiched in the middle of both can feel claustrophobic as fear starts to trickle in, suffocating the air out of your comfort zone.

Think about it. Are you really going to let a little four-letter word hold you back? Imagine that. A tiny word holding so much power over you. Over your decisions, your actions, your life.

What exactly is Fear?

It's anything that is holding you back. Fear could be worry that consumes you. Regret that eats away at you. Anxiety about judgment, ridicule, and rejection. The *what ifs … what if they don't accept me … what if it doesn't work … what if I make a royal fool of myself*. My personal belief is that fear, at its core, is simply the *uncertainty of the unknown.*

> It's the *fear* of not being in control of the result of a situation that keeps us perpetuated in the cycle of fear.

So I flip the magnet on fear.

I love fear. I think it is one of the most important driving forces in our lives. Anytime I feel fearful, I know I am playing it safe. When my fear barometer starts to rise, I know it's time to level up. Time to have fun with fear. Yep, you heard me right. It's like a game of facing your demons at each level, learning to overcome them so you can level up. And although each level may feel more challenging than the last, you've accumulated resources on your journey to prepare you.

But I didn't always love fear. I used to *fear* fear. In fact, I was probably one of **the** most fear-consumed people. I let fear dictate and even determine 85% of my life.

Did you know that studies reveal that approximately 90% of fears don't come true? That means so much time is wasted on worrying about things that never happen. So, essentially, our body is in a state of fight or flight 90% of the time for things that are not real.

And that's what F.E.A.R. is - False Evidence Appearing Real

Fear is just an illusion. It doesn't exist because it's not real. The only thing that's real is the present moment. The past is over; it no longer exists. It can't haunt you unless you allow it to. Don't recreate it in the present moment by bringing up past scenarios in your mind's eye and causing emotional chaos as if you're living it now.

> Disclaimer: I am in no way referring to past fears that are deeply rooted in trauma or any other life-altering event. I don't touch trauma. I only dabble in drama. I am also not talking about life-threatening fears. Only the ones that seem threatening because they loom in our minds and falsely pervade our sense of security.

Remember, your mind can't distinguish between what you are experiencing in real time vs. your thoughts about a past or future event, so it instinctively signals to the body to go into anxiety mode. Don't future trip about things that haven't happened yet. Your life is your movie, and you hold the pen to your script.

When I took pen to paper to rewrite the narrative of my life, I had to learn to write through F.E.A.R. – Face Everything And Rise – or I would fall to my default mode of –F*ck Everything And Run. See, it's all about perspective. And it's all about the acronym. Which one *you* choose to adopt and *adapt* to the story of your life.

The goal is to go from F.E.A.R. to Freedom.

F.E.A.R. leads to a Free. Expressive. Authentic. Reality.

When you allow yourself the **F**reedom to **E**xpress yourself, **A**ccept what is, and **R**elease resistance, you will ultimately unshackle yourself from the chains of **FEAR** and allow freedom to permeate throughout your life. Stop giving so much power to fear. What's the worst that can happen?

My motto for many years was "*Hope for the best but expect the worst.*" That was my self-preservation safety net of setting myself up for disappointment so that when things ultimately went wrong, I wouldn't be ... disappointed. Messed up, isn't it? I justified that if I'd hope for the best and expected the worst then I was covered on both ends.

But bookending my life left the pages in the middle empty.

When I was suffering all those years with physical ailments, I would literally walk into my doctors' office and say *give it to me straight*. Then I'd ramble on about the worst-case scenario I researched about my symptoms on the internet. I had at least three different doctors who banned me from WebMD back in the day! *True story*.

The truth is, everything I had was fixable, reversible, curable. The hardest part to fix, though was my mindset. I had to reset my thinking about fear.

> Fear is the gateway to freedom.
> It's the GPS of where we need to go
> versus where we think it's safe to go.

Again, I am not referring to any life-threatening situation that can cause any permanent damage. I am not talking about trauma, or grief, or the serious threat that can harm someone's life. I am talking about drama – the fear of the unknown, fear of failure, fear of success, fear of visibility, fear of judgment, fear of other's opinions, fear of rejection, fear of appearances, fear of embarrassment, fear of imposter syndrome, fear of unworthiness, fear of finishing, [insert your fear flavor of the day.] You get the picture.

And it's just a picture. *The only place it exists is in our minds.*

I hear you asking, "How come we are never done with losing fear? Why does fear continually show up in our lives, no matter how many times we overcome it?"

Have you ever noticed that once you finally overcame one fear and shot up the ladder to accomplish your goals, a new set of fears crept in? Maybe it's the thought of leveling up. Maybe it's a brand-new endeavor you are taking on. Maybe it's in an area that is out of your wheelhouse, and you are feeling inadequate, and a whole load of impostor syndrome gets dumped on you. Whatever the case may be, know that everyone must start somewhere. Read that again. *Everyone* had to start somewhere. And with each new venture, we must start over and over.

I was once in an online speaking room with Greg Louganis, who was talking about how he pivoted to a very different venture than his Olympic diving days. And I had the opportunity to ask him how he found the courage to start something outside his comfort zone after he had already climbed, *or dove*, to the top with a gold medal. His answer still resonates clearly. He said, and I paraphrase, "When

I have to climb a new ladder from the bottom rung, I transmute the energy of fear into courageous excitement, and it fuels me."

Game changer.

Your fear is in direct relation to your desire.

Think of the scales of justice in terms of a scale of life. When you weigh one option over the other – your desire being on one scale and fear being on the other – which energy tips the scale in your favor? My job as a lawyer is to tip the scale in favor of my client. I'm going for the win. Solutions require one side to prevail – unless you mediate and settle the case, and even then, it's a give-and-take to harmonize both sides.

In the scale of life, when the competing energies of desire and fear are each elevated, you have to ask yourself, *How badly do I want it?* When the regret of not going after it outweighs the fear of doing it, that's when the scale tips in your favor. And when the fear starts to dissipate, lightening the load, the scale tips even more in your favor.

And you don't need to start at the bottom rung each time you begin a new venture. *You can literally traverse laterally.* How? By bringing your experience with you. Everything you have done up to this point has set you up for success for the next chapter. Especially the failures. It taught you what not to do, how to take rejection and pivot, and how to keep forging ahead. Use that experience as a safety net when traveling up the ladder. Lose the baggage of doubts to lighten the load. Uncuff the shackles of anxiety to free your climb. Trust the process of the unknown.

> When you don't start at the bottom rung but traverse to another ladder mid-air, your past experiences serve as your safety net.

It takes dedication and commitment. Tons of failure. Laser focus. A willingness to keep going. It's often not the smartest or the most talented people that typically make it to the top; *It's the ones who never quit*, who never give up on themselves, who believe so fiercely in where they are going that they take one tiny step at a time, often at a painstakingly slow speed, usually slipping down a few rungs, clinging onto their dreams with sweaty palms. No one sees the blood, sweat, and tears it took to become an overnight success. As my brilliant father always said, *a disciplined, ambitious, and dedicated work ethic is a recipe for success in your craft.*

D.A.D. - Disciplined. Ambitious. Dedicated. *Thanks Dad*.

Imagine a time when you were filled with fear. So much so that anytime you wanted to go after your dreams, you were frozen in fear, stuck in analysis paralysis with all the thoughts racing through your mind of everything that could go wrong. Those thoughts are your mind's way of protecting you. The subconscious mind protects you *from rejection* so that it could save you from future failure, embarrassment, judgment, etc. And the more the thoughts swirled around like a chaotic frenzy in your brain, the more you *believed* that the storm was real. You may have experienced a physical response to those thoughts – anything from sweaty palms to a gut-wrenching knife in your stomach, to a full-on panic attack, leaving you with a racing heart and anxiety.

Whatever the case, was it enough to dissuade you from going forward with your dreams? I'm going to guess that for a bunch of you, it was. And for others, it didn't deter you, but it attached a heavy load of doubt, anxiety, fear, second-guessing, or overthinking to your endeavor. And that may have been enough for you to give up on your dream, or at the very least to pause it. Sound about right?

But don't worry, there is a way to flip the fear.

I'll tell you a little secret. I was terrified to start this journey. I even created a separate social media account because I didn't want to be judged by people. And I figured, *hey, if it didn't work out, then I'm no worse off. I'll just delete the account, and no one needs to know*. I started getting excited about posting. Having written poetry, lyrics, and inspirational quotes my whole life, I began to think that social media was created just for me!

So, I let loose, posting daily until one day, someone I knew from my *other* life, aka, my real life, started following me. Then another. And another. And instead of being excited for getting up to 50 followers (no shame in starting from scratch), I felt that old familiar feeling of dread wash all over me. What will they think? Maybe I should hold back. All 50 sets of eyes are on me. *I'm exposed.* They'll call me out for the impostor that I am. Yes…all those thoughts raced through my brain. But I gave myself a moment to acknowledge my analysis paralysis, and then I drew in a deep breath (or ten), exhaled, and charged ahead (albeit sweating droplets of fear along the way).

During that process, I was continually challenged. I posted videos. Did live postings. Created reels. And with each new "thing" that I did, I would come up against my old friend – fear. She and I did a dance teetering on the edge of giving up, so I decided to challenge myself. Instead of giving up, I was going to give up something that was holding me back. Just for a month.

The idea behind it was that it would give my mind a break from overthinking, my emotions a break from over-stressing, and my body a break from experiencing the tense sensations resulting from the first two. And the premise was that if I could give myself permission for just one month to give up, i.e., *fear of visibility*, then every time I was going to post a video and hesitated, I had a *get-out-of-jail-free* card that said *nope, not today*. And it instantly gave me permission to post fear-free. For real. It worked.

It provided a safe space within the parameters of a month to be free. I like a good challenge, and I like to win so my hungry side outweighed my fearful side. The result? I was able to be as creative as I chose with no filter. So freeing.

And the reason for giving it up for a month was because I thought that if I could do something for roughly 30 days, then what would stop me from continuing it after? I would tell myself, *if I really hated giving up fear of visibility for a month, then come next month, I'll go back to it.* Chances were in my favor that I wouldn't.

Even if I slipped, I would have built up the tools to get back on the proverbial wagon and *run over that fear*.

Each month I would choose a new fear to give up. And as each month passed, I added something new to the *"give up"* pile, and it accumulated over time. I ended up with a repertoire of outdated habits and beliefs that no longer served me. I was able to move through fear and show up online. I was able to authentically speak about topics people may not have expected from me without letting the fear of judgment get in the way. I was able to implement the dreams in my mind and manifest them to a tangible reality. Such as this book. How cool is that?

It didn't mean that the fear wasn't there. But rather, the energy of love was stronger. And as I ventured out into the world of visibility despite my fear, I had an epiphany. *You can't actually die of embarrassment.* But maybe a *death of the ego* is not a bad thing. Alchemize my embarrassed, burning cheeks to melt my ego. Watch my fears dissipate in a puddle of ego-driven thoughts, then mold that into love-based emotions.

One of my favorite lyrics I've ever written is:

> "When you lose your fear, you've got nothing left to lose."

Now I realize we can never truly lose fear, nor should we, because it serves as an emotional compass to where we need to level up. But – here's the thing. We need to lose fear as the driving force of our life, stick it in the back seat, and take control of the steering wheel of our life.

Losing your fear doesn't mean it will disappear. It means that your fear won't control you. To loosen its grip on you requires that you move through the fear.

In **Chapter 2** we touched upon the **3F Formula for Fear** –*Face it. Feel it. Free it.* Now let's delve into it.

Face it. Feel it. Free it.

FACE IT

Acknowledge it. Your old stories will stick in your mind. Acknowledge that it's hard to face fear. It is so much easier to make excuses for why we are staying comfortable in our chaos. Why we don't want to ruffle any feathers. Why we resist change.

Identify what limiting beliefs are coming up for you. When we ignore the root of our resistance, it doesn't just disappear. It festers silently within us, blocking our power to flow. When we dare to dive deep and acknowledge the uncomfortable aspects of ourselves, that's when inner change begins.

- In order to grow, we need to change.
- In order to change, we need to evolve.
- In order to evolve, we need to get uncomfortable.
- In order to get uncomfortable, we need to release resistance.

Imagine this. Resistance is like pushing against a door, so it doesn't open. You're essentially holding the door to your dreams closed. You believe that the **door of drama** has all sorts of scary things looming on the other side. When you release that resistance, you allow the door to open in its own time.

Friending Fear

> # Releasing the resistance is the key to unlocking the door of drama.

What's behind the door is a pathway to your destination, paved with opportunities that seem to appear out of thin air. I'm always confident that what we want, wants us, that when we send out an order to the universe, the universe always responds – either with what we want, or something better. And sometimes this is hard to see because it may come in the form of a rejection. But rejection is typically protection from the universe, and an opportunity to pivot to something we may not have considered before.

As one door slams shut, it causes such a force as to have another door fly open.

The trick is to keep on going.

But most people give up because they don't see any instant manifestation, and so their belief systems solidify their reality. You see, the method of delivery is directly related to the frequency of the request. And by *frequency*, I'm not referring to the number of times the desire is requested. I'm referring to the energetic vibration surrounding the request. I like to set my intention and let it be. *Set it and forget it.*

Much like if you have stocks and don't watch the fluctuations of the market on a daily basis but HODL– hold on for dear life. With faith, of course. Chances are that you will have a good rate of return. And in situations where you don't, maybe there's a good opportunity to cut your losses and invest elsewhere. There is no shortage of abundance, but there seems to be a shortage of patience and perseverance in our world. The era of instant gratification has killed progress.

But, if you are patient and confident, and set your intention with aligned energy that you are worthy of obtaining your desires, the faster they come. So, depending on your frequency, the delivery method could feel like it's coming by jet plane, by speed train, by car, by bicycle, or via snail mail. The boomerang effect of delivery is determined by your heart, mind, and soul.

Think of it like this. You want something but are afraid that *you'll never get it, you don't deserve it, you'll be completely out of your comfort zone, you'll end up failing, it's too hard to complete (current situation with me about finishing this book!)*

On one side of the door lies our desire. On the other side of the door lies the object of that desire trying to reach us. And in between there's a veil of fear separating the two. Have you ever felt that you were so close to obtaining your dream that you could just reach out and touch it? Or taste it? Or grab it? But then fear pops into your ego and you hesitate – just enough – to slow that momentum down or throw you off kilter. And now the veil between you and your dreams has thickened, further distancing you from your dreams.

You have two choices. Retreat. Or **face your fear.**

The more you face your fear, the thinner the veil gets. Until the **veil of resistance** becomes translucent. It's like a mirror reflecting back to you both your *desire* and your *dread*.

And the only way *to* your desire is *through* your fear. Stare into that reflection, face what you're fleeing, reach out and **feel your fear**.

Scan this QR code to watch my video.

https://lisastuart.com/qr-codes/5

FEEL IT

Address it. This is the sticky part that is so uncomfortable, when we sit in the muck and really feel what it is that's causing us to feel scared, worried, guilty, envious, small, or unworthy. Don't judge what's coming up for you. Just sit with it. Allow yourself to feel it like the *Indiana Jones* boulder of doom pummeling over you. Feel the pressure compress you and decompress you. Let it run through your body. The uncomfortable feeling of letting things be. The in between is where we need to breathe through it, move through it, dance, cry, and even laugh. We know that we must honor our emotions so they can move through us. If they stay within us, they will amplify. This is how we get to the *release*.

Emotions of non-threatening fear can trigger a cascade of physiological bodily reactions. Remember, scientifically, it takes 90 seconds for the chemical response of an emotion to run its course through your body. This initial surge of chemicals creates the physiological experience of an emotion. After the peak, the neurotransmitters involved in the emotional response will start to dissipate if not actively sustained by further thoughts or reactions. Any excess emotional response is due to the person choosing to stay in the emotional loop.

To simplify, an E-motion—Energy in motion— is only supposed to live in our emotional response system for roughly 90 seconds. But it's we who cling onto those emotions for dear life, as if they're some type of life raft. This emphasizes the power of addressing our emotional loops so that we can choose to manage our emotional responses.

So while we may not have control over the initial physiological reaction to a stimulus, we do have the power to control our sustained emotional response to a significant degree. This doesn't mean that we can automatically feel happy after we are triggered. It just means that we can embrace the uncomfortable response

The Drama Diet

and let it run through our veins. The emotions running through our veins essentially cleanse our system like an IV cocktail at your favorite med spa.

For example, if someone wronged you, it doesn't mean that you don't have a right to feel hurt. You can acknowledge it without the need to hold onto it. If there's a way of releasing it and being able to observe it knowing that the situation sucks, but not letting it permeate through you— you can just recognize it, acknowledge it, honor it, and be neutral.

Here's an exercise. Next time you face your fear and feel that impending dread ... give yourself 90 seconds. Set a timer. If you need more time, give it to yourself— even 24 hours. No judgment, shame, or guilt included. But promise yourself that once that timer goes off ... times up! And let it go. Like a helium balloon.

Here's another exercise. I want you to take a deep breath and imagine that whatever fear you are feeling, you are exhaling into a balloon. Breathe all your fear into that balloon, let it go, and watch it float up in the sky. Keep watching for 90 seconds, and as it rises, I want you to *feel* yourself getting lighter and airier. Then when the 90 seconds is up, I want you to watch that fear filled balloon pop. And with it, your emotion dissipates with the popped balloon.

If you give something your *attention*, it grows. If you ignore something, it festers. If you *address* something, it shrinks.

FREE IT

Accept it. Now the fun part. Let it go. Release it into the ether. Shake it off. You don't need it anymore. It's done its job, but it's not going to get in your way anymore. You've acknowledged it, now set it free. Once you decide to work through fear and leave it in the past, you can focus on the present moment without distraction.

Holding onto the fear is like wanting to replay a scary movie scene in your head on repeat. Holding onto the hurt, the guilt, the shame, the regret, anything that will hold you back is doing just that ... *holding you back.* You deserve more. Let go of the fear, let go of the drama. Release it. Use the **drama remote** and flip the station.

Your body can release it by feeling through that energy and moving that E-motion –*Energy in motion*– through you by any of the following modalities: movement, breathwork, journaling, walking, ice bath, hot yoga, singing, dancing, even screaming if that works.

And if you still can't shake that feeling, I have a quick movement tip that may help. Movement helps move that E-motion–*Energy in motion*– through and out your body.

Be like an Etch A Sketch. Do you remember that toy? You would draw something on it, and when you wanted to start over, you would literally shake the toy until the writing disappeared. Like new. Like it never existed.

Similarly, you can shake away the illusion of what's holding you back and keeping you stuck. Shrug off feelings of unworthiness, scarcity, and smallness. Let the past that no longer serves you drip off of you like raindrops on a raincoat. Let it go and don't look back. One of my favorite quotes is, *don't look back unless it's to check out your ass in the mirror.*

> Face forward. Face the fear. Move to it ... through it ... and past it.

This applies to relationships as well. If someone in your life is not treating you the way you deserve to be treated, or the way you *desire* to be treated, then you have to face your fear and address it head-on. Not only with the other person, but with yourself as well. Look yourself in the mirror straight in the eye, like a deer in headlights, and reflect the truth of what you need and why.

For example, if you feel like your partner, a friend, or a family member is not stepping up or does not have your back the way you expect them to, this may bring up feelings of anger, sadness, and resentment, causing you to spiral down a deep emotional and mental path. I'm no therapist, but a conversation with this person is warranted to prevent you from developing an ulcer.

Before you clear the air, you should first clear the air with yourself by implementing the 3 F Formula for Fear.

3 F Formula for Fear

First, **face** the fact that maybe the solid relationship is ungluing at the seams. That may make you feel that you're not in control. But facing the facts is vital to owning the situation.

Next, **feel** the pain. Don't ignore it, address it. Notice how it feels to finally express what you need to rather than suppress your feelings out of fear.

Then **free** it. Let it go. Tell yourself that you've given yourself a chance to acknowledge and address the impending conversation you need to have, but now you are ready to have that much needed talk with resolve in your heart to find a solution, rather than a lump in your throat blocking the words from coming out.

Recap:

- Face it. Acknowledge it and be aware of its existence.
- Feel it. Address it. This is not the same as giving it your attention. Attention makes it grow. Addressing it makes it shrink.
- Free it. – Accept it – accepting it is key to forgiving and releasing it.

Face it. Feel it. Free it.

But why stop at 3 F's? There's so much more fun we can have with fear. Here's a fourth F:

FLIP IT

Flip the narrative. Instead of imagining that fear is consuming you, imagine that these blocks of fear blocking your path to peace can disintegrate. Imagine you're pummeling over these blocks, and they evaporate into a cloud of dust, illuminating where you need to travel. But instead of this fear deterring your journey, you simply ride over the fear, leaving tire tracks of fear highlighting where you've been and what you've overcome.

Here is the fifth F, all five fingers of your hand so you can high-five yourself á la Mel Robbins for conquering fear.

FRIEND IT

You may face it, feel it, and free it, and even flip it ... using a certain finger. But your fear may be like that friend that just doesn't get the message that you are busy right now and that you want alone time. It shows up uninvited, usually at the worst possible time, and demands your attention.

In those situations, *give fear your attention*. Yes, you heard me right. Pay attention to fear. Make fear your friend. Bring it along on your journey, but stick it in the back seat. Don't let it take the wheel but *do* ask it for directions. It will lead you straight into what it is that you are resisting. It will guide you to where you need to go when you are trying to avoid going there.

When you *navigate with fear*, you need to move in the direction of fear. And through the fear. Free the fear by bringing it into the light with you. But as I said, stick it in the back seat. Oh, don't be fooled, it'll get loud and pesky, like a backseat driver from your worst nightmare. But you can drown out that noise by leading with love and tuning it out. Tune into a good station. Remember, you can tune into the vibration of love at any time. Just tune your vibration station to the frequency that serves you.

So next time fear rises up to block you, ask it "Are you going to

The Drama Diet

hold my hand as I move forward? Are you coming on this ride with me? Because whether you are or not, I'm going ahead...."

Chances are high that your fear will try to deter you, but once it sees your power and strength to charge ahead *despite the fear*, it will ultimately surrender and join you. Sure, it will think the ride is fun. Initially. But guaranteed, it will get bored at some point, so that it can't work its magic on you, and it will want to go home. Until your next "play date" together, that is.

Embrace the expression, *keep your friends close, and your enemies closer*. Don't make fear a foe. Make fear a friend. And give it a name.

Meet Felicia. The name I gave to my fear-mongering mean girl. Randomly (or not) another F name. I named Felicia as my alter ego because, well, I was told that I was almost named Felicia. So, I consider Felicia to be the part of me that never came to fruition, other than tormenting me with her mean girl ways. I let her come along with me for my wild rides. But I never let her take the steering wheel. Or choose the music we listen to in the car. Remember, music is energy, and in any given moment, we can lean into love or lean into fear.

> Keep a tight eye on fear,
> but never let it steer.

Fun trick. Next time your alter ego comes to talk you out of something because of fear, name it. Once you attach a name to it, you can separate that part of you from your true self. For example, when fear-provoking thoughts arise in me, it helps to say.

"Oh, hi Felicia. Thanks for the warning, but I'll let you worry about that as I focus on my goals."

Or "Oh hey Felicia. It's only you who's bringing those thoughts to the surface. No, thank you. I'm good."

Or simply "Bye Felicia." (Couldn't resist. Walked right into that one.)

It sounds silly, but trust me, once you disassociate fearful thoughts and compartmentalize them as the alter ego trying to protect you from rejection or humility or failure, you can easily identify where the fear is rising from and transmute that energy into courage. Remember, courage is acknowledging the fear but doing it anyway.

One trick I used years back is to take a Post-it Note and either write the name of your "ego voice" on it or draw a picture of what you believe that drama-inducing voice looks like. Then place it where you work, on your laptop, in your car, or on your bathroom mirror. Wherever you feel you need it. And when a drama-inducing thought comes up, look at the Post-it Note and have a catch-all phrase ready, such as "You handle this. I don't have time for drama now." "Oh, it's only you again." Or "You're still in time out." Whatever works. And crazy enough, it does.

I also dabbled with a sixth F.

F*CK IT

But it's not what you think. I'm not saying f*ck fear as a way to ignore it, because I believe we need to integrate fear into our lives to evolve and elevate. What I mean is f*ck it as in *who cares*. Who gives a flying F if you fail or F up, or something goes wrong on your journey? You ultimately will, and guess what, you should!

Success isn't a magic unicorn that comes without failure. You should be failing, flailing, fumbling, fixing, and figuring things out along the way. Yes, more F words. You should have fun, have faith, and feel good as you take messy, inspired action. Next time fear rises up like bile leaving a nasty taste in your mouth ... who really gives a f*ck? It's inevitable. To evolve, you must let fear guide you in the direction you *fear* to go. Fear is your internal GPS. Digest the fear and let it fuel you. Turn it to your advantage and flip all your fear-driven desires to excitement as it navigates you on your journey.

Let Fear Fuel You.

Even if it means you proceed toward your dreams one baby step at a time. When new fears start to creep in, you can creep your way to success. And it does take a minute.

When you C.R.E.E.P. you Create. Rise. Experiment. Evolve. Pivot.

As you should. That's the roadmap to freedom. Through the fear. To go *from fear to freedom*, you need to embrace whatever it is you are afraid of. As the adage goes, *everything is on the other side of fear.*

This is true, but most people don't know *how* to get through to the other side of fear without risking some emotional or mental bruising along the way.

You see, so far, we have been focusing on disrupting the drama to learn how to *navigate with fear.* The next two chapters deal with *deflating drama*, which teaches you how to *lead with love.* This requires facing your shadows and deflating them so you can walk through the door of drama, learning how to clear the cobwebs ingrained in you and around you, and get clear on why they exist.

Now that's not saying you won't be subjected to some spiritual scrapes. But once you learn how to flip the magnet and lean into love, you can take the lead in the **Drama Dance**. Do a spiritual tango and dip your fears to the back seat of your car, where it can travel with you, but you are watching fear from the rearview mirror, rather than through the windshield. It's behind you, fueling you like a jetpack.

We know that with the dance of duality, we need to dance with fear but lead with love. And by leaning into love, we are automatically *leaning away from fear.* The question still remains, though, *what are we truly afraid of?* Where is the **source** of our fear? How do you *lead with love?*

We are going to take a deep dive into this in the next chapter. Let's dive in.

RECIPE

Fear Fondue

Courage is infusing excitement into fear. Here's the recipe.

- Transmute fear to excitement:
- Inhale fear
- Exhale love
- A dash of courage
- A big breath in of faith
- A pinch of reality that if you don't go after your dreams you will suffer regret
- A glimpse of what's on the other side of fear
- Blend with excitement and proceed with confidence

*****

EXERCISE: Fear Flavor of the Month

Give up something each month. Example: fear of judgment, fear of failure, fear of visibility, fear of trusting your gut. And these are cute reminders that can help you each month. Put an emoji on your calendar daily for the month. Stick Post-It Notes on your mirror. Choose it as your password for your computer.

Practice daily for 30 days. Give yourself permission to be **fear free** for whatever it is you choose. For example, if you chose fear of trusting your gut, then anytime doubt rises up at the thought of following your instincts, shove it aside to revisit at the end of the 30 days. But for today, you are going with your gut. Then, at the end of the 30 days you can see how many "doubt days" you set aside to revisit, if they are still there. Chances are that you've moved past them. Now it's time to choose another fear to give up for the next month. Whatever flavor of fear for the month you choose, stick with it. Oh, and the fear flavors from the previous months ... you can decide if you still want to stay fear free on those or go back to living with those fears. What will you decide?

Tag me on social media with the hastag #fearflavor and let me know what fear flavor of the month you are giving up and how it's working out for you. I'd love to support you on your quest from fear to freedom.

*****

DRAMA DIARY JOURNAL PROMPT

Release the 3 P's: Perfectionism. People Pleasing. Procrastination.

- What is keeping you stuck in perfectionism?
- What is keeping you on the people-pleasing loop?
- What have you been procrastinating on?

Replace them with these 3 P's: Progress. Productivity. Pleasure.

- What can you do daily to track your progress?
- What can you take intentional action on to move the needle on productivity?
- What can you do for yourself that feeds you pleasure?

Release. Replace. Repeat.

8

DEFLATE PART 1

The Deep Dissolve

> **Case Law: *Dig Deep vs. Dive Deep***
>
> Ever notice that these terms are used interchangeably? But if you really dig deep or dive deep, you'll see that they are on opposite sides of the scale. Law of duality. When you *dig* deep, it implies that you've hit a hard patch and have some shoveling to do to remove the blockage. When you *dive* deep it feels smooth, like effortlessly gliding into water. Keep in mind while doing your inner work to differentiate between digging deep and diving deep. Digging deep indicates you need to excavate whatever is blocking the path to your inner peace, desires, or true self. Once cleared, you can dive deep fluidly and explore your true self freely like an underwater scuba diver. Let's dive in.

DEFLATE

Welcome to the second prong of the 3D Drama Diet Formula. **Deflate.**

Remember the hand movements? Here's a QR code in case you need a refresher.

The Drama Diet

https://lisastuart.com/qr-codes/6

Deflate means to squeeze all the air out of the drama you just disrupted that still wants to grab your attention.

You may ask, "But if I've disrupted it, then why does it come back for more?"

It's like those pesky ants that seem to appear in your kitchen from nowhere. That no matter how many times you spray, more keep coming. So what should you do?

- Determine the problem source.
- Dissolve the problem.
- Deflate the drama.

This chapter deals with the first prong of **deflate – to determine the problem source.** Where are the ants coming from? Where is the drama originating? Where is the judgment, victimhood, or fear stemming from? To diminish these issues, you need to understand the source and determine how deep it runs within you. Once you *determine* this, you can *dissolve* it at the source. **Chapter 9** deals with dissolving and resolving problems so you can *lead with love*.

> **Disrupt drama** = *navigate with fear.*
> **Deflate drama** = *lead with love.*

Disrupting drama only blocks the drama from getting in. Where does that energy go? It doesn't disappear, as energy can neither be created nor destroyed. It can only be transformed into something else. Therefore, it's important to understand where the drama originated from so you can transmute it from the energy source.

Deflating drama gets to the source of why you keep attracting it. Where is it emanating from? You must find the cage of what's keeping you trapped and stuck in fear mode. Once you pinpoint this, you can deflate the drama like a pin deflating a balloon. Squeeze all the air out and let it go. Don't hold onto anything that's holding you down. Release what's weighing you down.

My grandmother always said, "Never burden your conscience."

To piggyback on this, "When you have a clear mind and heart, and are in harmony with yourself, your beauty comes out in your face," says my mom who happens to have the most beautiful face. She also says "Be harmonious and happy with what you have. You can't wrinkle when you smile."

I am fortunate to come from a long line of strong, wise, and beautiful women. Beautiful inside and out. That's because they have taught me the art of letting things go. Yes, it's an art, and my mom happens to be an amazing artist who has metaphorically painted a picture of how to live a harmonious life despite strife.

Life has strife.

When things weigh you down with a heavy heart, guilt or regret, or you feel scared to tell somebody the truth, or you can't be honest with yourself about what you truly want— it's an indicator that you have not dealt with it. Once you deal with that unpacked baggage, it will lighten your load.

Trust yourself to open up and be real with yourself. When you hit a hard patch, roll up your sleeves and start digging through the drama.

Once you clear the *route* to get to the *root*, you can take a drama dive.

Grow from within. This is essential to evolve and transform.

Just like a tree. When you gaze upon nature's beauty and take in the majestic height of a tree with its trunk and branches spread wide, do you ever think about what that tree looks like beneath the surface? In the cold, dark soil? When you plant a tree, the seeds are buried in darkness, forced to grow roots to support the foundation of the tree before it emerges above, almost a mirror image of each other.

When a tree seed germinates, it sprouts a root that anchors into the ground. This ensures both stability and nourishment for the vital growth of the tree. As the roots grow longer downward, it derives its energy to expand from the soil's nutrients. When the tree is ready to grow upwards, nutrients supplied from the roots enable the tree's growth above, while the roots below expand to support it. This sustains the balance above and below, allowing the tree to thrive with a solid foundation.

As below, so above: A reflection of each other. Just as we are. What's buried dark within the recesses of our soul is reflected in our outer world. If we don't cultivate a healthy inner core, it seeps into our life.

Speaking of trees, I'm going to go out on a limb and disclose something very personal. There was a moment where I started shedding hair. More than normal. Was it stress? Perimenopause? Post COVID symptoms? All of the above? A hybrid? Who knows. But what I do know is to get to the source of the shedding I had to get to the root of my hair – *literally*. Was the follicle strong enough to support growth? Was my hair able to thrive in a healthy scalp environment? And spiritually – what was I trying to shed from my life? What did I need to let go of? What was not aligning with my desires? Sometimes we cling onto things long after their shelf life expires in hopes of keeping things consistent. Comfortable. Then life comes in and says "Nope. This isn't working. You need to release it."

Hair's the truth. (I couldn't resist.) But seriously, here's what I learned throughout this shedding process. When the hair follicle starts to contract, it can't provide a solid foundation for healthy hair to grow. In contrast, when the follicle expands, it creates nourishment for sustainable hair growth.

Contraction and Expansion. The ebb and flow of life. The law of duality. What are we resisting? What are we releasing? What are we holding onto so tightly in our life because we are afraid of what will happen if we let go? What are we not allowing to expand within us or in our daily life so we can let change in?

I want you to pause and take a moment to think how this may apply to your current situation and note what comes to mind.

When we think of *contracting and expanding*, we may think that the opposite holds true – that the tighter the follicle gets, the more it would hold onto the hair. And in contrast, when the follicle expands, it loosens its grip causing the hair to shed. But instead, when the follicle relaxes and expands, it is able to breed a healthy environment. And when it tightens and contracts, it squeezes the life out of it.

So now imagine your body reacting like this. When you are tense, anxious, trying to control things by holding onto them so tightly, what happens? Your body has a physical reaction. Those "contracting" emotions present as stored energy mass in your body, and maybe you get a tight neck or a tight feeling in your chest.

But when you exhale, let go, let loose, you expand your potential, your time, your energy. You allow your body to relax with ease. But if you feel tightness anywhere in your body, chances are it's a physical manifestation of an emotional block that needs to be addressed.

In **Chapter 6,** I discussed how to visualize your life as a blockbuster movie by building it block by block. Now we are going deep to dissect how to clear the blocks that are ruining the foundation of your movie. Start digging inward to clear the path.

The Drama Diet

Why inward if we have external drama? Because everything starts and ends with the relationship you have with yourself. And with opposing energies competing for attention all day long like sibling rivalries, it's no wonder your attention may get scattered and diverted. The secret sauce is to stay calm in the eye of the tornado, no matter what chaos is swirling around in your life. You deserve to thrive while alive, instead of just trying to survive.

As I detailed back in earlier chapters, I used to *go go go* every day. And I didn't want to stop because if I stopped, then all my thoughts and worries would catch up with me and I'd have to confront them. Instead, I would run myself into the ground until I had no choice but to stop. When I was running, I wasn't aware of the inner turmoil. The external noise was too loud. But when things got *silent*, that's when I was able to *listen* to the whispers of my soul without distraction.

Did you know that **silent** and **listen** are the same letters rearranged?

Filter out the noise, get **silent** within, and **listen** to what you need to focus on and filter out.

When I stopped running, it created an internal tidal wave. Picture a raw egg in its shell. Spin that raw egg on a countertop and the egg white and yoke will swish around the inside of the shell like an internal title wave. But while the egg is in motion, it may not be aware of the internal chaos because the external force that spun the egg caused the internal and external parts of the egg to spin in momentum together. This essentially cancels out any imbalance. They are equally in chaos.

Now imagine that you put your hand on top of the spinning egg to abruptly stop it from spinning. The outer shell becomes still. But what's going on inside? The raw egg didn't get the memo, and it is still experiencing an internal tidal wave.

Nothing has yet disrupted the internal chaos. How do I know? *Let go of that raw egg and it will go right back to spinning.* If you don't address the internal chaos, it will get caught up in the drama and keep it spinning. You must **solidify your inner core,** so you won't get whacked out of balance by external or internal factors.

> A solid foundation is the key to inner peace. If you keep calm inside this will reflect in your outer world.

Fun fact: When you spin a cooked egg on a countertop, abruptly stop it, and let go–*the egg stops spinning*. There's no internal turmoil thus proving that a solid foundation is key to inner peace. Furthermore, the internal energy alchemized the external chaos demonstrating that if you keep calm inside, this will reflect on your outer world. FYI, this is also my go to trick for determining if unidentified eggs in my refrigerator are cooked or raw. *You're welcome.*

But, if your inner core is not addressed - if the roots within you are blocked, causing internal chaos - you won't receive nourishment to flourish in your external world. You must get to the root of what type of environment you are thriving or wilting in. That is why the way to face your fears is within.

I.N.W.A.R.D.

I-nsecurity
N-egativity
W-orry
A-nxiety
R-egret
D-oubt

These are internal limiting beliefs that need to be *Acknowledged*, *Addressed*, and *Alchemized*. So, when your mind spins like a wheel stuck in muck, think of it as your personal AAA to give

The Drama Diet

you some roadside assistance on your path. Remember, there is no such thing as a 'bad' emotion. There are only emotions, and they are either positive, negative, or somewhere along the spectrum. Don't equate a *negative* emotion with being *bad*. Just because you feel angry, anxious, scared doesn't mean that it's a 'bad' emotion. On the contrary, negative emotions show you where you are in connection to where you want to go—they highlight the path away from that dark emotion. And that's a *good* thing.

And we love negative emotions. Yep. Put a positive spin on that wheel and get excited when negative emotions show up. Remember, you need to embrace your dark side in order to get to the root of things. And contrast brings clarity. So when you're anxious, out of sorts, and a total drama magnet, receive it as an opportunity to transmute it and say "This is my trouble spot. I got this." Then deflate that emotion like a flat tire by going down the rabbit hole of "What is this trying to teach me?"

> Everything you experience is either a lesson or a gift, and lessons are, in and of themselves, gifts.

So unwrap the present before you like it's Christmas morning or Chanukah evening, with anticipated excitement, present by present.

When you start ruminating and can't get off the cycle, determine why you are obsessing. I find that the optimal time for rumination typically happens in the middle of night when you're tossing and turning yet can't escape the truth. Or you find yourself staring up at a dark ceiling and feeling your world spin out of control as you hold on tightly to the carousel of life.

If you tell me this doesn't apply to you, that you've been sleeping like a baby, then I'm sorry to hear that. In my experience, babies don't sleep for very long stretches. Or maybe that's just all three of my children. But if thoughts are keeping you up at night, you need to be honest with yourself. Uncover what you have been hiding under the blanket of your ego. Somehow those truths have a way of peeking out when you're hiding. And yet, you really can't hide from yourself.

Are you worrying about the future? Obsessing over the past? Playing a conversation you had with someone on repeat in your mind? Analyzing a loved one's strange behavior towards you? Do you feel like you can't speak up? Or speak out? Or speak your truth? Are you telling yourself to keep the peace, so you don't have to deal with confrontation? Are you frustrated because you committed yourself to something for fear of saying "no" and disappointing others? Do you berate yourself? Talk mean to yourself? Did you slip on your diet or whatever personal goal you set out to achieve? Do you compare yourself to where others are in life? Are you hard on yourself?

Our thoughts are so powerful. When we have a negative thought stuck in the body, it can lead to physical manifestations of symptoms. Our thoughts can literally make us sick. Where do you think the expression *don't worry yourself sick* came from?

Confronting our shadows can be a scary thing. We were taught that our dark side is shameful, so we bury it deep, thinking we can disguise what lies beneath. The only way to free it is to accept it. So why would we want to open up Pandora's Box and risk exposing loose wires and toxic energy that's been festering over the years? Why unleash the beast of darkness, leaving us open, raw, vulnerable, and tainted?

By embracing every part of our being is how we can truly whittle away the fearful aspects and carve ourselves into the authentic beings that we are.

The Drama Diet

AAA: Acknowledge. Address. Alchemize.

First **acknowledge** and identify the feeling. Make a conscious effort to recognize those aspects of yourself that you may not be proud of. Understand that these traits are not flaws, but rather feelings you developed in response to life's experiences. If you acknowledge this, then you can start to change your emotional response system. Try to think of its origin.

Then **address** it by accepting it. Sit with your shadows and give it some love. Accepting your shadow is crucial. This does not mean that you are *approving* of your negative feelings or behavior. Rather, you are addressing that they are part of you. Once you take responsibility and *own your negative emotions*, you can then start the process of transformation.

Next, **alchemize** by finding a way to use the energy of your shadow traits in a positive way. This involves *integration* which transforms the shadow into something productive rather than *suppressing* it. For example, if you feel angry, channel this energy to create a piece of art or music. Use the negative emotions as a catalyst for promoting change in a positive way. Integrate your shadows, don't suppress them. That way you can lead with love for all parts of you, leaving no stone unturned within to fester.

If this seems intangible, I want you to imagine that a loved one came to you with the very thing that is causing you inner turmoil. What advice would you give them? What tone would you talk to them in? How patient would you be with them? *Why treat yourself any differently?* You are stuck with you and so you better learn to *love, accept, see,* and *hear* all parts of you.

Don't lash out on yourself. **L.A.S.H**. into yourself.

Love. Accept. See. Hear.

All of you. The light and the dark side.

Ask yourself – *What did the drama trigger in you? A feeling of unworthiness? Remnants of a childhood fear of rejection? Is it gnawing at your people pleasing habit? Does it eat away at your guilt?* There is an underlying feeling that is the root of why something affects you so deeply. If it affects your peace, it's worth digging deeper below the layers.

Once you identify the block – Sit with it. Accept it. Forgive it. Exhale it.

That will keep you **S.A.F.E.**

Sit. Accept. Forgive. Exhale.

EXERCISE: Place your hands on your heart and your core and feel into whatever emotion it brings up. If you're anything but relaxed, happy, and at peace, what are you feeling? Are you upset? Stressed? Nervous? Visualize the source of it and try the box breath method below.

Box Breath: S.A.F.E

- Breathe in for 5 seconds and silently chant "**s**it"
- Hold the inhale for 5 seconds and silently chant "**a**ccept"
- Exhale for 5 seconds and silently chant "**f**orgive"
- Hold the exhale for 5 seconds and silently chant "**e**xhale"
- Repeat as needed.

And while doing so, visualize yourself freeing whatever has been living inside you rent-free. Once you release it you make space for what aligns with you, so you can plant your seed of intent. Like a tree, you must first cultivate a healthy environment for it to grow roots and flourish in. Yet even in the healthiest of environments, *weeds* may suddenly appear in the form of other people's opinions, judgment, toxicity, or shade bringing on a new gamut of negative energies.

W.E.E.D.S.

W-orthlessness
E-nergy vampires
E-nvy
D-rama
S-tress

For example, when we rehash fights with a loved one, they tend to eat away at us. We then stew over "I can't believe they did that" and possibly drag that energy around with us. This regurgitation of the past will stew inside you unless you digest it and clear the block.

Whatever you don't digest, eats you.

By not letting it go you are keeping it alive. *This is one reason why problems keep coming back as recurring themes, and you're not getting any royalties for them.* You get what you tolerate. People are only going to meet you where you are. You have to meet yourself where you want to be. Don't let circumstances dictate your emotions. You can't control external circumstances, but you can control your response to them.

You do this by focusing on the solution, not the problem.

If you focus on the drama, the fight, the dilemma, the judgment, the shame, the frustration of what it is … *you will get more of what is.* Like attracts like. The universe will say, *oh, you are putting so much attention on the problem that you must want more of that energy.* When you realize you have all the power to transform a situation by focusing on the solution, things shift. The power of the problem seems to melt away while the strength of the solution seems to amplify. By no means does this mean the problem simply vanishes. It means that the *power* the problem holds over you diminishes.

So next time someone throws a mouthful of judgment your

way, remember what judgment is – *their perception from their vantage view limited by their life experience*. Looking at it from this objective perspective, you can gracefully focus on the solution. So, the person acted in spite. Or jealousy. Or maybe that person just couldn't see things from any lens but their own perspective. That's on them, not you.

> Don't stand in someone else's story. Stand firm on your story.

Remember the egg analogy – W.E.E.D.S. are not sustainable with a strong foundation. It starts at the *root*.

R.O.O.T.

R-emember
O-ur
O-ptimal
T-houghts

Be kind to your mind. Don't clutter it with negative self-talk. Imagine your positive thoughts as seeds, needing the right environment, energy and care to grow into reality. Think of your positive emotions, like happiness and love, as the sunlight and water that nurture these seeds, helping your thoughts grow strong and healthy. While sad or angry emotions will make them grow slower and weaker. The more you focus on planting positive thoughts and nurturing them with your positive emotions, the more beautiful your garden *"life"* will become. Change doesn't happen overnight. Be patient. It may get worse before it gets better.

You see one of the side effects from creating new thoughts resulting in new emotions is – **withdrawal**. Yes, you heard me right. Dr. Joe Dispenza brilliantly articulates how we are addicted to feeling familiar negative emotions. He explains that when we try to feel good in a situation, we typically don't feel good in, it causes us to experience symptoms of withdrawal. *Mind blowing.*

Dr. Joe Dispenza explains *and I paraphrase* that our brains aren't used to choosing a better feeling thought in familiar situations. In sequence, our bodies are uncomfortable with the "better feeling" emotion elicited by this new "better feeling" thought. We are not used to experiencing new emotions in old, patterned situations where we are accustomed to feeling a certain way – *bad*. So when we try to change this up and feel good in those scenarios, we end up feeling anxious, out of sorts, and uncomfortable in our skin. And so our bodies crave feeling our familiar emotions in response to those familiar circumstances, *which is to feel bad*. And we want to feel bad so we could – *get this*– **feel good!**

Essentially, it feels bad to feel good! Wild, isn't it?

But it's true, our bodies are not used to reacting this way. It makes our skin crawl. And so, when we try to interrupt the flow of an emotionally triggered response by training ourselves to feel better from that particular trigger, it actually backfires on us, causing us to go through withdrawal. The result is that it feels more comfortable to resort to our old ways. Your brain is like, "I know this pattern. It sucks. But it's safe. Let's do that again!" Our nervous system prefers *known discomfort* or *uncomfortable safety* over *the unknown possibilities of potential peace and joy*. **Drama addict**.

And believe it or not, this is your body's *safety mechanism* on autopilot trying to protect you from the unfamiliar. It says, "Hey, don't venture into unknown territory because then I won't know how to protect you." Your brain has stored accumulated files over the years, and is in desperate need for an upgrade, along with your *emotional response system*.

It needs to go beyond those files it's accumulated over the years. It's like an outdated computer system that hasn't been updated. It takes comfort in reverting to the recognizable thought patterns and emotional reactions because they feel cozy like a pair of worn in tattered slippers. Molded to the person you are with frayed threads and holes in the sole. It doesn't add quality to your life, but you take comfort in its familiarity.

Your amygdala is highly involved in detecting emotional stimuli. **Drama Detective.** It is responsible for the renowned "fight or flight" reaction to threats. The amygdala is essential for emotional learning, associating certain stimuli with emotional responses. Through neuroplastic changes, the amygdala can strengthen or weaken these associations based on new experiences.

But it will take time as it will feel uncomfortable, borderline unbearable, at first. As if you are tying a knot around the amygdala, and the tighter it gets, the tighter it chokes your confidence and squeezes your energy. Start pulling on the ends of the knot so it unravels before you do. The unraveling is the ability to sustain and feel new positive emotions and thoughts in situations that used to provoke negative ones.

Just like if you were a sugar addict who gave up sugar. Your body goes haywire, and you constantly crave that sugar hit. But if you could stick it out for a month, or even just a week, chances are you can pass on that Nutella fix (my weakness) without a second thought. It's not easy, but it's doable. And no one can do it for you. You have to be the one to interrupt the thought pattern. You have to be the one to change your automatic response. You have to be the one to retrain your brain. To be aware of when you're flexing your memory muscles on autopilot. To stop yourself from reflexively reacting to situations.

> Reprogram your subconscious beliefs. Once you crack the code, you can *Rewire* your beliefs and *Rewrite* the program.

Rewire and **Rewrite** have the same letters, except "Rewrite" as an extra letter "T." **T** for **Thoughts**.

To **Rewrite** is to **Rewire Thoughts**. *Neuroplasticity.*

But just like a new pair of jeans takes some time to break in, so does recreating a new pattern of thought and emotional responses when faced with trigger-provoking situations. So, when you start a *Drama Diet*, don't be surprised if things get worse before they get better.

What if you allowed yourself to be wrapped up in the uncomfortableness of the situation. Look the drama in the eye from a positive perspective rather than fear based. Attach a different meaning to it. It will feel uncomfortable like a stiff robe rubbing abrasively against your skin. But sit with it and don't judge it. *Give the drama some love.* It's going through withdrawal and it's probably starving for a little affection. Eventually that stiff robe softens, and over time turns into one of your favorite items of clothing – soft and cozy like a second skin. But don't forget to throw out the tattered slippers and replace them with new ones. It may be hard to let the old slippers go. The old pattern of thoughts and reactions.

When we D.I.G. at the R.O.O.T. of the W.E.E.D.S. we can *deconstruct inner grievances.*

D.I.G.

D-econstruct
I-nner
G-rievances

Let's analyze the root of the drama. If you stick a Band-Aid on a deep wound that needs proper attention to heal, you are covering the wound but not healing the source. You have to own your grievances, your shortcomings, your shadows, and *your dark side*. Give it some acknowledgement, then lovingly chisel away the negative residue built up within. It's like putting on a **mesh** bandage so the wound can breathe and heal, instead of festering.

Heal with the **M.E.S.H.** Method:

Mental. Emotional. Spiritual. Hygiene.

Time for a Spiritual Cleanse

Spring cleaning is a time to clear clutter, throw out the old, and bring in the new. Think of *deflating drama* as a **spiritual spring cleaning**, that can be done during the season of life where you are ready to rebirth your worth and clear the mental and emotional clutter. So, you can reveal your true essence and shine. And you, my friend, have the brightest light burning inside of you. When you ignite your light, it may be like turning on a light bulb in a dusty attic, where you will have no choice but to face the cobwebs – *the past* – and the caked-on layers of dust. But you got this. Grab a broom and start sweeping the cobwebs away. Not under the rug but out the door.

Just like showering, you need to do it daily. Spiritual hygiene is not a one-and-done.

Done for the day, not for your life.

You don't get good results by going to the gym sporadically. So why not apply this to your self-care? When you feel good, you may forget that you need to keep up the emotional maintenance, the mental motivation, the spiritual workout. It's all about consistency.

Here are some tools that I've used to dig deep.

Practice purging: Unclutter your thoughts and emotions like you're cleaning out those cabinets in your pantry. Let out your thoughts and frustrations so they don't linger inside you. You can do this by journaling, or you can spew into an audio or video recorder. The point is to purge it out of your system. One of my favorite practices is to go on a writing rant, get out any aggression, then light up that paper and watch it burn away all my pent-up energy.

Practice letting go: Drain your brain of chatter. Thoughts are just clouds floating in and out of your mind. Don't attach your emotions to thoughts or they'll stick to you like bugs smashing into your windshield when you're driving 80 mph on the freeway. Wipe them away. Be *mindful* of your thoughts or your *mind* will be *full* of thoughts. Let them float in and out freely.

Practice clearing: My grandparents, who worked their entire lives and built themselves up in business, always advocated for having a clean workspace. If there were a few pieces of paper on their desk, they would immediately address it to clear their space. They physically got rid of any clutter *before* it piled up. This was one secret to their success. They would say, even back in the 80's, *a messy desk will detract from concentration, but a cleared desk will allow you to focus.* They would emphasize the fact that if your mind is too scattered on too many things, you will not be able to focus on business. It was important for them to *concentrate* in a clean environment.

When you clear away the clutter you make space in your life for what you are working for. But with the law of duality, you could inevitably make room for more … clutter. So, practice clearing your physical space and see how that clears up any brain fog or distraction.

Practice shedding: Have others labeled you as something and it stuck? Did you label yourself with a limiting belief? Labels are for peeling. Peel back the layers of labels one by one like an onion. And don't worry if there's some shedding of tears in the process. It's cathartic. Besides, have you ever peeled an onion without crying? (Actually, for all of you contact wearers, you can now peel onions tear free.) Now if the labels won't peel off easily it's because the glue is stuck to you. The glue is the meaning you attach to the label. *The glue is the only thing attaching those labels to you.* Don't attach. Detach.

Labels are only as true as the person who identifies with them.

You are not defined by labels. Start chiseling away the layers of old truths. Deconstruct those labels. *Who put them there? Are they true? Do you want them?*

Once you free yourself of labels, you can continue this practice of shedding by sticking labels around you with positive affirmations. *I am enough. I got this. Not today, inner mean girl. Progress over perfection. I am perfectly imperfect. I am loved.* Whatever you need at the moment. If you love Post-It Notes as much as I do, go crazy. Stick those affirmations around your house, on your computer, your bathroom mirror, in your car. Wherever you are sure to read whatever it is to keep you on track.

I once needed a daily reminder of my worth and was told to write my affirmations in bright red lipstick on my bathroom mirror. At the time, I happened to have the most beautiful marble bathroom covered with mirrored walls. As an overachiever, I wrote the most loving affirmations and mantras to myself ... all over the bathroom. When my husband walked in one morning he exclaimed "This looks like a crime scene!" *The only crime was identity theft, and I was taking my identity back.* And it worked! Make your own lipstick crime scene and have fun with it.

Practice playing: And here's a bonus with spring cleaning. It's a renewing of energy. In the midst of digging and clearing, you may stumble upon a gem or two. A diamond in the rough you forgot about. Perhaps a hidden talent you were ridiculed for at a young age. Maybe a dream that you felt ashamed to share or scared to declare will emerge. Which leads to play. When we get lost in a hobby that inspires us, we get transported to a place of calm. We can feel something shift within us, opening up the door to a lost craft or project. Get lost in your passion and find serenity. It's also a good time to redirect your negative energy into something positive.

Practice surrender: Meditation is meant to slow down our racing minds, deepen our breaths, rejuvenate our cells, and bring clarity and calmness throughout our bodies. If you're new to meditation or have a love-hate relationship with it like me, start with practicing 5 minutes each morning. I suggest listening to a guided meditation, so your mind doesn't wander to your laundry list, then experiment on your own with different music.

EXERCISE: Here's something that helps me when I meditate. Turn on soothing music, get comfortable either sitting up or lying on the floor, and close your eyes. Start to envision you are at the theater and the movie playing is your desired life. The curtains are closed. Imagine you are on stage, and you spread open the curtains like you're spreading the curtains to your dreams.

The curtain is the obstacle that blocks you from your dreams. Shove those curtains to the side. Shoving aside is not the same as shoving them inside you by closing the curtain. By shoving aside, it exposes what's inside and shoves the blocks away. Take this visual and embody what it feels like to reveal the obstacle and remove it. Once you do, *what do you see on the screen? What are you imagining for your life with no obstacles to block your view?* Sit with this visual and embody the feeling as if you are watching it in real time. When you are ready, open your eyes.

Then take inspired action. That is key. Don't go backwards, that's just a distraction. And distraction breeds procrastination. Don't use procrastination as avoidance. Stop making justifications for your procrastination by thinking *it's not the right time* or *you don't have the time*. Just start doing. Hesitation is a motivation killer. Grab your latte, matcha, or whatever boosts your energy and get to it.

When I wake up, I **caffeinate and meditate**. In that order. Whatever works, right? My coffee is my non-negotiable. But so is my wellbeing. So even though I have a love-hate relationship with meditation – *it's either the most healing form of relief for me or the most irritating, abrasive torture–* I know how much peace and clarity it restores in me.

And luckily, I found meditation in other forms. Breathwork is my favorite. It is the most soothing way to restore inner balance within.

It can be done anywhere, anytime, quickly and effectively. It can be savored in a long, healing breathwork session. You can practice breathwork while walking, dancing, and singing. Singing is a great release in that it combines breathwork with musical vibrations emanating from our core. My theory is *don't confine yourself to what you think you should be doing.* Do what *feels good* to you. And be open to it changing. Maybe one day you need to take a hike with a walking meditation to get your frustration out. Or maybe you need a gentle sound bowl meditation to rejuvenate when you feel depleted.

Breathwork is the way home to peace. When we intentionally breathe, not shallow breaths, but the deep breaths that fill our inner spaces from our core to the top of our head, it rejuvenates oxygen to our cells which is so vital to a healthy body, mind and spirit. It promotes relaxation.

So **B.R.E.A.T.H.E.**

Being. Relaxed. Everyday. Aims. To. Heal. Everything.

Deep breathing activates the parasympathetic nervous system, which is responsible for the "rest and digest" state. This is important as the gut is often referred to as the "second brain" due to its production of neurotransmitters. It is estimated that 90% of serotonin– *a neurotransmitter that contributes to feelings of happiness and wellbeing*– is produced in the gut. This can influence mood and emotional wellbeing. The brain-gut connection may explain why you might get "butterflies" in your stomach when you're nervous. This connection also underlines the concept of a "gut feeling," suggesting that our intuitions or emotional responses can be deeply tied to our gut.

An imbalanced gut may have difficulty digesting food. *What impact do you think this has on digesting emotions?* I'm not a doctor but my bet would be that when we don't follow our gut, it makes processing situations more difficult - *harder to digest.* When we have a **tug** in our **gut** [same letters rearranged, similar energy], we need to pay attention, listen to our intuition, and process whatever emotions come up. As you dig deep beneath the surface be careful that you don't get lost in the abyss. Come up for air. Take a breath. Digest what you uncovered. Then go back to excavating.

I know this is a lot to digest. But once you clear the route to get to the root, you can take a **drama dive.**

D.I.V.E.

D-evelop
I-nternal
V-ibrational
E-nergy

It's all about energy, and where we focus our intention, attention, and time. *Hi spirituality. Meet science.* Everything is energy. We know that water is made up of the same chemical components as ice cubes and vaporized steam. Yet their energy components differ by vibrating at different frequencies. That is why water can turn to ice or steam, and vice versa.

In the same vein, we know that emotions are *energy in motion* and therefore we can alchemize the emotion of what we are feeling into a higher vibration. The way to transmute that emotion is to change the vibration of that energy by tapping into a different frequency. Using the analogy from the last chapter, both **fear** and **excitement** trigger similar physiological responses– *fast heartbeat, a release in adrenaline, butterflies in the stomach.* Imagine you're faced with a daunting presentation versus you're riding a fast and bumpy roller coaster. You may present with these same physical sensations, yet what is the key difference?

Your perception of the situation you are in.

Riding a roller coaster, you may feel scared, but you are probably having fun. Whereas presenting in front of others may feel like you want to cringe in the corner. There is a perceived sense of **safety** with excitement that may be absent with fear. But if you can learn to switch the flip, *to breathe into the unknown and feel that you are safe even in an unfamiliar situation*, you will start to transmute the energy of fear into excitement. And when you do, you will learn to regulate your emotions, which in turn will trigger neuroplasticity in your brain. With practice, your regulated emotions will produce a different perception in your brain to situations so that, little by little, those "scary" situations will not trigger fear. Thanks amygdala.

So similar to the water, ice, and vapor analogy that shape shifts the same matter into different energetic components, you too can shape shift your physiological, emotional, and mental responses into different energies. Just tap into the right energetic frequency in order to manipulate energy to your benefit.

How?

Be the Butterfly.

The next chapter will take you on a transformation journey of metamorphosis so you can F.L.Y. - First Love Yourself.

RECIPE

RECIPE FOR A CRIME SCENE: Lipstick (or Post Its) on a Mirror Challenge

My mirror looked like a crime scene with all my affirmations written all over. But it was helpful. It worked.

Write out whatever affirmations you need for the week all over your mirror. You can write it with lipstick, use colored Post Its, or anything that will immediately grab your attention as you wake up in the morning and throughout your day. The brighter the better - not just the form of how you present the affirmations, but the affirmations themselves! Be positive and specific!

*****

EXERCISE: BUBBLE WRAP DANCE

Get some bubble wrap. Imagine all the air-filled bubbles are droplets of drama. Then dance on it. Deflate the drama. Let the air out. This is like grounding. Get grounded. Have fun!

*****

DRAMA DIARY JOURNAL PROMPT

Nature has a way of bringing us back to ourselves — and gardening is the perfect metaphor for emotional clarity. It's meditation. It's movement. It's messy and beautiful, just like growth.

Today, think of your inner world like a garden.

1. **What are the weeds in your life right now?** *(List the beliefs, habits, or patterns that are cluttering your joy, clarity, or confidence.)*
2. **What do you need to gently pull out by the root — not just trim on the surface?** *(Fear of failure? People-pleasing? Self-doubt?)*
3. **Now dig deeper:** *(What hidden seed — a dream, desire, or gift — have you neglected to water?)*
4. **What does that seed need to grow?** *(Self-care? Space? A little faith? A bold step forward?)*

Bonus: Take your journal outside and write this in the sunshine or under a tree. Let nature remind you — everything blooms when it's nourished.

9

DEFLATE PART 2

Dark Light

> **Case Law: *Dissolve vs. Resolve***
>
> **D**issolve is generally known as the process of melting a solid *(a solute)* into a liquid solvent forming a solution. Resolve means to find a solution to the problem. But as we saw in **Chapter 8**, before we can dive deep, we need to dig deep through all the solid, the mass, the heavy energy. We need to *dissolve* the dense matter in order to turn it into a "solution" so we can *resolve* it. And guess what – ***U*** are the so***U****lution*.

Welcome to the second prong of **Deflate**. The last chapter focused on *determining* the root of the problem. This chapter delves into *dissolving* it at the source. *Deflating drama* is finding the source of the problem and being solution oriented.

The 3D Drama Free Formula is *shaping* you into the person you inherently are and getting you into the best *shape* to handle situations.

Get into S.H.A.P.E.

    S-urrender to what you can't control
    H-eal what is still controlling you
    A-bandon your outdated mindset

P-ivot towards your desires
E-xercise your mind, body and soul each day to stay in total shape

So, get into your warrior position!

Be a Warrior. *Not a Worrier.*

Worriers focus on the problem.
Warriors search for the solution.

"What's the big problem?" my daughter likes to say, and what she means by that is *there is no problem*. And she's right. In a sense.

For a problem to exist, a solution is always available. Even if it's something completely different than what you'd expect. And it may require a change in perception or a shift in perspective. Oftentimes, a solution isn't even fixing the problem but rather changing your relationship with the problem. With these concepts in mind, when you are faced with an *overpowering problem*, you must *empower yourself* by focusing on the solution.

Dissolve what stands in your way.

But here's the thing. You navigate with fear, excavate your dark side, and leave no stone unturned. So why do obstacles still build up like a stone wall?

Why do recurrent themes keep coming up?

Maybe you feel confident in some settings, and then run into an old childhood friend and crumble into a former, insecure version of yourself?

Or walk into a family gathering and revert to your role of who you were back then, rather than who you have become?

Or have an internal power struggle with trying to control an uncontrollable situation?

Or sit at the table in a professional setting, feeling that someone is going to figure out that you don't really belong there because you haven't "earned it" yet?

Or linger on that one person who "changed" and doesn't support you the way you feel you deserve to be treated, wreaking havoc on your self-worth?

Why do certain situations cause us to unravel the fabric of our identity that we have woven over the years? Why do they make us feel so vulnerable, self-conscious, *exposed*?

> We haven't dealt with droplets of drama that left deposits within us accumulating like plaque over the years.

Instead of chiseling away or sloughing it off like an exfoliant, we keep our drama buried within, thinking it's gone, only to resurface when a triggering situation presents itself. It's as if our imposter syndrome takes off its costume to reveal all our imperfections and self-perceived flaws. Calling us out on our fraudulent ways of "putting up a show to the world" when really, we feel like our younger selves are dressing up to play the part of a grown-up who is still figuring it out.

Well, guess what? You're not alone. Most people don't have it all figured out. Many times, they have to wing it – just like a butterfly, fluttering around, making it look easy and breezy when really all that winging it is causing them to feel physically fatigued. Have you heard the term "Fake it till you make it"? That got me through a lot of my early years in court. I would envision the best possible outcome in my head as I stepped into the courthouse – head held high, briefcase in hand, the clicking of my heels echoing as I walked down the corridor.

I don't recommend you *fake it till you make it*. A high stiletto cannot mask low vibrational feelings forever. Especially when it comes to unprocessed emotions, inner conflict, and unresolved wounds. When recurrent themes keep showing up, it's because we haven't resolved our emotional imbalances, our childhood wounds, our adulthood wounds, or whatever wound that still festers to remind us of our imperfections, fears, and unworthiness.

It all boils down to the beliefs you hold true about yourself.

- Where do they stem from?
- Why do you believe them to be true?
- Why do you hold onto them like a life raft?
- Why do you attach them to your identity?
- What will it take to believe a new story about yourself?

These cringeworthy scenarios trigger the parts of us that need healing, that we have not *resolved*. They bring us back to moments of our past where we may have felt berated or put down, ridiculed or mocked, dismissed or rejected, unimportant or irrelevant, unworthy or unloved.

You see, what you believe about yourself is the truth, to you at least. Whether it's true IRL (In Real Life) is irrelevant if you put so much weight on it. I am here to give you permission to *lose the weight* of untrue beliefs, and that begins with the emotions triggered by those beliefs.

You've got to face 'em, feel 'em, free 'em.

Once you face those stuck emotions within, are you able to free them? The way to release stuck emotions is to *feel them*. And it's not a fun process to feel them rising to the surface, bubbling over before you can purge them. The deeper into the abyss of your being that these beliefs based on emotions are ingrained, the more uncomfortable the process, much like a butterfly going through a metamorphosis.

Deflate Part 2

Feeling is healing.

The path to *healing* is by *dealing* with how you're *feeling*. But are our outdated beliefs and thoughts causing the stuck emotions? Or are our stored emotions causing the ruminating thoughts? Remember from **Chapter 5** the carousel *(thought loop)* going round your mind, with the horses *(emotional response)* going up and down? What comes first? The thought or the emotion? It's the classic chicken and the egg conundrum.

My untested theory is that when we encounter a situation, our emotions pick up things with their "spidey senses" faster than our brains can think. Although scientifically, thoughts and emotions are transmitted through neurons by electrical pulses at the same speed, it's their perceived speed that we consciously experience. We can *feel* a situation subconsciously before the mind can translate it into thoughts.

For example, people suffering from PTSD automatically react to situational triggers even if they can't explain why. The majority of clients I deal with in my law practice suffer some sort of trauma or PTSD. I do **drama**, not **trauma**. So, I turn to the experts to explain the effects of trauma.

I was privileged to have a conversation with trauma expert Dr. Russell Kennedy, aka the Anxiety M.D. He opines that the amygdala never forgets — for better or for worse. He believes that emotions create our thoughts much more so than the other way around. Dr. Kennedy's theory is that thoughts are the effect of emotions, therefore the underlying emotion is the driver of thought more than the thought drives the emotion. He said:

"You can never think your way into feeling better. You need to feel your way to feel better. The way to heal is to feel. You can redirect your energy and calm yourself with modalities such as breathwork."

And breathwork works. All the cells get filled up with oxygen, making you feel relaxed, calm, and maybe a little lightheaded. It's almost as if your body can float up effortlessly like a helium balloon getting pumped with air.

But if you haven't untethered the string attached to the balloon, it will not rise.

In order to make that balloon float higher, you don't add more helium to the balloon.

You don't **inflate** the drama; you **deflate** the drama.

You release whatever is tethering it to the ground.

In your case, for you to elevate, you don't add more to your plate, keeping you distracted, busy, and depleted. You get to the root of what is tethering you down, and you release them. You let go of the heaviness that weighs you down – *trapped emotions that you've been lugging around from recurring stories and labels that no longer serve you*.

But maybe you've tried the techniques in the previous chapters – meditation, breathwork, burning your journal – but you still feel something gnawing at you. It's like a **drama dagger** stuck in your side and you just wanna pull it out to stop the pain. Have you inflated the pain or deflated it?

P.A.I.N. is — Positivity Alchemized Into Negativity

Take the **drama dagger** and stab the pain to deflate it. Alchemize negative emotions into positive ones.

Remember, there is no such thing as a bad emotion because negative emotions are road signs that you are going in the wrong direction. They are your own GPS indicators of catching yourself going off-road so you can pivot. But if you haven't addressed the gnawing sensation in your emotional response system, *if you aren't breathing* **into** *the pain,* then you can breathe all you want, and that **drama dagger** will not budge.

In **Chapter 8** we touched upon the concept of putting a pin in the balloon of pressure and letting out the air of negative energy.

- You've got to deflate the inflated negative emotions.
- Finding the root of fear-based emotions requires sifting through the beliefs that are holding you back and getting to the root of that story.

Who dissuaded you? Criticized you? Made you feel small? When? How long have you held onto that outdated story and carried it around with you? Why are you still so attached to it? Why are you afraid to let go? *What do you think will happen if you do?*

Take a hard look at yourself in the mirror. If what is reflecting back anything other than peace and joy, grab the **drama dagger** and start digging. Get *clear* on what belief is chipping away at your worth and *clear* it out.

Or take a hard look at your relationships. *People are reflections mirroring back what you have yet to learn.* Get excited that the universe is highlighting your lessons. Remember, everything is either a lesson or a gift, and lessons in and of themselves are gifts. What can you learn from this situation? What nerve did it hit that needs healing? How do you *feel* about it? Insecure? Dependent? Worrisome? Envious? Stressed?

Start healing by feeling, forgiving, and freeing your fear-based emotions.

Forgive the chatter of the peanut gallery. Maybe it's your own mind chatter that plays on repeat, or it's other people reacting to your life. These narrow opinions show you what hit a nerve. If it strikes a chord, it's because it is not aligned with what you truly believe about yourself. *Forgive.* Feel how freeing that is.

Dissolve those old stories within you. They ran their course and don't define you now. You are not the same person unless you actively *choose* to be. You decide whether you want to carry those stories into the next part of your life or leave them in the last chapter. This is a *choose-your-own-adventure* moment. Don't make it a cliffhanger. Decide now. Feel how good it is to forgive your outdated beliefs.

Face imposter syndrome and free it. Why do you believe you aren't what you project? If you *feel* you are … then you *are*. No one starts out with the finished product. There's no overnight decision to be something with an instantaneous big reveal. There's a whole BTS (behind the scenes) action that takes place, *for as long as it needs to take place* before the imposter syndrome feeling wears off. But by no means does that mean that you are an imposter! Believe in your worth wholeheartedly and feel it cultivate confidence in you.

Hug your inner child and thank it. It highlights where you have been. Are you still in the same place? Are you still the same person? Your inner child is rooting for you to finish what was started. Give some love to yourself. Tell yourself you did good with what you had and knew. And let you remind you which parts need attention, love, and forgiveness. Look at how far you have come and feel the progress.

Disintegrate past pressures. Maybe you're still trying to fulfill someone's expectation of you that was planted years back. *Would completing that complete you?* If not, it was never yours to complete. Deflate those pressures and feel them alleviate.

In the same vein, deflate any pent-up stress, anger, or guilt. Release that stale energy to change your E-motion, energy in motion, otherwise you may have a different E to deal with – you may **explode**. Don't explode. *Exhale*. Feel your breath release. Feel the tension dissipate.

We must **stand on our story … not in it.**

This is when we know we have come through the other side

when we use obstacles as stepping stones instead of letting them step all over us. Believing in yourself is the secret ingredient. Transmute negative emotions to positive ones.

Tip the **Drama Diet Scales** in your favor.

All you need is a 51% preponderance of the evidence. That's all you need for self-conviction. *You don't have to be all in– just believing the positive 1% slightly more than the negative is enough to tip the scale in your favor.*

To sum it up, you must **face** your unresolved emotions. Next, you must **feel**, sit with, and let them envelop you. And finally, **free them** like a butterfly. Let's explore the transformation process.

Fear to Freedom

Do you feel that you live in an invisible cage of restrictions that are either self-imposed or created by others?

We are silently chained to the **S.E.A.** – something **S**afe. **E**xpected. **A**cceptable.

- Every time we look for validation from others we add another bar to our cage.
- Every time we wait for others to give us permission, instead of believing we are worthy, we add another bar to our cage.
- Every time we stop ourselves from taking action in the direction of our goals for fear of failure, we add another bar to our cage.

There are no limitations – only those that are self-imposed.

We always have two options: *Be a prisoner of our past. Or…be liberated by our free choice.*

The Drama Diet

Most of the time, when we feel claustrophobic within the confines of our mind, it's a product of our own doing. We then make up stories that these self-created walls are meant to shield. But it's the total opposite.

Those walls confine us.

We may talk ourselves into false stories of our limitations. This is our ego talking, and our heart and gut are listening, creating a trifecta of harmonious agreement.

- "It must be true if I feel this way."
- "I can't override my gut that is trying to keep me comfortable."
- "It doesn't feel safe to ignore my heart that is pounding so deeply every time I dip my toes outside my self-imposed cage of familiarity."

Does this sound familiar? Are you waiting for someone to come along and save you? Tell you what's waiting for you outside that cage? Give you permission to take messy, brave, and imperfect action to find out? Allow you to be someone other than what's expected of you? Validate your worth to try something different? Tell you it's ok to create a new version of yourself? Step out of your comfort zone? Open that locked door for you? *Unlock your life to freedom?*

Can you see how you are the creator of your own prison?

Do you realize that if you are the creator then you also hold the key to your cage?

You have the ability to free yourself at any time! It just takes courage to take the first step and unlock yourself from what's holding you back and venture into the uncomfortable unknown. That is where all the growth awaits you.

When you stay complacent in your comfort, or worse, *in your chaos*, you know it's time to evolve.

Change is growth, and growth takes change.

This requires courage, strength, and a willingness to just do it. Then, when you muster the confidence to unlock the door to the cage, you make another discovery.

The cage was never locked!

It was always open, waiting patiently for you to just open the door. Take a chance on yourself, your dreams, and your curiosity to explore uncharted territory. Because it finally dawns on you.

You are the Key!

K.E.Y.

Keep **E**mbracing **Y**ourself.
Keep **E**mpowering **Y**ourself.
Keep **E**levating **Y**ourself.

Loving yourself is the key to everything, and you are the key to self-love.

You are the one to release your inhibitions. You don't need permission or validation to live your true authentic self. The fact that you exist is enough for you to unapologetically live your life. Once you understand this, you can courageously step beyond the cage. And although you may want to retreat into the comfort of the cage instead of the uncomfortable unknown, you make the final realization.

There is no cage!

It doesn't exist. It never did. The walls, the boundaries, the edges, they were all fear-based borders confining you, dimming your light. When we build those invisible cages in our minds, *bar by bar*, we set our own self-imposed limitations. The cage in our brain keeps us *feeling* trapped ... but are we really trapped? Or is it an excuse?

For example, I tend to be a huge procrastinator. I believe that the 11th hour was created just for me. When the clock strikes 11, I strangely dissolve any pressure, and I get laser-focused and complete whatever it is that needs to get done. Why do I wait? Maybe I use perfectionism as an excuse for procrastination – *it's not the right time, I'm not in the right frame of mind, I'm not ready*. But I've learned to dissolve this limitation by implementing progress over perfection. That's one bar that I am constantly actively dissolving.

Another way to dissolve the bar is to *feel* what it is like on the other side of that bar before we get there. *A little taste of freedom.* The bar is an illusion, thinking it's keeping us safe and protected. But it's just another excuse driven by fear-based limitations. Get past the fear by feeling what it's like to get past that obstacle. That's how we dissolve the bars that have kept us trapped in an **emotional drama dungeon.** Find the root of the limitation and ask yourself, *is that story true?* If it's fear-based, *dissolve it.*

> The bars creating the borders of the cage were built on beliefs that were never yours to latch onto.

The cage you created is too small for the person you have become. There's no room for you to grow. You've outgrown your past stories.

As they dissolve ... you understand ... you were free all along. When I first came to the realization that not only was I the key, *but that the cage never existed,* it was like mist clearing right before my eyes. Then I saw the truth so clearly. *I really am free.* And yet, I so willingly kept myself chained to a past version of myself, to my stirred-up emotions that kept me shackled to an identity I created to keep me safe. Even when others place bars on us, it's still our choice whether to leave the barriers up or kick them to the curb alongside our limiting beliefs.

We break barriers by loving ourselves.

The only **B.A.R.** you should construct is to **B**elieve. **A**chieve. **R**eceive.

- Believe that you are worthy of Achieving what you desire.
- Believe that you are worthy of Receiving what you desire.

You set the B.A.R. to how high you want to succeed. You are the center of everything, like a nucleus. All roads in relationships lead back to the relationship you have with yourself.

> The greatest relationship you will ever have is the one you have with yourself.

When you dim your light, you are actually being selfish. You are depriving the world of your gifts. Someone out there needs the very thing you may feel unworthy to put out. And that not only deprives them, but it also deprives you of living your purpose. So the next time you hesitate speaking your truth, or walking your authentic walk, think of how many people could benefit from you just being … you. When you realize your own strength, courage, and bravery that you've always had within, you can push beyond your own limitations. Don't play small anymore. The world needs your greatness.

It's time to **F.L.Y.**

When you First Love Yourself you F.L.Y. and elevate your life.

Can you feel how trapped and confining it is to shove yourself into a box with little to no movement? You were never meant to fit into formulas like an equation. You were meant to expand your wings like a butterfly and F.L.Y. - First. Love. Yourself.

From Cage to Cocoon

Years back, I ran a webinar series called **Be the Butterfly**. It was based on the premise that we can deflate our former beliefs and transform ourselves – *mind, body, and spirit*. And I had every age group of people from around the world. The consensus I had was that it felt *"freeing"*.

Think about it. Look at the person you were one year ago, six months ago, last week, or even yesterday. Do you recognize that person? Do you like where you are now in relation to where you were then? You have the ability to transform yourself and *your life* into your wildest dreams.

It seems normal these days to put so much pressure on ourselves— on our appearances, our status, our goals, our successes, our timelines. The real pressure we should be applying is for the purpose of transforming our lives. And I'm not talking about negative stressful pressure. I'm talking metaphorically, like a diamond that is revealed when the proper amount of **positive pressure** is applied to coal.

Embrace positive pressure to transform.
Deflate the negative pressure of drama.

Do you want to **RELIVE** pressure or **RELIEVE** pressure?

The difference between these two words is adding an extra **E** – for **E**nergy. You will experience increased energy when you **relieve** pressure rather than **relive** it. Conserve your energy. Can you feel how freeing that is?

Get **relief** from your old **belief**.

Shed the layers that don't serve you. Shed the stories from your past. Shed the identity you have outgrown. *Shed your old skin.*

The human body regenerates new cells all the time. For example, did you know that your skin, the epidermis, renews itself roughly every 30 days? That means every month you naturally exfoliate to reveal new skin. You are essentially *shedding your old skin* each month. How cool is that? Why not take that as an opportunity to shed your old identity each month? Like a snake, let go of what you have outgrown. Remember when I told you my trick of *giving up a new fear each month*? Likewise, you can take each month as an opportunity to take inventory of what isn't serving your emotional wellbeing. What prior version of yourself trapped within should be left in the past?

Recognize what needs deflating so you don't boomerang forward then revert back to your past self.

Each moment serves as an opportunity to leave something in the past and transform. This requires two things:

- You need to pan out and expand your vision with a bird's eye view of the limitless possibilities.
- And, you need to start moving in the direction of that vision, *even if it's at a slow crawl.*

When a caterpillar crawls, it inches its way by anchoring itself, using the ground as resistance to move forward. You could say the caterpillar is *grounded*. But its view is limited to what it sees from ground level. Its perspective is hindered in this way until the caterpillar undergoes its transformation to emerge as a beautiful butterfly, light and free, floating above and expanding its perspective.

Butterflies represent the epitome of transformation.

Butterflies are ethereal, free, living their best lives. They represent an ease in the world. But they don't start out that way. They start out slugging along the soil, trying to find their place, until one day they're wrapped up in a cocoon, confined to their silent world of metamorphosis. In that isolated darkness cut off from the outside world, they undergo the most difficult yet miraculous transformation.

The caterpillar has to physically and *metaphorically* **deflate and dissolve** its prior form in order to recreate itself. Did you know that during the process of metamorphosis, caterpillars, or *chrysalises*, literally *liquidate* themselves to rebuild themselves? They have to decompose their essence and rebuild a new identity.

They have to deconstruct themselves in order to reconstruct into the butterfly they never knew they were meant to be … *or did they?*

To top it off, the butterfly must push against the inner wall of the cocoon with its delicate wing in order to emerge. The featherlike wing must muster all its strength and faith to push against the suffocating cocoon it is entrapped in. This is a slow and uncomfortable process, but it builds up strength in their wings so that by the time they create an opening, their wings are ready to fly. If they enter the world before they are ready, their wings will be weak, and it will be an effort to fly. *Butterflies are light, but if their wings are weighed down by the stress of drama, they can't fly*. Once their wings are strong, they can fly freely from their confined cocoon.

A complete transformation – *the before, middle, and after*. Similar to the *face it, feel it, free it*. The caterpillar must *face* its inevitable truth – that it must shed its prior identity in order to transform. Then it must *feel* the pain and discomfort of shedding its old existence in order to make space for the new. Then it must *free* the old in order to emerge lighter and freer.

It must die a sort of death of its old self so it could rebirth its worth.

I like to refer to this process as **dark light** –- only in the lonely darkness where it can undergo an uncomfortable transformation can a butterfly find the light to alchemize into a beautiful lightness of being. *This* **dark light** *process in the cocoon best represents the emotional inner work.* It's not a pain-free process, nor is it comfortable by any means.

The reason I named my webinar *Be the Butterfly* was to encourage people to find the light in the darkness, to spend time in their personal cocoon, transmuting, transforming, and metamorphosing. We are all born from a dark womb, where we spend months forming into the person we become. We sleep at night when it's dark, forcing us to spend hours to recharge, reset, rejuvenate, and re-energize. We can learn to do the same in the darkness of our lives. Take it as an opportunity to go within and dissolve the drama. Just like a caterpillar must dissolve itself in order to transform into a beautiful butterfly, and fight its way out of the darkness in order to fly.

Beware of Poisonous Butterflies

Sometimes when we dive deep to discover our stuck stories, our ego tricks us into thinking it's better to bury the baggage of the past instead of sifting through it. So instead of allowing ourselves to go through the painful transformation process, our shadow self drags the negative emotions deep into the dark abyss. But in doing so, the shadow self also suppresses the positive emotions. See, it's a package deal. You can't fully embrace your positive emotions because there's an anchor of negative emotions attached pulling it down. I call these *"poisonous butterflies"* because although the ego thinks it's keeping us safe, it doesn't appreciate that the unprocessed negative emotions don't disappear simply because they're being ignored. They linger, festering in the darkness, preventing us from doing the inner work. The ego denies the shadow the opportunity to face the negative emotions, feel them, and free them.

Everyone encompasses light and dark. Which means that everyone must be held accountable for their choices. It's the dark light. But you have a choice which energy will guide you. Choose light. Love.

> Dance with your darkness
> but let love take the lead.

Be The Butterfly

Butterflies are reminders from the universe that miracles can happen, that change is good, and that nothing needs to remain as is. A butterfly will not revert to crawling on the ground just to appease someone who can't wrap their head around the fact that they have transformed from the inside out and can fly. Once it's transformed, no one turns to it saying "Hey butterfly, you're a fraud. Turn back into the low crawling creature you truly are."

No one looks at the butterfly and says, *"You're just a caterpillar in disguise."*

No. People look at the miracle of butterflies in awe of their power to transform. *And the butterfly certainly doesn't suffer from imposter syndrome.* It embraces its transformation and emerges confidently in its new skin. It doesn't hide but rather shines, unapologetically, spreading joy and flying effortlessly.

But that butterfly had to go to hell and back to metamorphosize. And yet, all we see are the results. And to us, it seems effortless. We forget the agonizing hours it spent trapped in a tight cocoon, motionless except to liquidize itself and regenerate into another version of itself. We forget the miracle of this creature that crawled on the ground and can now suddenly fly. It takes work BTS (behind the scenes), like an actor performing on stage who has to go behind the curtains for a costume change. We don't see the chaos ensuing in the wardrobe department. We only see the finished product.

Why would you think your transformation would be any different?

It's all a process. Nothing comes overnight. Nothing worthwhile at least. Remember, life is a journey with many destinations. And each destination is unique to each individual. But a journey means you have to go from point A to point B, no matter how long or short that is.

And I guarantee you ... someone will ask "How did you do it? It seems like you did it overnight?"

And you will smile, knowing what you went through, what you overcame, and how you thrived in the process.

Why do we sometimes see our friends, family, or coworkers as the people we've always seen, rather than the people they have become? Because the receptor in us is how we perceive things, people, and situations, as we are accustomed to. So when *you* start to transform, don't expect people to automatically accept the new version of you. It's okay if someone cannot appreciate the updated version of you.

When people say you've changed, say "Thank you. I've worked really hard on it."

Always be conscious that you are operating from the updated version of yourself– *butterfly* – and not the outdated version you're still dragging around that's dragging you down – *caterpillar*.

And remember, a butterfly earns its wings not by forcing flight, but by surrendering to what is and trusting the process. A butterfly strengthens its wings by uncomfortably pushing against the inner walls of the cocoon, breaking the barrier to find an opening to spread its wings to fly.

So, break barriers and fly! Get comfortable in the uncomfortable. It's never too late.

> There's no statute of limitations on starting over to reach your goals.

Don't ask *"Who am I to do this?"* Who are you *not* to do this!

Confidence is a choice – *a mindset* - not an emotion. But we waste emotion by expending energy on why we can't do it. And while energy can neither be created nor destroyed, it can get depleted as there is a finite amount in us that needs to be recharged. Like a draining battery. So next time you feel scared to do something, and you experience butterflies in your stomach, know this ...

Each butterfly in your stomach represents a mini transformation!

Butterflies in our stomachs are the antithesis of the free-floating, fearless creatures they typically represent. So why are these *"inner butterflies"* trapped in our gut when we are nervous about something? My theory is when we feel scared, we are in the midst of transformation, and those are our inner butterflies that have yet to come out of their cocoon, aka, our stomach. Our inner butterfly is stuck inside of us, fluttering around because we are not quite yet at a place where we can release it and be free.

So now, when I get butterflies in my stomach, I remind myself that I *am* the butterfly. And to *be the butterfly*, I need to remember the end result is that I am going to emerge free, transformed, and at ease. I have learned to embrace my *"inner butterflies,"* tell them not to be scared because they will soon be free (*when I* **face** *my fear*), take a deep breath (**feel** *into the uncomfortableness*), and release them as I exhale (**free** *them*).

Caterpillars Crawl. Chrysalises Transform. Butterflies Fly.

And you F.L.Y. by **First Loving Yourself**.

Deflating Drama means that you **lead with love**. The most important type of love is *self-love*.

Give yourself *butterfly kisses*.

Butterfly kisses are when you take your lashes, and you gently rub them against someone's skin. When you do this to yourself (or others) it's an indicator that the person on the receiving end of the **L.A.S.H.E.S.** is:

L.A.S.H.E.S.

Loved. Accepted. Seen. Heard. Enough. Safe.

- Spread your wings and expand your life past your preconceived expectations.
- Spread your limitations wide open pushing past barriers that no longer define or confine you.
- Spread your love to create a ripple effect.

The butterfly effect.

RECIPE

THE DRAMA DIFFUSER

- Diffuse Drama by letting it dissipate and dissolve
- Get to the source and find the solution
- Infuse Love into everything you do

When you approach life with excitement and curiosity – even the hard parts– you "get" to do things that may feel tedious rather than you "have" to. You end up experiencing the fullness of life.

*****

EXERCISE: *Wing It*

When you allow yourself to *transform* and set your past free, but you're not sure how things will *transform* – **wing it!**

Here are the ABCs to **Wing It:**

A. Approach life with lightness like a butterfly's wings
B. Believe you can elevate yourself with the same grace that a butterfly can flutter
C. Carry yourself with confidence that the winds of change can guide you in the right direction

*****

DRAMA DIARY JOURNAL PROMPT:

When you say Y.E.S.
You. Expect. Solutions.
When someone else says N.O.
It is Not. Over.

- What's something you will say YES to?
- What's something you will not accept a NO to?

10

DETOX PART 1

Surrendering to Chaos

> **Case Law: *Sucked into chaos vs. Surrendering to chaos***
>
> We are all just magnets, sucking energy into us or letting energy get sucked from us, either drawing or repelling good and bad experiences to us. You can be a magnet for what you want and flip the magnet for what you don't want. It's a matter of either attaching to the energy or detaching from the energy. And I'll spill the tea on how you do this.

Detox is the third component of **The Drama Diet 3D Formula - disrupt, deflate, detox**. Remember the hand movements? Scan the QR code to watch the video.

https://lisastuart.com/qr-codes/7

- Disrupt = stop the drama in its tracks
- Deflate = squeeze the air out of the drama
- Detox = flick away the drama so it can't inflate

Recap: Each "D" of the Drama Diet Formula has 2 prongs – what you need to delete and what you need to add. In order to detox drama from your life, you need to **delete attachment** (this chapter) and **add loving boundaries (Chapter 11).** The first prong of **detox** is about releasing old attachments and detaching. Like a detox tea.

Here's the T.E.A.

We attract what we get depending on our T.E.A. – **Thoughts. Emotions. Actions.**

Although all components of the **3D Drama Diet Formula** deal with *thoughts, emotions, actions*, each is more prevalent in one prong.

- **Disrupting drama** deals more with *Thoughts*
- **Deflating drama** deals more with *Emotions*
- **Detoxing drama** deals more with *Actions*

Chapter 9 highlighted how drama *boils* down to the beliefs you have about yourself. Here's a visual of how it's all *boiled* down. Imagine you are boiling water in a pot on the stove.

- What happens when you add an egg to the boiling water? *The egg hardens.*
- What happens when you add a potato to boiling water? *The potato softens.*
- What happens when you add a tea bag to the boiling water? The tea transmutes the water to … tea.

Be like T.E.A. - Transmute. Energy. Around.

Chapter 9 demonstrated, through the butterfly's transformation, how to transform energy *within* by alchemizing emotions.

This chapter will focus on how to alchemize the energy around you to create a life of freedom. You can't change people. But you can change your energy, your responses, your thoughts, your actions, your beliefs. When you love yourself, and come from a place of *Compassion, Forgiveness, Observation* – you become the C.F.O. of your life, shielding yourself and setting loving boundaries. Like an invisible dome. I call it a **drama dome.**

Alchemize the room like T.E.A. with Thoughts. Emotions. Actions.

- Thoughts attract mindset.
- Emotions magnetize manifestations.
- Actions create freedom.

The 3D Drama Diet Formula in Sum

Disrupt thoughts – *attract mindset* – **navigate with fear**
Deflate emotions – *magnetize manifestations* - **lead with love**
Detox actions – *create freedom* – **become a Drama Ninja**

Your inherent right to create freedom is in your **D.N.A. - Drama Ninja Action.**

And believe it or not, the greatest action to freedom is the act of **surrendering.** Yes, you heard me right. Letting go will propel you forward. How? It releases the weight of the past, and it frees the burden of future fears. It teaches you how to **detox drama** by *detaching* instead of *attaching*. It allows you to surrender to the drama rather than get sucked into it.

Surrender

Surrender is a word to which I was completely *attached* in 2007 and didn't know why. Yet, it was in that year that I started creating music. Songs poured from my pores onto paper, and for some unexplained reason orchestrated by the universe, the word *surrender* was splashed across my lyrics. The crazy thing was, I didn't understand what it meant to surrender. I went on a quest to comprehend the concept of *letting go, releasing resistance, and accepting what is.* It didn't make any sense, until years later, when I learned, through challenging inner work, what it meant to surrender from past beliefs, ingrained stories, and constant mind chatter– not to mention the subconscious emotions that rooted themselves so deeply that my cluttered mind was not even aware of them.

When I look back now at lyrics written in 2007, I'm a bit shaken at how I was able to write about things I hadn't yet experienced – *how I was able to express myself in ways to help my future self.* But then again, I believe I was just the vessel channeling what my higher self knew. (Looking back, I also incorporated the following words and phrases – *Shine. Clarity. Prisoner of Fear. Believe. Consume.* Do you see a common theme?)

So here we are, over seventeen years later, and I can finally say with certainty that I truly understand *and greatly appreciate* the concept of surrender.

In its simplest terms, surrendering is relaxing your grip on whatever it is you cannot control and trusting the universe to take over as you objectively observe without judgment or expectation. Surrendering is an inward journey. It's acknowledging that you don't need to control a situation. It's learning to "be" instead of "do." It's allowing space to expand instead of feeling confined. It's giving in to self-trust and choosing to trust in a higher power. It's operating from a place of faith instead of fear.

> Faith over fear is one of the strongest energies you can operate from.

I want to quickly differentiate between *faith* and *hope. Faith* comes from a place of trust and belief that things will work out for your highest good. *Hope* stems from a feeling of lack and desperation. I don't believe they are interchangeable; I believe each signals a different energy. I can personally feel the difference in energy when I use these two words. [Sidenote: These are my interpretations of these two words. You may agree or disagree and that's ok. No judgment.]

When we loosen our grip on things we can't control, and trust the process, it allows us to flow through life without resistance or force. This doesn't mean that we grab our yoga mats and flow through Ashtanga all day without putting in the work. It means that we take action on things we can control, and don't focus our stress on things we cannot control.

> Know what you can control so you don't let it control you.

Attaching feels sticky, like you're entangled in a web. Or stuck with glue. For example, you are not responsible for holding your family together and keeping the peace. You are not the glue. Glue is an illusion. It doesn't bond people. It's a temporary fix. Glue is sticky. Glue hardens. Glue gets dried out. Glue doesn't hide cracks—it just keeps them closed so the light can't get in.

Try not to be like glue. Try to be like water. It's fluid. It ebbs and flows. Surrender to the flow without resistance. When you're swimming in the ocean and the tide— *the ebb and flow*— is strong, it can suck you into a dangerous situation. If you swim *against* the **current**, it can pull you in. But if you swim *alongside* the **current**, surrendering to it and trusting it to move you along to safety, it has no power over you. **Current** also means belonging to the present time. When you stay in the present, in the now, you let go of the past and release resistance about the future. Eventually, you will find a soft ebb and flow that can easily bring you to shore.

Being like water can mean saturating love, being a flood of light, and being powerful like a waterfall, trusting its path over the edge. Water isn't *dripping in drama*. Water has no defined shape or constraints. It flows effortlessly, not controlling its destination, but surrendering to it in trust.

Don't drip in drama.
We can only control our actions, not the outcomes.

But remember, without action, the outcomes won't happen. *Drama Ninja Action*. And sometimes the only action we need to do is to focus our energy on the creation and not the result.

Don't attach yourself to the outcome.
Attach yourself to the process.

Attach yourself to the vision, the feeling, the day-to-day actions. Pour your emotion into that, or it'll drain your energy every moment you haven't attained your results. Have you heard of the catchphrase "work smarter, not harder?" I feel that many people have taken that as an excuse to *work less* and *expect more*. But that's never going to work because they're missing a key ingredient – **intention**.

When the focus is on the outcome, not the process, the energy comes from a place of *obligation* rather than a place of *inspiration*. Or even worse – a place of *desperation*. Can you feel the difference in these energies? *Obligation* and *desperation* feel heavy and burdensome, causing much *perspiration* and *exasperation*. *Inspiration* feels light and passion-filled, causing *celebration* and *elevation*, definitely fueling *motivation*.

When our intention comes from our inspiration, we allow ourselves to surrender and let things go. This creates space to allow the floodgates of creativity to pour in. Doesn't that taste like freedom?

> You create freedom which gives
> you the freedom to create.

Flow in the direction of what you *can* control. Operate from a place of **F.A.I.T.H. – *Flow. Alignment. Inspiration. Trust. Harmony***, like a beautiful symphony of music, vibrating effortlessly, touching your soul. Can you recall moments in your life when you felt glimpses that you were limitless, unstoppable, magical? That is your true self.

Speaking of music, I was having a conversation with a friend of mine who's a musician. We were talking about how it's counterintuitive to force art, but when you feel the stress of time constraints squeezing you, it's tough not to feel the external pressure. She was saying that when she *has fun and enjoys the* **process**, she can tap into creativity.

It's so true. When we tap into the energy of fun, we become the **equal energetic frequency** to receive the very thing we ask for. The universe is tapping its foot, waiting for you to relax and receive. Whether it's a download of music, painting, poetry, or any other vessel that expresses exactly what we want to convey, it should feel easy. Trying to get the same outcome from a different energy won't work.

When you feel pressure, make sure you're **pushing** yourself, not **punishing** yourself.

Pushing and PuNIshing have the same letters, with the additional letters of "I" and "N" in punishing. When you push yourself, it comes from a place of motivation that you desire. When you punish yourself, you are saying "I Need" it, which is a different energy connoting a lack of it.

N.E.E.D. = Nervous. Energy. Enticing. Drama.

Change *need* to *desire*. Desire is belief that you *can* have it. Need emits a belief that you can't have it, but you *need* it to feel better. That feels like pressure.

Release that pressure and Let. It. Flow. Easy. – That's **L.I.F.E.**

That's how you **detox – detach** – from the outcome and attach to the process.

The Tornado of Chaos

But as detached as you are, the tornado of chaos keeps swirling. Whether it's relationship drama, work drama, family drama, or self-created drama – it's easy to get sucked right back into the chaos. The swirling of drama creates frenetic energy within you and around you. If you engage with the frenzy or even poke your little finger at the swirling drama, it is guaranteed that you will get swept up into the tornado, whether you intended to or not. It will suck you in and suck the energy from you.

Now, imagine you are standing in the center of the tornado - the **eye of the tornado**. There's a slice of peace within the storm that is completely calm and unaffected. *Can you feel it?* From that place, you can turn and look at the drama from any angle, 360 degrees, and not get affected. *How?*

You are observing rather than engaging.

You are coming from a place of neutrality rather than judgment or defensiveness.

But just one little outstretched finger making contact with the chaotic energy of the tornado will pull you right in. Why? It's the law of momentum. *Once you start engaging, drama tends to escalate.* Even if your intention is to try to de-escalate the drama.

So, what do you do? How do you stay out of the drama when it's ensuing all around you and you feel trapped? How do you not poke the bear that consumes you? **You surrender.** You melt right where you are, in the eye of the storm, and you breathe. You look that drama right in the eye and you don't waver. And it will have a fit! *A meltdown!* It will try to draw you in, get you tangled in the web of chaos by throwing shade on you, or guilt, or blame. And it will enrage you. It will trigger you. It will anger you. It will shame you. It will entice you. It will egg you on. And you may slip and fall right into the drama trap where you will wrestle with all sorts of sh*t that you didn't sign up for. But you can always escape to the sweet surrender spot in the eye of the storm.

**You can always come back to your center
by surrendering to what is.**

Surrendering doesn't mean you are giving up or giving in. It's not about giving at all. Surrendering means you are taking back your peace of mind, your power, and your freedom. When you're detached from drama, you're free from attachments. Only then do you become the observer instead of the victim.

Bee the Observer

No, that's not a misspelling. That's my reference to the time I had to walk through a swarm of bees. Now, as a qualifier, I'm not afraid of bees, even though I've been stung a few times. But a few years ago, I was taking a walk in my neighborhood when suddenly I was faced with a situation that was bee-yond my control. There I was, with my destination about twenty feet ahead of me, and the only thing separating me from it was a swarm of hundreds of bees.

Immediately, I felt F.E.A.R., which I believed to be the appropriate response in this situation. I realized I had three options:

Option 1. Face. Everything. And. Run. I could face the fact that I was terrified and run back in the direction from which I came.

Option 2. False. Evidence. Appearing. Real. I could pretend it was an illusion, but in this situation, the fear was valid and not some illusionary mindset.

Option 3. Ferociously. Elevate. And. Rise. I could trust that if I believed I would be okay, even in the thick of the swarm, and I could just observe the bees without attaching my fear to them, then they would not, *could not*, touch me.

Which option would you choose? Well, I chose Option 3. I walked through that mass of buzzing, half expecting the bees to part the way, much like Moses and the Red Sea. Although that didn't quite happen, what *did* happen is that I walked right through completely unscathed. And unstung. It was a surreal moment. I'll never forget being in the midst of it, noticing the bees around me, hearing their loud buzzing, and feeling no fear whatsoever, as if I tapped into some universal secret of how to detach and bee-come the observer without the chaos sucking me in.

As I got to the other side, I looked back so proud of what I had just overcome. It was such a metaphor for life. It may sound silly, but it was one of those moments in life that taught me how to remain calm and centered in the middle of a storm. Just because there's a storm brewing doesn't mean you have to attach yourself to it.

It also taught me how to Bee more and Do less. We are human beings– not human doings. If I were to try *doing* something – swatting the drama *(bees)* away – I'm sure that the drama would be compelled to sting me, because I gave it attention, albeit negative attention. By just bee-ing calm and releasing resistance, I was able to move effortlessly and freely. I'd like to think that my energy alchemized my surroundings. And in the same vein, my surroundings did not affect my energy. Law of duality.

That's the F.A.T. truth.

- I had **Faith** – I believed I would be ok.
- I took **Action** – I took the steps forward, literally.
- I had **Trust** – I trusted that I would get through to the other side … which I did.

I did not disempower myself by playing into fear. I surrendered to what was and I had faith. I detoxed the drama by flicking it away and moving forward with **E.A.S.E.** Everything. Aligns. So. Effortlessly.

But it took a positive mental attitude. Which is not always easy to maintain. So, I turned to my mentor. I asked my grandmother how she was able to stay positive despite adversity. She would say that she always **"lived with confidence."** And she meant it. My grandmother was the most confident person I ever knew. She took the phrase *confidence is your greatest accessory* to a new level. She truly trusted her **Belief** that she would be able to manipulate life to get what she wanted. She always **Expected** things to work out. No matter what.

She lived her **B.E.S.T.** life because she **Believed. Expected. Surrendered. Trusted.**

She was a master at manifesting without knowing it. The art of which is knowing what you want and then letting it go. Surrendering it. This doesn't mean you're letting go of your intention. It means you're not holding on to it so tightly that you're suffocating all the air out of it. When you **Surrender**, you **Trust** that you will get what you want ... or something better. You believe that what you desire will come to you in some form or other. You expect that what you're taking action on will materialize. You live with confidence that things will work out.

I used to think that confidence was an emotion. That if I felt anything but confident, I was insecure. I was confusing a confident *feeling* with a confident *mindset*. My husband often says that confidence has nothing to do with emotion, but rather it's a mindset. He says it a little more blatantly, but the gist is "Nobody cares if you're feeling confident. Just put your mind to it that you'll get the job done and go and do it." Eventually, practice turns into progress and progress turns into confidence.

Confidence. My favorite accessory. My secret shield.

Shielding Your Energy

Detoxing drama is not only alchemizing the energy around you, it also acts as an energy shield. Whether you're the subject of drama or just an innocent bystander, when someone is angry, you become susceptible to being the target of their negative energy. Imagine their words, emotions, and energy spewing out of them and *attacking* you, *attaching* to you, and *affecting* you. The 3 A's. Imagine those 3 A's as arrows, or rather *drama daggers*, triggered from them and pointed at you. What do you do? How can you get out of harm's way?

Be A Matador

In **Chapter 5,** I talked about wearing a raincoat and letting words slide off of you, taking off your coat, and shaking off that energy. *Disrupting drama.* Now imagine you use that coat as a shield, much like a matador uses his cape as a prop to coax the charging bull. When someone throws shade at you, take off your coat, *or cape*, and use it as a shield. That way when the drama charges at you, simply move the cape out of the way *à la matador style,* and the *drama daggers* will just rush past you, never touching you. Now you're simply an observer of those words, emotions, or energy as they pass you by. You can acknowledge their existence without allowing them to attach to you. Superhero cape style.

I imagine this like the scene from the original *Spiderman* where Peter Parker is at school the day after the infamous spider bite and someone throws a punch at him, and misses. The camera shows us how Peter perceives the punch. It looks as if it is in slow motion with Peter having time to look back and forth multiple times at the fist and the person, as he effortlessly moves out of harm's way. The punch never touches him. That's how I envision negative energy passing by, without letting it touch us. We just stare at the negativity and see it for what it is – *someone else's drama, not ours.*

> You always have a choice to either *attach* the drama to you or *detach* from it and let the daggers fly past you, taking away its power.

Sucked into Drama

What if a drama dagger pierces your shield and drags you with it?

Let's choose the dagger of criticism. When someone tries to poke holes in you with a *drama dagger*, it can only affect you if they succeed. And they can only poke holes where you have thin skin. So, in order to get thick skin ... know this.

You're simply the mirror reflecting someone else's perspective.

People meet you from their level of perception. It's nothing personal. You know the line, "What people think about you is none of your business." It's really never about you. It's a reflection of what someone else is going through. Everyone is dealing with things you know nothing about. People get triggered by things that get triggered in themselves. Happy people don't want to put others down. They don't need to elevate themselves by lowering others. It's generally people who are insecure, jealous, and unhappy, hence the term *misery loves company*.

Happy, confident, and successful people want to see you thrive. They know rooting for you doesn't mean less of the pie for them. They know there's no shortage of abundance to go around for everyone. So, when someone attacks you or tries to discredit you, know that they're coming from a place of fear or jealousy or limiting beliefs. And that's not on you. So don't let their negative energy attach to you. Don't give these energy vampires a host. Draw your boundaries, let it go, and move on. Don't be a *drama dweller*.

What if something in your life happens, and when you need the support of your closest ones, they turn their backs on you?

When the drama hits the fan, people you trust may show their true colors and throw you under the bus. That's when you need to rely on yourself. Realize how strong you truly are. And when the tornado of thoughts and emotions throws you into a tailspin, stay calm and centered. Detach and observe.

Sure, it stings when people turn their backs on you. But just like my bee story, if you have a positive attitude in life and trust that you will get through the other side unscathed, you will. It starts with you having your own back and trusting yourself and your decisions— *without attaching yourself to the outcome*. When you do this, the wrong people fall aside, the right people come to your side, and in time, those who have let you down will reveal where they stand with you. And by then, you will be so grounded in your truth that no matter their decision, you will be able to handle it gracefully. This is not only a form of self-preservation, but it also assists in conserving energy, which is so vital to your well-being.

What do you do when you want to alchemize the climate in a relationship, but the other person is being stubborn?

There's a certain person in my life who constantly thinks I gaslight them. But all I'm doing is holding up a mirror to reflect what I feel they are not giving to the relationship— or themselves. The fact remains that they can't face the truth about themself and so they deflect or lash out. My intentions come from a good place. If you can relate, how would you handle this situation?

It sounds counterintuitive, but instead of harping on the issue, you have to let it go. That's right. Release it and exhale, trusting that once the situation is detached from your energy, you can focus on maintaining positivity. You see that person may or may not come around. I have done this enough to find supportive evidence that once you let go of the negative, stop giving it all your attention, and see it for what it is— a negative attitude— then you can alchemize the situation. Bring down the temperature in the room where cooling heads can prevail and surrender to the situation. Not fighting back doesn't mean you're weak— it means you're protecting your peace by failing to engage in a fight you know you can't win. Or rather, a fight in which *no one* can win because it's set up to be a lose-lose situation from the get-go.

So instead of engaging— detach. Simmering down the situation allows the other person an opportunity to change behavior in a de-escalated climate rather than you accepting their sparring match. People change to meet you where your energy is vibrating— at a higher level— rather than you lowering your vibration to meet theirs. And if they don't, it won't bother you because you will be vibrating from such a high energetic level that you won't allow anyone to pierce your happiness bubble.

What do you do if someone is acting like the puppet master of your emotions?

- If they're stringing you along – cut the string.
- If they're attaching things to you – cut the cord.
- If they're dangling the carrot in front of you – buy your own carrots.
- If they have a tight leash on you— detach the leash.

Stop letting them be the puppet master. No one is pulling the strings but you. They want to be in charge of charging your emotions. Don't charge their power with your energy. Don't give an excuse as to why you're cutting their drama loose. Stop explaining yourself. That's like putting a suction cup on your energy and literally draining it from your body. **Explaining yourself gives away your power.** Conserve power. Let it go.

Mirror Mirror

But what if you can't let it go? Or what if it's self-criticism that's keeping you a prisoner of your past? What if you can't stop fixating on past regrets, attaching yourself to that story, holding on for dear life?

What are *you* reflecting in the mirror? What are you reflecting *on*?

> People and situations are mirrors reflecting to you what you are rejecting in yourself.

The world is your mirror. It's the view, perception, and the illusion of what you perceive to be real. Of what you believe to be true. When you look at yourself in the mirror and see a frown, you don't tell your reflection to smile. No, *you* smile to make your reflection smile. That *is* the world.

What you are experiencing around you is a reflection of what you are experiencing *within* you.

Drama is a reflection of what's going on inside you. Where you are at. This gives you a good indication of what needs some internal rewiring. What have you not given love to lately within yourself? The drama pokes at your inner compass to wake it up, saying you've veered off course and need a course correction stat. As you move through your journey, remember that the rearview mirror in your vehicle is reflective of your past. And it's a small mirror for that reason. It should not take up too much of your attention span. It shows you what you've already passed. You need to focus on what's present— through the windshield in front of you. It's large and clear for a reason. It focuses on the now.

Another tip for letting go: if you can't get something out of your head, put it in an imaginary container. Or *drama dump* about it in a letter and stick that paper in a jar. Drama doesn't seem so big once it's confined to a little space. It also seems removed from you. See it for what it is and let it go.

When you can't let go of a past situation, remind yourself of the following: Are you going to *Relive* the Drama or *Relieve* the Drama?

When this happens to me, I remember my favorite quote from Peter Crone, a brilliant mind architect. He eloquently puts things in perspective and says:

"What happened ... happened and couldn't have happened any other way because it didn't."

Game changer! I can't tell you how many times I have used this phrase and felt instant relief because it immediately detaches any feelings of guilt, remorse, or agony. That instant relief is priceless. *Thanks Peter!* This, in conjunction with my favorite tagline— *it is what it is*— are both tombstone worthy. That may sound dark, but this *is* a book about dancing with darkness and leading with love.

And when you stay centered in the eye of the tornado, you operate from the energy of love, despite any fear of the past swirling around you. You're letting it go in a way that it can't touch you, even though you may be able to see it from all angles. Remember, you can't have competing energies at the same time, so by leaning into love, you can observe the fear from a neutral perspective. You can forgive yourself for feeling fear, as well as forgiving the fear itself for fearing it.

> Forgiveness is key to leaning into love. Forgiveness allows us to move on, and this includes forgiving ourselves.

Giving ourselves grace. Being kind to ourselves. Forgiveness is not a form of weakness. It's the total opposite. Forgiveness requires immense strength. And it doesn't mean that when you forgive, you allow others the same access to you. You just aren't tolerating the toxicity to reside in you anymore like poison. Forgiveness frees you. Forgiving yourself releases a part of you that was stuck, tormented, and full of regret.

Let's talk about what happens when you attach yourself to future outcomes. If you pull the thread on future tripping and start unraveling it, *you* may start unraveling. Have you ever found yourself caught in a tornado of *what-ifs*? Don't unravel. Instead, detach from the thread by unraveling your attachment to it.

Let's take Lucy. Fictitious name, real people pleaser. Lucy tends to get caught up in making decisions based on other people's reactions, opinions, and judgments. She doesn't handle criticism well because she wants to make everyone happy. So, I asked her to consider the following:

When you think twice or hesitate about taking action because you're concerned about what someone else would think, ask yourself– would that person not take action because they're worried about what *you* would think? Do people take *your* judgment into account when they decide to do something? Then why take *theirs*?

You do you. Be the mirror and reflect to the world who you want to be. The world may not understand it, and that's ok. Give yourself permission to believe in your worth so wholeheartedly that everyone has no choice but to believe in you, too. Or not. Either way, it doesn't matter as long as you are detached from others' opinions.

It's so important to navigate life focused on the present. That's the only thing that's real at any given moment. The past is a memory. The future is a vision. The present is a gift of the current moment.

> Being *present* is the best "*present*" you can give yourself.

Surrendering is the key to mindfulness. The butterfly doesn't try to reverse the metamorphosis process. It surrenders to each stage of life. Responding to the chaos by transforming from the inside out. Literally.

Be mindful of where you put your time and energy. There's a lot of talk about work-life balance. Unfortunately, self-care tends to fall at the bottom of the list because *how can you balance it all in just 24 hours?*

You can't.

It's hard to balance everything in life. Something always happens that you don't fit into the equation of your day. When things are out of balance in your life, you need to stay balanced—*internally*. It's about inner balance rather than balancing external circumstances. When your mind, body, and soul are in harmony, you will feel at ease, confident, and able to accomplish things from a place of serenity instead of frenzy.

I wrote this poem in October of 2020. It pretty much sums up everything I want to say on balance:

> *Balance should come from the inside out*
> *Prioritizing is what it's all about*
> *You can't give your external circumstances equal attention*
> *But when you come from a place of deep intention*
> *You focus on each category one by one*
> *And you're able to accomplish what needs to be done*
> *So while you can't give everything the same attention each moment*
> *You prioritize what needs it the most in the present*
> *And you can come from a place of feeling centered and at ease*
> *That keeps you balanced internally with a sense of calm and peace*
> *So while external factors may be swirling all around*
> *Knocking your focus off kilter so you're standing on shaky ground*
> *As long as you remain balanced inside*
> *You can handle anything that comes your way outside*
> *So keep it real and know what you can take on*
> *And still remain at peace, centered, and calm.*

Enough said. So now that you're operating from a place of inner balance, how do you juggle all the curveballs life throws at you?

The Drama Diet

The Juggle is Real.

As a retired multitasker, I don't believe in juggling more than one thing at a time. Have you ever tried to juggle multiple things? You may be nodding your head in pride, saying, *yes*, you've managed to drive and put your lip gloss on at the same time, while conducting a meeting on the phone and avoiding a traffic ticket. Or maybe you bring your laptop to your child's sports game in an attempt to get in some work while supporting your kid. Or maybe you hide your phone on a Zoom call and scroll through social media, all while staying "present" in the meeting at hand. This *was* me and I used to wear multitasking and "doing it all" as a badge of honor. And guess what? I got a trophy of burnout, fatigue, and brain drain. Fun times.

Stop the juggle.

Imagine that all the things you multitask are assigned individual balls. How many of those balls do you think you can juggle until you start to drop one ... two ... all of the balls? Well, I've tried it. And let me tell you, *juggling ain't my jam*.

Scan the QR code and watch my video.

https://lisastuart.com/qr-codes/8

I don't believe you can do it all, *at least at the same time*. But I *do* believe you can *have* it all. Again, it's not about balancing your life - it's about prioritizing your time with **intentional mindfulness.**

It's about inner balance when the juggle is real, especially when things get overwhelming.

I don't believe you can balance things in your life. I believe that you need to be internally balanced in order to handle all the things out of balance in your life. Otherwise, you will feel as though you are walking on a tightrope all the time, trying to balance it all while moving with stability. It's just not sustainable.

I balance my energy by giving all my attention to whatever is needed at the moment. When I'm working, I don't stress about my laundry list of things I have to do for my kids. When I'm watching my kids perform in sports or plays, I don't worry about the hearing I have the following day because I know that I gave my legal brief 100% of my attention and effort.

I **prioritize** so I can be more **present**.

And that not only keeps me calm despite the chaos, it also decreases my stress level. I'm able to shake things off and let them go instead of dragging that energy throughout my day.

It's exhausting to try to do it all, to try to be it all, and even more so to add the pressure of having it all be perfect!

As a quasi-recovered perfectionist, I've learned over the years that perfectionism is boring. It's not relatable. People don't connect with perfectionism because it's usually an unattainable standard, so you are setting yourself up for failure before you even start.

Now take *imperfectionism*. There's simplicity in imperfection. It's authentic. Real. Raw. *Relatable*.

Let's crush the stigma of perfectionism. *Perfectionism is the dis-ease to please.* There's serenity in being real and there's release in acceptance - it's called **progress over perfection.**

Mindfulness vs. Mind Clutter

So now we've touched on multitasking, but what about filling up our calendars with *stuff* just so we don't feel that we are being lazy? Filling up the time slots in our day becomes a sport. Yet over-scheduling until our calendars overflow is a major cause of stress and is highly unproductive when the goal is to be more productive.

I was always the type to pile up things on my plate because I thought I could handle it. *Filling the void with more things was like literally stuffing down my feelings with food.*

So, I would say "yes" to that fundraiser, or event, or commitment, even though it meant squeezing time into my already pinched off day. And guess what— it made me feel even more pinched off. Squeezing in the time was like squeezing into an extra-tight wetsuit. I couldn't breathe, literally and figuratively. My day had no air, I couldn't breathe, and it caused tension. Yet, it was very hard for me to say "no" to others because a "no" to others was a "yes" to myself, and that came with a side of guilt and shame.

So, what's the antidote?

I started prioritizing my energy. I realized that I couldn't function at my full capacity unless I filled up my own tank first. It's the classic *'put your oxygen mask on first'* airplane analogy, and it's meant to save lives! I started saying "no" to things that were not as important as I had thought. And I started saying *"yes"* to myself, guilt-free. I gave myself permission for self-care without the big ugly G word. Now I have wiggle room to move with ease from each meeting, appointment, activity, or obligation. When I have a small window of time, I take it to decompress, reset my mindset, release built-up tension, or just breathe and relax.

I learned to take a daily *retreat*, so I don't *deplete*. Then *repeat*.

Donate your time and energy to things that fill you up instead of things that drain you.

What you give your attention to is so vital to the preservation of your energy. When you donate your time, you are doing it with the intention of not receiving anything back. The byproduct of this is that it fulfills you with joy and gratitude. But if you're giving your time and energy away, free of charge, to energy vampires and other people's opinions, you are sacrificing yourself. Notice the difference. **Donating** your time vs **sacrificing** your time. Both require expending time, energy, and attention. But it is the *intention* behind it that makes the difference.

Is the intention to serve others from a place of love or do you sacrifice your time from a place of fear?

This is an important distinction. Oftentimes sacrificing comes wrapped up in the disguise of donating. It's when we think we are doing something helpful to others, but the way we feel at the end of the encounter tells a different story. You will know the difference because there will be an ***unequal exchange of energy***. The scales will be predominantly tipped in one direction, making you feel internally imbalanced. Everything in life is energy and therefore everything has to have an *equal energetic exchange* to feel balanced. So, beware of energy that only flows in one direction. If the pipes are not open, then the energy will get stuck in the emotional transaction. It will only flow one way, towards the other person, thought or situation.

You can detox this by learning to say "no" ... without guilt. Which leads me to this: I also decided to detox my calendar. I wasn't going to allow worry, guilt, shame, fear, judgment or any other limiting belief, cloud my calendar. I made a conscious decision not to give them a time slot in my day. This freed up my energy to be more productive.

I also discovered that depriving myself of self-care and self-love was only destructive to me.

Self-Love

Self-love gets a bad rap. It has been called *selfish*. It emits a connotation of being *self-absorbed* for people wrapped up in themselves. There has been a lot of shame and guilt thrown around the subject. And the concept of self-love has often been reserved for people who pamper themselves. Yet oftentimes the same people who are indulging themselves are simultaneously shaming themselves in guilt. Why? Because of the stigma that self-love is bad, we need to pour everything out of ourselves for other people, because living a service-based life is what we are supposed to do. Right?

Partially.

> Serving others and giving back is an important part of life, but not at the expense of yourself!

Read that again.

You can't pour from you if there's nothing left to pour!

Sacrifice is old school. Martyrdom — that's *so 1900s*. It is so important not to neglect yourself. You are your best judge of where you're at energetically, physically, emotionally, mentally, and spiritually. You are responsible for making sure that you keep yourself fully filled with self-nourishment on all levels — mind, body, and spirit. No one else is responsible for that. My grandmother always told me, "No one will love you the way you love yourself." What she meant was that no one knows you like you do. You need to differentiate between what nourishes you and what depletes you.

Self-Love isn't Selfish.
Self-Love is being Self-*ish*.

I used to think self-love was selfish until I realized it wasn't about choosing to love me or you. It wasn't even about putting one of us above the other. It is about honoring ourselves so that we don't deplete our energy for the sake of pleasing others. It's so we can come from a place of wholeness. It's being **self-invested**. It's *essential* to being **self-interested**. When others aren't interested in you … take more interest in yourself! You do this with self-care.

Self-care isn't a luxury. Self-care is a necessity.

But self-care feels better if you make it feel luxurious. *Aren't you worth it?* If you don't take care of your needs – mind, body, and spirit – who will? You know the phrase, *"If you don't make time for your wellness, you will be forced to take time for your illness."* Self-care and wellness should have a daily time slot in your calendar. Check in with yourself and ask what you need. A ten-minute walk around the block to move that energy? A matcha with a friend? A fifteen-minute breathwork meditation? A dance party for one with your favorite song? Or luxuriate with a massage, mani-pedi, facial, or simply a bubble bath. Do you need some one-on-one time with your partner? Children? BFF? Or maybe some alone time with yourself and a good book. Whatever fills your cup to the brink is what you need to do for yourself. Don't pour from your cup. Give from whatever spills over. Give from the overflow.

- *Do you give so much to others that you forget to prioritize yourself?*
- *Do you feel like your cup is filled to capacity with what you "should" be doing?*
- *Is your cup overflowing with stress, guilt, and fatigue with little to no time left for you?*

Go from OverFlow to OverGlow!

First, prioritize self-care and fill your soul with renewed passion and joy. When you are in harmony – mind, body, and soul – you glow effortlessly.

It's time to Glow Up.

Slough off the drama like an exfoliant and reveal your glow. *Shed who you are not to reveal who you are.* Give yourself permission to *shine!* Notice when the voice shows up – the chatter, judgment, opinions. Forgive the voice – it's all it knows. After all, the voice is just noise.

Light doesn't make noise. Light shines.

Light travels faster than sound. Know that when you shine you are emitting a greater and more powerful energy than any noise that may attempt to destroy it. When you shine, you're not taking the spotlight away from anyone. You're not diminishing anyone else's flame. Just like when one candle flame lights another candle, it does not dim the light of the giving candle. It can burn just as bright as the next, and the next. In fact, you can light endless candles with the flame of just one candle and they'll all burn bright. True, eventually the candles will burn down and burn out. But that is different from another candle stealing its flame and in doing so blowing out that first candle.

Shine bright – the world needs your light. And don't dim your light just because someone else wants you to or feels that your light is casting a shadow on them. Everyone can shine just as bright without casting shadows on each other. Yet inevitably, there will always be those who *want* to cast shadows.

Those people want to see you shine, as long as you don't outshine them.

Illuminating. Don't block your blessings by shrinking yourself.

When you dim your light, you are blocking not only your blessings but those around you who are being deprived of the benefit of the light you have to offer them.

You're not helping by hiding. Be seen and shine!

In the same vein, when you forgive and shower others with love, you are shining your light on them. But you are not giving away your light as you do when you let energy vampires suck your light. You and you alone get to choose whether you are dimming your light. When you shine a light on others you are allowing them to ignite their own flame.

When you own your worth, you win.

Own It — To Win

Own it and *to win* have the same letters rearranged. And they both derive from the same energy. In order to win in life, you need to own all aspects of yourself. Remember the **L.A.S.H.** method – Love. Accept. See. Hear. All aspects of yourself. You're worth it.

Who wrote the rules anyway?! You wrote the rules. Now own the rules!

- Own your worth!
- Don't hand it out like party favors.
- Don't ask anyone to validate it for you like parking tickets.
- Don't shove it under the rug for others to walk on.

The keys to self-worth are *self-acceptance, self-validation, and self-love*. See how self-*ish* you deserve to be?

Self-worth isn't earned. Self-worth is an inherent right.

The ugly duckling is a symbol of knowing one's worth. Remember the **S.W.A.N.** that you are.

Self. Worth. Attaching. Nothing.

Be detached from limiting beliefs. As a lawyer, I urge you to stop defending your limitations and start advocating for your worth. Self-worth detoxes *guilt, judgment, and victimhood.* All wasted emotions.

Got Guilt?

Surrender that story. Guilt is giving someone or something the power over your peace of mind. *Are you guilty of feeling guilty?* Lose the guilt. The fastest weight to drop is the unbearable heaviness of guilt.

Do a Guilt Drop.

G.U.I.L.T. — Give. Up. Investing in. Lost. Time.

Stop wasting time on a dumb emotion like guilt. If you have regret, do something about it. If you can't, forgive yourself and move on. Don't stay stuck in a moment. I like to say "FIAMO" when I'm stuck in a sticky emotion. FIAMO stands for *Forgive It And Move On* or *F*ck It And Move On* depending on your mood. Both work. And it's fun to say in an Italian accent. Somehow, that makes it feel more powerful.

Judgment

Unless I'm in a court of law, I stay away from judgment. Everyone messes up. People are trying their best, and if they're not, then they have a choice to step it up or step away. If someone is criticizing you and it's not constructive, then it will end up being destructive if you don't detox it and flick it away. Next time someone judges you, say, "Go ahead. Finish that sentence. I don't break that easily." And mean it. *Even if you are only saying it to yourself under your breath or in your mind.* Their judgment can't break you unless you allow it to. You've established a strong foundation that they can't shake. If you still feel the sting, remember the 3 F's: *face it, feel it, free it.*

I'm in no position to judge others, and therefore, I gave up judging myself. Self-judgment is the gateway to self-loathing, and

I'm not walking through that door. When my inner mean girl has the audacity to judge me, I tell her, "That's a mouthful of judgment." Then I remember my craving for success, joy, and peace, and munch on those instead. I feed myself self-love.

Victimhood

There are no victims, only volunteers. Of course, this does not apply to criminal acts. But it is criminal to waste your emotions on victimhood. Instead, pull yourself up and pull yourself together. *The blame game* is so 2020. It's time to be accountable for your own actions, choices, and decisions. If you feel wronged by someone, accept that it happened and do something about it other than complain. Take your power back.

When someone continuously treats you badly, whether or not they're consciously aware of it, instead of falling into the victim mentality, look at them as if there's something wrong with them, as if they have an illness or uncontrollable symptom— *like a puppy who pees everywhere and can't help himself!* You feel sorry for him. It's not his fault. That's how you have to look at it. People are urinating all over you, but it's not their fault. Unfortunately, they're wired that way and can't help it. Detox yourself and don't let their uncontrollable actions leave a stain.

Instead, be mindfully observant, as though you're watching yourself on TV. Vested in how you feel yet disconnected from the events.

T.V. –Thoughts. Visualization. You have your own TV program in your consciousness. You're in control of the remote. Don't go back to the antiquated **V.C.R.** version of your life –your **Victim. Consciousness. Reactions.**

The VCR records old memories, reactions, and emotional responses and keeps them on a time loop set in old patterns of behaviors and thoughts. This also allows you to replay them on demand.

The TV alchemizes the frequencies and vibrations into pictures and sounds –into tangible realities. Stay conscious in the present and create your reality.

Let's play devil's advocate that you can't get out of victimhood. Well, did you know that the word **devil** is the word **lived** spelled backward? Do you want to live from a place of darkness? Or light?

When you choose to **L.I.V.E**. *–* *Love. Ignites. Vibrations. Effortlessly.*

As your *Drama Diet* advocate, I suggest you choose to live with love. Because to choose otherwise would feel illegal, as if you were robbing yourself of joy. And as a lawyer, I advocate to be **L.E.G.A.L**.

Let. Everything. Go. And. Laugh.

Yes – laugh – because W.T.F. – Where's. The. Fun?!

Let. In. Fun. Energy. – L.I.F.E. should not be that serious.

And don't take yourself so seriously either. Laugh at yourself, at your imperfections, even at your drama. Let loose and let them loose. When you're tethered to the drama, imagine it's just an airplane flying in a moment of time that sucked you in. Detach from it like you're jumping out of that plane. Surrender and trust the process. You're always waiting for someone to give you a parachute when you take that leap of faith. Or for a safety net. You can't have it both ways. You can't take a leap of faith and expect someone or something to save you. Falling, *failing*, is saving you because it's teaching you how to rise up again. Otherwise, you'll always stay in the gray zone, the comfortable chaos of being complacent, where you safely inch forward and back but don't gain any true momentum.

Life is a rhythm of flying and falling. Once you trust to flow with the music, you will fly with fear and fall with faith. The harmonious balance of life.

RECIPE

The E.A.S.Y. Shake

The recipe to make life feel E.A.S.Y.

ETCH. A. SKETCH. YOURSELF.

Literally, shake it off. Like the game. I like to give my body a little shake and imagine that I'm erasing whatever was attached to me that was not aligned with me. Like it just disintegrates into thin air.

The antidote to agonizing over something or the past

Etch A Sketch Yesterday - shake off the past.

*****

EXERCISE: The M.O.O. Method

Mindful. Objective. Observation.

Be a **C.O.W.** – a **Conscious. Objective. Witness** of your thoughts, feelings, and reactions.

Sometimes, drama tries to stampede your mind. The M.O.O. Method helps you slow things down, ground yourself, and respond from *awareness*, not autopilot.

Here's how to practice it:

1. Mindful

Pause. Breathe. Notice what's happening *right now* – in your body, your emotions, your environment.

Ask: "What am I feeling?"

"Where am I feeling it in my body?"

"What triggered this?"

This step is about presence – not fixing anything, just *noticing*.

2. Objective

Detach from the swirl. Pretend you're simply curiously studying yourself with compassion

Ask "Is this a fact, or is it a story I'm telling myself?"

"What else might be true here?"

"What would I say to a friend feeling this?"

This step helps you move out of reactivity and into clarity.

3. Observation

Zoom out. Witness your thoughts like clouds passing or cows grazing (C.O.W. vibes). No judgment – just gentle awareness.

Ask: "What patterns am I seeing?"

"Is this an old reaction or a new moment?"

"What choice do I want to make now – from love, not fear?"

When you're a **C.O.W.** - you're a **Conscious Objective Witness**, you don't *become* your thoughts or emotions – you observe them. You give yourself the grace to pause, reflect, and choose your next move with intention.

Try It: Next time you're triggered or overwhelmed, take a M.O.O. Moment.

Write down what you noticed in each step – or just say it out loud. Let yourself slow down, feel safe, and lead from clarity.

*****

DRAMA DIARY VIDEO JOURNAL PROMPT

Shed who you are not to reveal who you are.

Are you the same person you were 10 years ago? 5 years ago? Last year? Even last month?

- We evolve through our seasons, and every season demands a different version of ourselves.

- And when you evolve, you start stripping away the exterior labels that were given to you, so that your authentic self emerges.
- You don't truly change.
- You simply reconnect with who you really are.
- And when you align with who you truly are, all the pieces connect.
- You can reinvent yourself at any age. You can recreate your life at any stage. But the closer you get to your true life's purpose and passion, the more lit up and inspired you will feel!!

Record your manifestation goals in a video and watch it weekly. Then watch yourself transform. After a while, you won't recognize the person on the other end of the video as the current you - *that's how much you can evolve in such a short time*!

This is not only to inspire you and keep you accountable ... but also to see how far you've come and revel in your transformation.

The Drama Diet

11

DETOX PART 2

Fall with Faith. Fly with Fear.

> **Case Law: *Faith vs. Fear***
>
> On the scales of justice, are you leaning into faith, or are you leaning into fear? Now this is sort of a trick question because it begs to be asked – Do we want the scales to be even? We know that from contrast comes balance, so does that mean that the law of duality requires equal opposing forces to bring us balance? Or do we tip the scale in favor of one side, preferably faith? But then that makes the scales imbalanced. Perhaps it's in the teetering of the scale - the journey through the light and dark - that leads us home.

    Living in faith or fear depends on whether we are leaning into light or dark energies. We know the energies of love and fear cannot exist without each other. Same with faith and doubt. One defines the other. However, they can enmesh in the same space, forming a mix of emotions and situations that can cause inner turmoil or outer chaos. For example, you can adore someone and constantly walk on eggshells in fear that something will set them off. Anxiously awaiting their next episode. When these energies are commingled, they co-exist in a swirl of drama. And while one energy will always prevail in any given moment, it may present as strong fear or just a flicker of faith. We don't live in a vacuum. We are meant to experience the range of all emotions. So how do we measure the energy we need to balance our lives? Let's weigh our options.

Now that you've taken a *leap of faith* and jumped out of the drama airplane, you are able to pan out and see it from a bird's eye perspective. From that view, everything seems manageable, drama seems small, and you are able to rise above the drama. **The Drama Diet** encourages you to be firm, yet F.L.A.B.B.Y. in your decisions – Free. Like. A. Bird. Be. Yourself.

So with this bird's eye view, let's take a look at **The Drama Diet's** last prong in the *3D Drama Free Formula:* **Detoxing Drama – decide** to **dance** with your **drama.** When you dance with it, you embrace it and keep it close, but lead with love. This is how you become a *Drama Ninja*.

Decide to dance on the edge, along the tightrope of love and fear.

Sure, you can slip up at any given moment and lead with fear. But you can regain your balance and let love lead the way. So again, is your balance dependent on keeping the scales even? Or leaning one way or another?

For example, you've just heard juicy gossip about someone. Your first instinct may be to spread this tantalizing news, because it's just too much fun to keep to yourself. What do you do? You weigh the pros and cons of gossip on a scale and measure the results. If that tidbit your friend gave you slips out of your mouth because you want to share it with your other friends, think about how the object of gossip would feel. Would the hurt that person would feel outweigh the fleeting moment of sharing it and "bonding" with your friends? If your answer is *yes*, you may walk away feeling unsettled in your core. You could thus feel internally imbalanced, knowing that you've rocked the scales of justice in an unbalanced, and even unkind way.

This is because you made a decision – you *judged* that person you shared gossip about, and now you are *judging* yourself. The last chapter explains how judgment is a wasted emotion. But did you know that **judgment is also the absence of love?**

Judgment divides. Love unites.

For every decision, there is a consequence. *Cause and effect.*

Can I decide? *Have you met me?* Someone once said to me, "I know you're an Aquarius because you can't make up your mind." LOL. Life of Lisa. I like to weigh my options – on the scales of justice. But I've decided to be decisive. There's no wrong decision because a decision *is* a decision. If it doesn't work out, shake it off and choose another.

My grandfather always said that the greatest power is the power to choose. Choose faith over fear, love over judgment, peace over worry, confidence over doubt, happiness over envy. These are all choices we have at any given moment.

What we decide defines our reality. And in order to make decisions, we need clarity. In order to get clarity, we need to take action and believe in ourselves.

Here's the ABC's of it. Action + Belief = Clarity. Clarity leads to Decisions.

Let me spill the T.E.A. again. Thoughts. Emotions. Actions. are encompassed in all three prongs of the 3D Drama Free Formula – *disrupt, deflate, detox.* Yet **action** is prevalent for the **detox** prong. You need to take action to actively draw boundaries. The last chapter discusses how to get *clarity from chaos.* Freedom is derived from clarity, and clarity is derived from clear boundaries.

"Wait. I thought we were now free? Boundaries are confining! How does that make us free if we are restricted by borders?"

Boundaries *create* freedom.

The borders distinguish love and fear. It's the tightrope of life.

It's always a delicate balance of where to put that line because you want to keep exploring and expanding while at the same time keep protecting your peace.

Where do you draw the line?

Be a Kind B*tch

The day I stopped being nice was the day I started to shed my drama. I **decided** to be clear, firm, and resolute with what I was willing to tolerate. You see, I've been called *nice* my whole life. People often told me that I'm the *nicest* person they know. I'm not saying this to be boastful. I'm saying this to show a point.

Being told I am the *nicest* validated my worth and I would eat it up. But at times I was left feeling taken advantage of, and *that* would eat *me* up!

I didn't realize at the time that being nice was just another way of saying "Hi, I'm a people pleasing doormat. Feel free to step all over me."

> People pleasers want to control how others feel about them ... instead of controlling how they feel about themselves.

Being nice meant handing my heart over and letting people pour their emotions into me without boundaries. It meant doing everything to please *others* at my own expense. It meant saying *yes* when I really want to scream *hell no*. It meant feeling guilty if I chose self-love over sacrificing my time for others. It meant feeling torn and split anytime others expressed disappointment at my choices. It meant doing something to appease someone else when that person would probably not reciprocate if the roles were reversed.

Eventually, I had enough. I finally jumped off the loop of that stale soundtrack. I decided to stop being nice, and instead, decided to be kind. You see, *nice* does not equate to being *kind*. Kindness means serving others from a place of love, not fear of losing their "likes"– IRL not social media. It comes from a place of *wanting* to help others, not *needing* to keep the peace.

What kindness does *not* mean is doing something at our own expense, depleting our energy, or needing external validation.

Don't be *nice*. **Be a Kind B*tch.**

Say yes to yourself without fear.
Say no to others without guilt.
Set loving boundaries.

A Kind B* says *no* – *lovingly* – and if not lovingly to others, it's at least lovingly to themselves. Self-love. Self-preservation. Self-compassion. Give with your full heart to help others, but not at the expense of your own wellbeing. If that sounds b*tchy, well, so hence the term Kind B*tch.

A B*tch with Boundaries.

Nice = a slippery slope to being a doormat.
Kind = compassionate with boundaries.

Now when people call me *nice*, I cringe. Instead of equating to *worthy*, being called *nice* equates to *cringeworthy*.

K.I.N.D. B.*.T.C.H.

K-eep
I-nspiring
N-o
D-rama

B-oundaries
I-nstilled
T-o
C-ultivate
H-armony

And don't mistake kindness for weakness. Kindness is love with an edge. Don't be all rainbows and sparkles. Put on your *drama ninja* suit and protect your energy.

Be compassionate, not empathetic.

Be wary of the difference between compassion and empathy. They have opposing energies. Compassion holds space for others, preserving your energy with loving boundaries. Empathy takes on someone else's energy, so you feel it, which is draining. It basically makes you a host of other people's emotions. Compassion still has an element of kindness, but without the soul sucking drainage of letting your energy run out of you and pour into someone else through some invisible IV line. Being compassionate means you can hold space for those who need it, without letting that space invade your energy shield.

> Compassion alchemizes the room with your elevated vibration. Empathy sucks the energy from the room into you, so you become it.

As a prior empath, I not only felt other people's emotions, I took on those emotions. In fact, my brother used to tell me that my mood was based on other people's emotions. As much as I hated to admit it, he was right. There was no hiding it. I didn't just wear my emotions on my sleeve ... my emotions were dripping down my arm ... like sweat after a hot yoga class. *I was literally dripping in drama.* I thought that I was being compassionate. I wasn't. I was being empathetic. I now know the distinction and can draw the line.

Freedom Lines

Life ebbs and flows like the ocean. When nothing disrupts that flow, there is no resistance. When someone or something blocks that flow, it causes a jam such as a comment from someone that stings, or an action from someone that annoys you. Blocks are created by people who drain your energy, time, or emotions. Be smart like a smartphone and block them like a blocked call so they don't spam you and waste your precious time. Keep the line open. *Keep the channels clear.* Surrender to what is, release resistance, and let that sh*t go. E-motions – energy in motion – are only supposed to last 90 seconds. Use the 90-second rule – *face it, feel it, free it.*

Remember – you can sit in the emotions without letting them sit in you.

Don't give anyone or anything permission to be a block in the flow of your life.

There needs to be an *equal energetic exchange* for everything in life.

We see this energetic exchange in all relationships. Relationships with partners, friends, and family members. Relationships with money, jobs, and opportunities. Relationships with movement, emotions, and consumption.

Everything is an energetic exchange, and when it's imbalanced, *you will feel imbalanced.* You'll experience a tug of war with the invisible cord attached to your and someone else's energy. Or even between you and your inner mean talk. Or between you and your job. Or between you and your gym membership that you keep on hold. An imbalanced energetic relationship will feel like resistance which is an instant red flag to what is not aligning in your life. We know from the last chapter that when you release your hold on the cord and surrender, it does not mean you are giving up or giving in. It means someone has crossed the line and attached their cord to you. But you can draw a new line that they cannot cross.

Set those boundaries where you want. It's important to decide how close or far away you want to draw those lines from you. **Decide** who has access to you, your time, your energy. What are you willing to tolerate from people? From yourself? What decisions can you make without drama dwelling on negative self-talk?

The first question is whether the relationship is vibrationally equivalent. You'll know by the angst you feel in relationships. Maybe you've been the energy vampire and sucked people's time and energy. Maybe it's caused you to step up and fix it or step out and free it. And when other energy vampires sunk their teeth into you, were you their victim?

There are no victims, only volunteers.

Filter out who has real interest in you and who is just draining your surface. True friends keep it real. They have your back even if they don't agree with your decisions. They support you because *it's about you – not what you are doing.* They root for you on your path to finding the door to your next chapter ventures. They not only applaud you for finding that door, but they also *hold that door open for you!* They don't make you feel bad for not knowing where the door was in the first place. They believe you deserve to have your opportunity. Those are the people you should hold close to you, cherish, and never take for granted.

Then there are people who feign interest. They may seem interested, but it's not genuine. When you encounter these people, you will feel an imbalance of energy in the relationship, where one side is predominantly the giver or the recipient of that energy. You know the type – sometimes they lurk on your social media account but never comment when they see something new in your life. They call you up and pretend they don't know what's going on. They're not playing stupid. They're just disinterested, or insincere, or jealous, or judging, or just choosing to acknowledge what serves them. *Silence speaks volumes.* It's the absence of interest. Filter these people out of your energy sphere.

Then there are those who try to squeeze all your dirty laundry out to hang, while theirs smells all fresh and rosy. Do you know those "perfect" families? The ones where the kids just seem to fall into line, and every time you ask the parents how everything is, they always have a cheery smile and say, "Everything is wonderful." Ya, those are not my friends, lol. My friends are real … raw … honest. We don't gloss over the dark spots. We dig them up, dissect them, and then detoxify them.

Do you have those types of ride or die friends like that in your life? If so, be so thankful for them. And be reciprocal. You would never want to be the subject of anyone else's drama. It should be an *equal energetic relationship*. Don't worry about the non-supporters and the non-believers. If you can count on one hand how many people have your back, you are doing phenomenal. But you have to discern who these people are.

Focus on those who root for you, no matter what is going on in their lives. Focus on what you can control no matter what is going on in *your* life. Control what you eat, watch, listen to, and tell yourself. Control who you spend time with, who you confide in, what you give your attention to, and what you spend time on.

By controlling what you consume on a daily basis you are in

charge of your wellbeing. You get to decide where to draw boundaries on what you consume. As within, so without. *You become what you consume.*

Be a Conscious Consumer

I may be a Drama Dietician ... but while I'm neither a health practitioner nor a nutrition expert, I do know this:

What you consume consumes you.

Mentally. Emotionally. Physically. Spiritually. In the last chapter we talked about not just filling your time but being *intentional* with your time. Likewise, don't just fill your mind, body and soul mindlessly. Be *intentional* with what you put in. This is the secret to **detoxification.**

We consume with our bodies. Be mindful of what you are putting into your precious vessel. Fill yourself up with nutrients and goodness rather than toxicity. Junk food is easy to consume because it's effortless and quick. But it wreaks havoc on your gut. And gut health is so important. Not just for your physical health, but for your emotional health. You've heard of the brain-gut axis. A balanced gut microbiome directly affects your emotional wellbeing. A healthy gut helps reduce inflammation which aids in preventing inflammatory emotions. The gut produces about 90% of your serotonin which is the neurotransmitter that regulates mood, anxiety, and happiness. It's your "feel good" neurotransmitter. The gut also produces other neurotransmitters like dopamine. That's why your gut is considered your second brain. Feed your gut, feed your brain. Isn't that food for thought?

We consume with our emotions. Don't consume other people's emotions – don't give other people easy access to you with empathy – create loving boundaries with compassion. Loving relationships are like nourishing food for the soul. Toxic relationships are like junk food with a quick sugar high before your energy comes crashing down. When feelings present like a block in your gut, flip it by *facing, feeling, and freeing it*. Otherwise, that buildup of pressure will make you implode, like a pressure cooker. And no one would know but your insides, that gut wrenching agony of emotional pain. Here's an example.

I had a really tough week. I mean a brutal week. But I stayed calm. I kept my optimism. I know that the universe has my back. I know that everything happens *for* me, not *to* me. Until the last straw that broke the camel of the week's back, and I completely erupted. We all have a breaking point. Mine happens to have a large threshold. Not so good: allows too many things to boil up and boil over. I need to constantly clear out the drama clutter before it has a chance to erupt.

Instead, I imploded. We all have a tipping point on the emotional scale, and I was over my daily chaos caloric intake. And then, with absolutely no shame or regret, I vented to a friend, because even though I know the number one rule in stopping drama is to kybosh the venting in its tracks so as not to add fuel to the fire, I couldn't help myself. I needed to let it out.

I couldn't contain my emotional consumption without it consuming me.

Within a couple hours, I was back at base level. It was as if all the pent-up frustration bubbled over all at once and needed to be released. *Drama overload* I call it. I needed to drama dump. So, I made a **P.I.T.** stop to my friend and then **P**ut. **I**t **I**n. **T**he **T**rash. In that moment, I knew what was best for me, because I knew that to get over it, I had to get *through* it. And I know my limits. I know what I can handle. I know how much steam I need to let off in a healthy manner until I can bring myself back to neutral.

I'm human. Not plastic. I don't melt with drama. I escalate. As we all do. And it's a matter of knowing my own inner boundaries to know what I need for myself so that I don't bury drama deep within to fester and lay eggs. I already did the inner digging to dredge up

The Drama Diet

buried drama and crack it (and me) wide open. I'm not interested in adding layers to what I already chiseled away.

> A good friend is like a venting vault.

I'm also very lucky to have friends who let me vent without judgment, *and* without judging anyone about whom I may be venting. And if you're lucky enough to have one or two *venting vaults*, you are extremely lucky.

And this is my point. Humaning is hard. Partnering is hard. Parenting is hard. Friending is hard. Working is hard. They're all hard when they're not easy. And that's the plainest way I can say it.

So when we can't stop the drama without it infecting us, we need to let it go through and out of us. Like the E-motions. The facing, feeling, and freeing it. Sometimes the 90 seconds turns into 90 minutes, and that's ok. I have a one-day rule. Whatever you feel today, you need to shake off and release by the next day.

> My philosophy is that with the rising sun comes a new story, so don't drag yesterday's toxicity to poison today's potential.

If you do, that's on you. A little tough love, yet love, nonetheless.

I want to spend a little time here on the concept of venting. Yes, it can be destructive because the more we harp on something, the more we allow that toxicity to fester and spread. However, if we don't let it out of us, that same toxicity can fester and spread within us.

So, to **detox** that here are a few options:

- Journal it out.
- Dance it out.
- Walk it out.

- And if all else fails, talk it out.

With a safe space friend. Again, having a *venting vault* allows us to detox the drama out of us, but into a confined container which stops the outbreak of contaminating others with the drama. Make sense?

We consume with our souls. Be mindful of what you ingest each day. Choose to love yourself fiercely with daily self-care – *guilt free.* Be neutral and observe what is. Don't attach; shake off the non-essential drama that won't matter the next day. Focus on soUlutions, not problems. Fill yourself up with things that bring you joy. Listen to music that fills your soul, or podcasts that add value to your life. Take a walk in nature. Listen to the birds sing. Sit at the beach. Breathe. Play. Paint. Dance.

We consume with our passions. How hungry are you? It's typically not the smartest, most talented or gifted person that becomes a success ... *it's the hungriest!* And people who are hungry want to satisfy their appetite before anything else. They don't ask if it's the right time to eat, or whether they deserve to eat, or if they need to stand in line until it's their turn to eat. They have a voracious appetite that fuels their ability to surpass others who are more qualified. They believe they deserve success. They commit to their belief, and they are certain of it. Follow your passion without judgment. Do what you love so you love what you do. Don't deprive yourself of nourishing your joy. Don't starve the world of your gifts.

We consume with our minds. Be mindful of what you are feeding your mind and what you are allowing to penetrate your thoughts. What are you reading? Watching on TV? What are you absorbing by mindlessly scrolling on social media? What are you listening to? You're like a sponge, whether you consciously realize it or not. It seeps into your subconscious mind. You get to be in control of what you serve your brain. And what you serve your brain should serve you. Make sure that what you are feeding your mind is true. To make any change in our lives, we need to start with a thought. One simple thought can set the wheels in motion. It can simply be a thought of possibility, of "what ifs".

Once you accept that thought, you can allow it to simmer in the back of your brain, melting in your mind, and dripping down into your soul, feeding your desires.

No matter what you are consuming, make sure that it's bite-sized, digestible servings of whatever satisfies your craving. You are in charge of keeping your vessel – mind, body, spirit–healthy and vibrant. Your cells have memory. They listen. They keep score.

How you talk to yourself, *your cells*, is vital to your vitality.

Talk with gratitude, appreciation, and love. Stay calm and centered. Stress is a huge component of dis-ease.

You are too *blessed* to be *stressed*.

When you S.T.R.E.S.S. you have to:

Stop. **T**hinking. **R**uminating. **E**nergetic. **S**oulsucking. **S**tories.

Whenever I would stress about something, my grandmother would say with her infamous smile, "This isn't going to matter in 50 years." She was right. It probably wouldn't matter in 50 days or 50 hours or maybe even in 50 minutes. But in the moment, it seemed like the most pressing thing in the world, and the weight pressing down on my shoulders felt unbearable.

Still, I saw her point. *From a bird's eye perspective, is this really going to matter in the whole scheme of things?*

Then I began to think of all the things I had worried about in the past *that never came true* and realized how silly I was to worry about those things. Of course, hindsight is 20/20. When you break the hamster wheel habit of stressing, that hamster will not know where to go, and will inevitably go home.

Whenever I stress, my son loves to tell me "Mom ... it's not that deep." And he's right. When I take a step back to peer into the depth of the problem from a bird's eye viewpoint, it's relatively shallow. Interesting how a different perspective changes things.

Starve yourself of non-serving stress.
Feed yourself choices of happiness.

Yes. Happiness *is* a choice.

Are You Happy? This was a constant question my grandfather used to ask me. And he was genuinely interested in whether I was *a happy girl.* I wondered, what did it mean to be happy? We hear so much about the **pursuit of happiness**. *Life, liberty, and the pursuit of happiness.* Why is it always a pursuit? Why isn't it the *pursuit of life* or the *pursuit of liberty?* Life and liberty are assumed to be guaranteed. But happiness? It's dangled before us like a carrot on a stick waiting for perpetual pursuit. That makes happiness feel as though it's within our grasp yet still out of reach. What if we just grabbed it? Would it slip out of our fingers, endlessly waiting for us to chase it like the *Roadrunner?* Instead, what if we simply **decided** to be happy – in the moment – instead of waiting for something to *make* us happy?

This made me think. *Be like Tink. Think Happy Thoughts.* That's how *Peter Pan* and his friends fly. With happy thoughts. And to F.L.Y. you must First. Love. Yourself.

You are responsible for your own happiness and no one else's. In the same vein, no one else is responsible for *your* happiness. That is on you, dear friends. Others may add or detract from it, but no one can steal your happiness. You'd have to willingly give it to them. Happiness is a choice, and the choice is always yours to make. No matter what may disrupt your life. Remember that you are the key to your happiness and that you are the key to the energy that propels it forward. There is no spare so don't spare your time or energy on negativity.

Filter your Energy

I believe that energy gets projected through a filter. Our internal filter is either aligned or misaligned to the beliefs of our core. When we are aligned with our true selves, the energy filters through, emitting joy, love, peace, and light. If we are misaligned to our true selves, then the energy will be filtered through our ego and will reflect fear, doubt, heaviness, and darkness.

Fear is filtered through the ego.
Love is filtered through the true self.

While lightness and darkness can exist in the same space, they overlap in their constant fight for the front row seat.

Something happened in the midst of writing this book. I got stuck. Not just a bump in the road. The *heavy-can't-move-your-feet-forward-dragging-your-energy-with-a-500-pound-rock-attached-to-it* kind of stuck. So, I did what anyone in my position would do. *I freaked the F out.* Yep. I completely and shamelessly freaked out. I cried. I complained. I walked in circles. Literally. I couldn't figure out how to get unstuck. Nothing I pulled out of my usual bag of tricks was working. My go-to methods failed me. From movement to meditation. *Nothing seemed to be working.*

Until I accepted that I wasn't meant to fix myself. I was meant to feel all the feels. Not numb them or dumb them down. Instead, allow the shadows to take over for a minute and block the light– *without fear* – because I knew the light was always there. Blocking it didn't eliminate it. It was just a dark cloud covering the sun temporarily, allowing the dark aspects a moment in the spotlight (irony intended).

That's how I learned how to flip the magnet.

Flipping the Drama Magnet

I have a confession. When I first started talking about flipping the drama magnet to either attract or repel energy, I thought it was a cute metaphor. Repel darkness and attract love. But then it hit me – *magnets only attract its polar opposite*. This would mean that fear repels fear, and love repels love. It would also mean that love attracts fear, and fear attracts love.

This just completely blew my theory!

But then I thought about it. If **The Drama Diet** is about dancing with your darkness and embracing the drama, then it **must** *attract love and light*. It took me a minute to wrap my head around this, but I came up with a digestible explanation.

Since a magnet attracts its opposite polarity, *if you have love, you attract fear*. Likewise, *if you have fear, you attract love*. One cannot exist without the other. To repel drama, you essentially have to embrace it so you can alchemize the energy of fear into love. On the flipside, if you're not careful, you can transmute the energy of love into fear.

You embody both competing energies – *light and dark, peace and drama, love and fear*.

- Two positives *repel* each other. There's no contrast to define it.
- Two negatives *repel* each other. Again ... no contrast to define it.
- It's the positive and negative charges fighting for the attention that *attract* each other.

The contrast defines the energies. They're both vying for attention. It's the push and pull. Which pull or tug is stronger?

You attract what you are by repelling what you are not.

> It's the fusion of opposite polarities that determines what we attract.

You **attract what you love** with an element of **fear** because you are leaving your comfort zone thereby repelling what you don't want. On the flipside, you **attract what you fear** with an element of **love** because you think you are keeping yourself safe in your comfortable chaos.

We need the darkness in conjunction with the light in order to attract what we desire – *or magnetize what we fear* – depending on which polarity of the magnet is stronger.

This is how you flip the magnet.

Embracing the dark with the light keeps you balanced on the tightrope of life. Otherwise, you will lose your balance and fall off.

The contrast keeps you balanced.

- We need boundaries, but boundaries can be stifling.
- We need direction, but direction can be limiting.
- We need defining but defining can be cage-like.

So, to be truly free, we need to test the boundaries to see how far we can wildly swing while staying centered within. Like a pendulum swinging back and forth while weighted in the middle. It's all about the yin and yang, the law of duality, the equal exchange of energy – *that's the true balance*. That's how the scales of justice tip in one direction or another while maintaining balance.

Tip the Scale in Your Favor

How do you know whether you're not moving forward because it's not the right opportunity, time, or investment versus you're not moving forward because you are stuck in procrastination, perfectionism, or doubt? Or whether you're not jumping into that relationship because of red flags that are real versus imaginary ones you've created for self-preservation? Or not taking a leap of faith with a new career opportunity because of the security your current job provides versus fear of the unknown?

Weigh your options on a scale. Then envision what your life would look like down the line if you moved forward *regardless* of the outcome. That is the key. You cannot attach yourself to the outcome - only to the process of taking the steps in the direction of your goals.

> When the heaviness of the fear of regret outweighs any fear of failure — you have to go for it!

It may feel scary at first, like you want to sit in the middle of a teeter-totter, not wanting to tip it in one direction or another. Otherwise, you might feel wildly out of control. I imagine it like a pendulum swinging back and forth, much like with a metronome keeping the beat. The yin and yang of our thoughts swinging wildly between rockstar status and hiding under a rock. Where's the sweet spot? Do we stay in the middle? Some would think finding the midpoint is where we are supposed to be. But that's actually keeping you comfortably neutral. Vanilla. And if you're a chocolate person like me, vanilla just won't do.

We need to hit the barriers on each side, bouncing off wildly and freely. It's where we feel alive! When the pendulum oscillates in an undisrupted flow, it can be analogized to a stable heartbeat. When we surrender to that rhythm, no matter the disruptions, we feel free. The dark and light always vacillate, just like the sinus rhythm of a heartbeat. That's life. And without a heartbeat, there is no life. So, we need to embrace the highs and lows of life. *This is how freedom is found in both rising high and dipping low.* How do I know this?

> Life has to be up and down. Just look at a heart rate monitor - it fluctuates up and down. You don't want it to be a straight line—otherwise, you flatline!

Scan the QR code to watch my video.

https://lisastuart.com/qr-codes/9

The sinus rhythm of a heart rate monitor must go *up and down* like a wave to reflect that we are alive. It shows the peaks and the valleys of the heartbeat, much like a pendulum. Now, a pendulum's tempo can be manually adjusted by moving the position of the pendulum weight. Much like the scales of justice, with love and fear weighted at either end, the rhythm of our life's tempo can adjust depending on how much pressure is exerted on each scale.

It's the roller coaster of life. When we rise, we can also feel a pit in our stomach. The exhilaration of launching upwards can give us butterflies in our stomachs. As you rise higher, you get a rise. Remember from **Chapter 9** how butterflies in your stomach are like mini transformations waiting to be released? When the roller coaster finally tips over the edge and dips down, you release and express your energy. When we fall, we can feel free on the way down. It's a scary but good feeling. That's how you should feel in the dips of life— positive that it's a good release and knowing that it will go up again, just like a sinus rhythm wave that keeps on going.

If we flow with a wave in an ocean without resistance, it will move us forward. What happens if we try to push against the current of a wave in an ocean? We will probably get slammed down into the water. Not fun and definitely risky.

Ride the W.A.V.E. – With. Aligned. Vibrational. Equivalence.

Remember, there must be an equal exchange of energy in order for any relationship in life to be balanced, harmonious, and fluid. It's found in the surrender of the dips and highs, the tug and pulls, the give and take.

It's like an arrow pulling us back in the dark seasons, the winter, where we are nurturing that seed we planted. We are constantly rebirthing our worth, rebirthing our purpose, shedding our skin. So when that arrow is finally released, it's never in a trajectory going straight up. It's up and a dip and up and a dip - just like the stockmarket. Things fluctuate. It's never just straight up. What goes up must come down. It's the law of duality. Hell, *it's the law of gravity*.

So if you know it's never a straight line up, you can relax and trust the process.

Fall with Faith. Fly with Fear.

Our spirit wants peace. *Our ego wants spice.* We crave the peak of the struggle, waiting for that moment of triumphant victory against all odds. Just look at the top blockbuster movies. There's a common theme of epic struggle with the spirit somehow finding a way to prevail despite the odds. You know – the big lead up in a movie where there's a major break up and then one partner runs after the other and in the nick of time catches her before she leaves on that plane and they fall into each other's arms in a long passionate embrace. Or the thriller where the tension rises as the action hero jumps out of the burning plane just as it explodes, with no parachute, and somehow manages to survive.

It's the hook.

How many of you would go see a movie without conflict? Without contrast, where it's just smooth sailing? You'd probably take that time to catch up on your emails or catch up on your ZZs.

Why *do* we enjoy watching other people go through heart-stopping circumstances? Because we are the viewers, the observers. We are removed from the situation. We can safely experience life vicariously through them without actually having to go through those experiences ourselves. We like the emotional thrill of the highs and the lows because it makes us *feel* something.

In our own lives, however, we may not be so brave. Although we need the lows in order to root for the highs, we may have a fear of unfamiliar heights and crave the grounding of the familiar lows. It's one of the many cycles of life.

And it's a *dichotomy*.

When you fall, your first inclination may be to lean into *fear*. The unsupported feeling when you free fall, when things are failing, when you're feeling less than – *they all feel like you're falling into the abyss of the unknown*. On the contrary, when you fly, you feel elevated, powerful, confident: destination – *success*.

Flying with fear. It would seem that when you fly you should lean into the energy of love, and when you fall you should lean into the energy of fear. *But it's actually the opposite.* If you lean into the energy of love when you fly, you may not soar as high because you don't want to enter the unfamiliar. You need an element of fear to break barriers and push boundaries. That's how you fly higher. When you *F.L.Y. with fear* – you First Love Yourself but still push out of your comfort zone. That's a very different energy mixed with love.

Falling with faith. When you fall, you may be filled with fear, as if you have a brick of limiting beliefs weighing you down, causing you to pummel to the ground. But when you *fall with faith*, you have peace of mind that whatever circumstances you are facing you can handle with grace, ease, and confidence. There's serenity in the surrender. Your soul is rooting for you, waiting for you to sprout your wings and soar. When you fall ... *just get back up*. The only true failure is in never trying and never getting back up. Who says you're supposed to fly the first time or even the 100th?! Do you scold a toddler for not learning to walk the first time or for falling hundreds of times in the process?

> Balance is learned. Remember this when you feel unsteady. It's a practice.

So, encourage yourself like you would encourage a toddler learning to walk. Give yourself grace when you fall. Humaning is hard. And we can be hard on ourselves. Instead, let's lighten the dark spots in our life. It's all in a mixing pot called the seasons of life – and we can season it with the truth, or pepper it with lies, saying everything is ok, everything is perfect, when it's not. So next time you feel like the floor has been pulled beneath you and you are walking on unstable times, afraid to fall - *fall with faith*.

> Have certainty in your faith. Know that everything happens for you, not to you.

Then trust the unknown so you can *fly with fear*.
Remember, fear is filtered through the ego.

F.E.A.R. Feel Ego Always Resisting

So you alchemize the energy of FEAR by Alchemizing the "A" to "E". Now you can spell **F.R.E.E. Finally Release Expressive Energy**
This is how you fly freely.
And love is filtered through the spirit.

L.O.V.E. - Leap Out Venture Everywhere

That's how you leap with faith, and know you'll be ok when you enter the unknown, expand, and evolve.

It's like bouncing on a trampoline: you jump high with a bit of fear as you are free-floating in the air, and you come down with a bit of faith because you trust the trampoline to catch you and propel you up high. Have you ever noticed that the harder and the more you jump, the higher you will go? This is because you start to trust the process of the highs and lows, the ups and downs. And this is a good analogy for life – *even though you bounce back to the surface, it will propel you to jump higher.* Like an arrow traveling in an upward trajectory of 45 degrees, no matter how many times it dips and rises.

Here's a more spiritual interpretation of this. When you think of highs and lows like energy—the higher you vibrate, the higher you fly, and the lower you vibrate, the lower you fall. Now, imagine every height you reach when you fly is a new destination you've achieved.

Remember – Life is not a destination with many journeys. Life is a journey with many destinations.

When you've reached your desired destination and are moving on to the next venture, or you're still trying to make it to the desired destination and facing many hurdles, you will inevitably rise and *fail* many times. But the more you transmute the lower frequency energy with the higher vibrations you've experienced in the high points, you expose the shadows and alchemize them. You need the elevated vibration of faith in order to dip deep into the lower frequencies of darkness when you fall. That's how you have the ability to transmute it and bring it up into the light. Then when you fly with fear you reach beyond the boundaries again. But because it's new territory, you are bound to fail, aka fall, and thus the cycle continues.

**Don't depend on the highs to feel good,
and don't attach to the lows when they feel bad.**

A good rule of thumb is not to get too excited in the highs or too down in the lows. That's the trick of life - to maintain inner balance despite how erratic our outer circumstances swing in either direction. That's how you keep the scales balanced and stay centered. You allow yourself to feel the bookends of life - *the vacillating energies* - swinging wildly back and forth like a pendulum. It's about not getting affected and simply observing the extremes.

You're free to ride the ride knowing you can, *and will*, always come back to your centered inner peace. Like a palm tree. No matter how much it sways in the wind, it trusts in its strong foundation and stays resilient in its roots.

Keep calm like a palm. No matter what disruptions you face.

Norm Disrupted

When anything throws our lives out of balance — a breakup, a move, *a pandemic* - it not only interrupts our lives, *it disrupts it*. It's not just a blip or a glitch throwing us off track. It changes the trajectory and takes us on a whole new track. A complete course correct. We will never go back to a new normal. We are not supposed to. *Norm disrupted.* Maybe we were meant to tear down the walls and break down the foundation that was holding up broken pillars of society and ancestral baggage. Maybe we were shown that there is a higher power that controls everything, to show us that even when we think we are in charge, we are not. Maybe it is our inner selves, our higher selves, shining through, light warriors to show us that there is a better way. That there is no norm. That society feels comfortable in the confines of its complacency, its familiarity.

> Change is progress and progress means change.

But we innately don't like change, it feels sticky, uncomfortable, it twists our minds and unsettles our spirits. But we must evolve, revolve, and get involved in living our truths.

When your authenticity spills out, it may look different than the next person's. It may conflict with your upbringing. It may cause chaos, pain, and confusion. But after you work through the fear, through the dread of what's to come, a new world emerges, full of wonder, magic, and hope. But this new world is not the new norm. It's not to say that you will go back to the old ways, the old patterns, although many will try and fight to go back. But you must move onward. There is never a new world – it is constantly moving and changing and evolving and ever expanding - and it begins with each and every one of us. Each of our own tiny universes that we live in, breathe in, and swim in a mixture of fear and delight. You are responsible for your own *norm disrupted* so that you may emerge as your truest, shiniest, happiest self.

The simple fear of change can be so daunting. I say it's simple because change is constant. It's how you grow. The world, its structures, and people – all evolve. And if you resist and try to stay stagnant in the current energies, never wanting to explore more, you will plant your roots deeply into the present and cease to evolve. When you're stuck in the past, it's typically because you wish you had a different outcome. But just the fact that you are aware of that shows that you have evolved. It proves that you are not the same person you once were. And this holds true for your future self. Why would you stress about the future when you can realize that you– as you are now– are not who you are *going* to be. You are constantly changing, and so should your thinking and emotional response system. You haven't even met the future version of yourself!

Life is an ebb and flow of remembering who you are and releasing who you are not.

When you move through **F.E.A.R.** you are **F**ree. **E**xpressive. **A**uthentic. **R**eal.

I don't have life figured out, but I have love figured out – As long as you lead with love you have life figured out.

When Everyone Vibrates LOVE ... That's how we EVOLVE

EVOLVE spelled backwards is E.V. Love - Everyone. Vibrates. Love.

We need L.O.V.E. to expand – Leap Out Venture Everywhere. We need love to evolve past our upbringings. To grow exponentially in infinite directions. We are meant to evolve. We are designed to evolve. We can't expect the previous generations to want us to stay the same. We want the next generation to surpass us in all areas of life.

That's the Revolution of Evolution.

We know our limitations by what pushes us to the edge of our boundaries. As we teeter, looking over the edge, do we have a fear of falling? I always imagine it's like sitting on a pointy rooftop, with a bird's eye view of what's around us. The decisions we make are teetering on the midpoint of that pointy rooftop, deciding whether to roll in one direction or another. There's always a tipping point – *love or fear*. Which side will you bet on?

Bet on yourself – When you bet on yourself, you place a **W.A.G.E.R.**

- Approach life with **W**onder.
- You live your life with **A**uthenticity.
- You handle situations with **G**race.
- You move through chaos with **E**ase.
- You don't hold on, but rather, **R**elease.

When you truly know how to acknowledge, accept, and embrace your drama, your fears, your dark side – you will know how to acknowledge, accept, and embrace your freedom.

Trust me – from one former **Drama Magnet** to another – this works!

You have now learned how to **Disrupt, Deflate, and Detox Drama.**

Congratulations! You are now a Drama Ninja, ready to navigate with fear, but lead with love.

Ready to take on the world. But actually, you were born ready. You just needed to remind yourself who you truly are. *Welcome home.*

The Drama Diet

Here's a poem by me from years ago, before I came up with *Fall with Faith, Fly with Fear*, and it's a perfect end to this chapter about the decision to dance with our drama.

CHOICES

*The choices we make, Day in and day out
Shape the lives we live, No regret...no doubt*

*The people who we are, And that we wish to be
Is something that we know, We feel it so deeply*

*Voicing what we want, Doesn't get us what we need
Action needs to be taken, To get us up to speed*

*The anchor pulls us down, The guilt draws us back
The future left to hang, Throwing us off track*

*Set a major goal, Then make a minor change
Follow with the next, And cover every range*

*Fear is not an option, Tho it may be a choice
Listen to your heart, Follow your own voice*

*The truth is screaming loud, Listen and you'll hear
The things you want are real, Reach out cuz they are near*

*Blink too long and then, You'll teeter and you'll fall
Reach beyond the stars, Go after with your all*

*Confusions merely smoke, It clouds and dims the mind
Settle in your thoughts, Leave the rest behind*

*Nothing left to say, Plenty left to do
No one's gonna judge, As long as you stay true*

*Finish what you start, Take it step by step
Stand with your head high, Know that you're adept*

*Choices aren't so hard, Once you pick and choose
Feeling strong in that, You're never gonna lose*

Recipe

The Drama Dip

Dip your toes and/or face into something uncomfortable i.e. freezing water, Jello, mud etc. then tag me with your photo on social media #dramadip

- Do a spiritual tango and dip.
- Show me your drama dance. Transmuting energy. Releasing resistance.
- Video it and tag me with the hashtag #dramadance

What goes up, must come down. And like a wave —go back up. Dip your toes into the uncomfortable unknown.

Embrace the dips in life.

D.I.P. - Do. It. Positively.

*****

EXERCISE: Spiritual Botox

- Botox your emotional nervous system
- Let your stress melt away
- Less reaction, more neutrality
- Just like when you get Botox in the face - you can't move your face. You can't give a facial reaction - only a neutral (and relaxed) expression.
- When you get spiritual Botox - you can't react.
- You can just observe neutrally. Can't react, can't move face, can just observe neutrally.
- Let your energy rise instead of your negative emotions.
- Release. Relax. Rise.

*****

DRAMA DIARY JOURNAL PROMPT
Fall with Faith & Fly with Fear

- Life isn't about choosing between fear and faith – it's about learning how to hold both.
- Falling with faith means trusting the descent, the pause, the unknown.
- Flying with fear means daring to rise anyway – even when your wings are shaking.
- This is how we tip the drama scale in our favor and become grounded, graceful, Drama Ninjas.

Let's explore:

1. Where am I being asked to Fall with Faith right now?
What part of my life feels uncertain, out of my control, or in transition?
Action: Write one sentence of surrender. Something like: "I don't know how this will unfold, but I trust that I'm supported."

2. Where am I being called to Fly with Fear?
What dream, truth, or next step is asking me to rise – even if I feel unready?
Action: Write one bold sentence that starts with: "Even though I'm scared, I'm willing to…"

3. What does my inner scale feel like today – tilted toward drama or balance?
Action: Name one small, loving choice you can make today to tip the scale toward peace. This could be a boundary, a breath, a kind word, or a moment of stillness.

4. What's one mantra I can carry with me to lead with love – even when fear is in the room?
Action: Write your mantra three times and speak it out loud.

Remember: Being a Drama Ninja doesn't mean being fearless. It means feeling the fear, honoring the fall, and choosing to fly anyway.

F.L.Y. - First. Love. Yourself.

12

DRAMA DIET DESSERT

Function with Freedom

You've made it. Not just to the last chapter of this book, but to becoming an official **Drama Ninja.** What does your life look like now? More importantly, what does your life *feel* like? Can you breathe a little deeper? Do you feel a heck of a lot lighter? Does it feel like freedom?

Function with Freedom

Now that you're free, how do you function with freedom?

If you're used to living in the confines of your mind or the prison of your fears, or being shackled to your outdated stories and belief systems, *freedom can feel strange.* It's like swimming in the vast ocean for the first time without floaties. When we label ourselves, it feels stifling. We've peeled those layers off, layer by layer, like an onion. Now we have reached our core - exposed, vulnerable and detached. When we implement clear boundaries, we lose the risk of feeling chaotic and frenetic. So, here's a little *cheat sheet* on how to function with freedom.

Freedom Cheat Sheet

- *Freedom from the mind* – the ability to lose the mind chatter and mean talk so you can choose your thoughts and words.
- *Freedom from the past* – the ability to forgive and not drag the past with you.

- *Freedom from obligation rather than inspiration* – the ability to do what you desire vs what you feel like you must do.
- *Freedom from future fear* – the ability to transmute fear into excitement.
- *Freedom from fear of judgment* – the ability to accept that not everyone will like you or approve of what you are doing and that's okay.
- *Freedom from fear of failure* – the ability to fail fast and fail forward, always getting up each time you are knocked down.
- *Freedom from regret* – the ability to let go and not relive past experiences that don't exist anymore. You can let go of your "regrets" by understanding them and opting not to repeat them. In doing so, the possibilities are endless!
- *Freedom from fear of the unknown* – the ability to live with faith knowing you are the creator of your life and can write your script mindfully.

Freedom from drama – Disrupt. Deflate. Detox. The ability to navigate with fear but lead with love.

3D Drama Diet Formula

Here's a recap. First, you have to *disrupt* the incoming and oncoming drama. It's like stopping an inflated ball of drama. Then you *deflate* the ball, squeezing out all the air. Then you *detox* it by flicking it away. Use the hand movements— it ingrains the process when you need it in a pinch. Sometimes someone says something to me that really ticks me off, and I subtly do the hand movements down by my side where they can't see, and I don't get affected. Or I don't get *as* affected. Remember what I said way back in the beginning of this book - *the 3D formula is to help you get drama free .... or at least live in the space of* **drama lite!**

Disrupt drama: Respond, don't react. Become aware of the drama. Don't let the thoughts get past your mind's bouncer. R.I.P. up the outdated checklist and write your own. It's your movie, and you get to direct your life in the vision of your dreams.

Navigate with Fear: You need an element of fear in order to transmute it to courageous excitement and live your life authentically. Just don't let it take the lead. Be aware of it so you can face it, feel it, free it.

Deflate drama: If the drama keeps coming and showing up no matter how many times you try to stop it, you need to get to the root of the inflated emotions and beliefs and dissolve those stories at the source. Bring the darkness to the surface and transmute it. This process may feel agonizing at first and then so purifying, like a cleanse.

Lead with Love: The greatest relationship is the one we have with ourselves. Self-love is not selfish, it's self- *ish*. You need to be self-interested in order to elevate your life. To F.L.Y. you must First Love Yourself. Remember, the supreme L.A.W. is that Love Always Wins.

Detox drama: Surrender, let go, release. Stay centered in the eye of the storm and observe. Detach and find inner balance. Take action and set loving boundaries. Fall with faith. Fly with fear.

Become a Drama Ninja: Flip the Drama Magnet. Dance on the edge. Dance with your drama, but let love take the lead.

- In a world that is united by love, we are also divided by fear.
- In a world that is fueled by light, we are also separated by darkness.
- In a world that is bonded as one, we are also fragmented by diversity.

The law of duality has been prevalent throughout this book. It's so important to highlight that contrast unites because it's only in the polarities that we can define what we truly want. We need one to distinguish the other. From chaos comes clarity.

The more you clear your inner world, the more your outer world clears.

The more you clear the outer clutter, the more your inner world is clutter free.

When you're conflicted, you create inner turmoil. You're entangled in drama and can't detach yourself from the web. When you have inner peace, despite what's going on, you are okay with the uncertainty, the unknown, and the uncomfortableness.

> Faith is the antidote to uncertainty. In the recesses of our hidden shadows lies the truth of what will set us free.

You need to be able to walk just as comfortably through the labyrinth of darkness as you do in the light. The darkness within reflects back the light.

Take *Dorothy* from *The Wizard of Oz*. All she wanted was to go home. But to get there, she needed to pick up a few items with some friends she picked up along the way.

- *Dorothy* wanted to go home - home equates to our true selves.
- *The Scarecrow* wanted a Brain - brain equates to our thoughts.
- *The Tinman* wanted a Heart - heart equates to our emotions.
- *The Cowardly Lion* wanted Courage - courage is taking action *despite* fear.
- And *Dorothy's* fashionable red shoes were the key all along - a bright and sparkly reminder to believe in ourselves.

They all had what they wanted all along. They were just relying on external validation to prove it instead of trusting that if they face the drama, they will find what they are looking for within.

When we have a switch in perspective in our thoughts, emotions, and actions, we can achieve anything as long as we believe in ourselves.

Dorothy and her crew had to embark on a journey to *follow the yellow brick road*. It was riddled with fear, a wicked witch, and ... yes ... flying monkeys. It was a dark walk in a vibrant, colorful place.

You too need to take a walk on the dark side of light. Follow the breadcrumbs to see where you are accumulating an excess weight of drama. A little bit of added pressure, doubt, worry, anxiety, and drama each day does add up. And don't *eat* the breadcrumbs. If you consume them, that's a lot of pounds! A pound can also be written as "LB." LB in drama stands for Limiting Beliefs. LB in law stands for Liability.

Limiting Beliefs *is* a Liability. Pound (LB) for pound (LB).

When you drop the weight of limiting beliefs, you drop the pounds - LBs. That's where freedom lies.

In law, once you establish liability, then you need to assess the damages.

D.A.M.A.G.E.S.

D-oubt
A-nxiety
M-ind chatter
A-ngst
G-uilt
E-nergy drain
S-tress

Exception: In this scenario you are not in a legal proceeding where you can get compensated for your damages. And the only claim you can make is to re-claim your life. And now, with **The Drama Diet**, you know how.

- *Leave* the emotional baggage you've carried over the years.
- *Lose* the pounds of mental weight you've packed on over the years.
- *Let go* of the heavy burden of trying to please others that feel like boulders accumulating on your shoulders.

Don't carry your drama with you throughout the day. Drop off that luggage before *it* lugs *you* around.

You don't need to know where you're going, but you do need to know where you don't want to be anymore and what you want to leave behind. That's how you drop the weight and gain freedom. As you know, it's not clear cut. Life is like figuring out a puzzle. And we are all just pieces of the puzzle that is our life. And yet, the picture of the puzzle keeps changing. It's not always constant. So, the pieces don't always fit, leaving us with an incomplete puzzle – a distorted portrait of who we are and where we are supposed to go.

The missing piece is the part of your soul that you are ignoring. Don't ignore it. Ignite it. Remember – **ignore** and **ignite** have overlapping letters. The remaining ones, spell **riot.** When you ignore the whispers of your soul, you create a riot. That's when you need to see if the puzzle pieces of your life still fit the picture of your life.

Don't be discouraged if the puzzle pieces don't fit. You can create a new landscape on which to build the foundation of your life. You are allowed to morph, transform, transmute, change, move on, expand, and evolve. It is through the evolution of your spirit, the elevation of your energy, the elation of your soul, the vibration of your heart, and the cognition of your mind that you're able to start weaving the intricate tapestry of your life into a new picture. When you dig deep and dive deep into the complex labyrinth of your core, you re-emerge stronger, braver, lighter, and freer.

Lean into the lightness of your being.

Come play in my **spiritual sandbox** for a minute.

A few years after I created this 3D Drama Diet formula, I realized something very interesting. *Rabbit hole warning.* If you are familiar with the concept of spiritual awakening, you will understand that the dense energies of the 3D paradigm - the ego world we are living in - is consumed with fear. Whether you subscribe to this notion or are just beginning to digest it, you may realize that there is a need to shift out of these heavy energies and into lightness. Instead, elevate to higher frequencies of energy that transmute fear into love. That's where the sweet spot is. Since there are no coincidences, then isn't it synchronistic that **The Drama Diet** formula is a "3D" formula to disrupt, deflate, and detox the drama?! *That it's meant to navigate with fear (3D ego) but lead with love (5D self)?* Food for thought.

I'm excited that you've embarked on this journey. I'm celebrating your freedom from drama. You should too.

Be the CEO of your life – Celebrate. Elevate. Operate.

Celebrate the **wins** and the **failures**. Failures are simply clues on what hasn't worked (past tense) so you don't waste time and can move on to focus on a solution (future based).

Elevate your vibration to the frequency of what you desire to attract and where you visualize yourself going.

Operate from a heart-centered place of inspiration rather than from an ego-based driven standpoint of obligation … or desperation. This is the place where passion meets purpose.

Remember – You are the director of your life.

You are the star of your movie. You are the creator of your realized dreams. You are the writer of your story. Never forget the power you have within you. It is stronger and more potent than you can imagine.

When you focus on **how** it feels to have the "thing" rather than focusing on the lack of it, it tricks your mind into thinking that you already have it. Your brain doesn't know the distinction between past, present, or future when you are in your **imagination.** Your body will follow suit and emit *the same emotions as if you are experiencing it in real life.*

The word **IMAGINE** rearranged is **IN IMAGE.**

You are IN the IMAGE of whatever you IMAGINE.

Once you're in that image, you gain yourself. How do I know? Rearrange the letters again and you get **I GAIN ME.**

So let your imagination expand, evolve, and illuminate your life.

You never get there because once you do, there is always more that you desire. There is always upleveling. That doesn't mean you shouldn't appreciate where you are. On the contrary - gratitude is the key to receiving more.

So, live your **E.P.I.C.** life! **E**volve. **P**lay. **I**magine. **C**reate. That's what we are all here to do.

Own Your Power

(Written in 2010 by a prior version of me.)
This is the hour
To own your power
Fly higher than the sky
Soar past your last goodbye
Stand strong and hold your ground
Never let 'em push you down
It's easy to sink in the pool of your tears
Its effortless to swim in all your fears
But rising above and taking a chance
Is freeing, it's living, it's laughter and dance

When you own your power, you have mastered **The Drama Diet** L.A.W. that Love Always Wins.

T.H.E. D.R.A.M.A. D.I.E.T. L.A.W.

Owning your power means owning your:

T-houghts
H-appiness
E-motions

D-ecisions
R-easons
A-ttitude
M-indfulness
A-mbitions

D-reams
I-magination
E-nergy
T-ime

L-ife
A-ctions
W-orth

Worth. Not coincidental that it's the last word on the acronym since there are no coincidences in life. Owning your worth is key.

You are the **K.E.Y.** - **K**eep. **E**levating. **Y**ourself.

Elevate your worth. How high do you value it? **Step on the Scale of Self-Validation.**

Never go hungry again, for self-worth, that is. Nourish your soul. Live a sustainable way to thrive. Don't wait until you feel comfortable to start living your purpose.

The fear may be louder, but the regret will be stronger.

Have you ever gone hiking and looked at the top of the mountain from the base and wondered *how the heck will I get there?* Well, imagine that mountain is your life. Only there is no top, because you are limitless. So, you keep moving upward towards becoming who you really are— full of joy and passion and purpose, vibrant and energized. And every time you reach the so-called peak, and feel that you've finally plateaued, suddenly another more arduous mountain surfaces.

Does that sound daunting or exciting to you? Can you feel the sweat dripping down your back, your legs burning from exhaustion, while blisters form on your aching feet? Can you allow yourself time to rest and reset or are you on a burning mission to make it to the top before you burn out?

The Drama Diet is not about a mini retreat for yourself after which you return to your normal life, after a couple of weeks. It's about making small changes in your life, which will result in a total transformation to a version of yourself that you aspire to be. This type of D.I.E.T. is not fleeting. It's everlasting.

D.I.E.T. – **D**on't. **I**nterrupt. **E**volving. **T**ransformation.

Remember – Life is not a destination with many journeys. Life is a journey with many destinations.

Rest when you reach them. Celebrate. Rejuvenate. Then proceed to your next destination with renewed energy. Let your fear fuel you. Let your faith inspire you.

You've got this! There's no deadline.

Transformation has no deadline.

It's a lifelong process, and the good news is the more steps you add, the more steps you'll take up the mountain of **L.I.F.E.** - **L**ove **I**ntegrates **F**earful **E**nergy. To balance life, we need to *dance with our darkness, and lead with love.*

Don't have a **Drama Duel. Dance**. A duel is just a fight dance. And you already have the tools to dance with your drama. So, you got this. Put on your dancing shoes and dance your heart out. You don't need fancy moves or slick maneuvers. You just need to stay on your own beat. Follow your heartbeat. Follow what fills your heart.

Keep on dancing! The music never ends. We never truly get *there*. We are always *here*. And so, it's the constant shedding of the weight that's keeping us down, the continual leveling up, that will keep us moving forward even when the winds of change are pushing against us. *Again, I believe that the closer we get to our dreams, the more obstacles the universe throws in our path because it is testing us to see how bad we want our dreams.* When you're tested, keep the faith, keep charging ahead, and keep a copy of this book with you as a tool of constant source of inspiration and guidance.

You A.R.E. what you E.A.T.

So **A**ctively **R**ecognize the **E**nergy of your **E**motions, **A**ctions, and **T**houghts.

Always remember your power. You have the power to control what you consume and how you respond. You have the power to decide which direction you want to go. You have the power to expand your world. You have the power to think big and dream bigger. Let yourself open up to the endless possibilities, the awaiting opportunities, and the magical experiences. Your journey is waiting for you.

Dream. Dance. Thrive on The Drama Diet!

CONTINUE THE JOURNEY BEYOND THE BOOK

Pair *The Drama Diet* with the companion **Motivational Card Decks**— designed with actionable tips to control your drama so it doesn't control you. This 51-card deck is divided into categories of quotes to inspire you, recipes to empower you, and exercises to motivate you. Each card offers a bite-sized reminder to keep you calm, light-hearted, and aligned. Pull one when you need a vibe check, a drama deflector, or simply need to kick your limiting beliefs to the curb. Grab a deck, ditch the drama, and become the calm despite the chaos.

Scan the QR code for The Drama Diet Card Deck
https://lisastuart.com/qr-codes/10

Follow me on Instagram. https://www.instagram.com/lisastuartofficial
https://lisastuart.com/qr-codes/11

For more motivational videos, follow me on Instagram.
https://www.instagram.com/thedramadiet
https://lisastuart.com/qr-codes/12

ACKNOWLEDGMENTS

People these days start off thanking themselves. I sort of did way back in the Dedication section of this book. But my original dedication was different. It was to my beloved Grandparents, Martha and Herman, of blessed memory. They truly shaped my reasons for this book on so many levels. My grandfather always wanted to write a book with me ... he was a pioneer of a healthy lifestyle– mind, body, and spirit–even back in the 80s before it was mainstream. My grandmother was both a Queen ... and a Drama Queen ... which made her a fierce, funny, and fabulous force unparalleled by anyone I had ever met. You both were a driving force throughout my life, and throughout this book, and helped shape me into who I am today, and I am so grateful for that. I hope you are smiling (and dancing) above.

Thank you to my beautiful mother, who has consistently been my biggest cheerleader, advocate, and sounding board. Mom... I may be a writer, but even I can't find the words to fully express my gratitude for the way you believe in me, not just with this book, but with all my endeavors. You are genuinely my rock ... or rather ... a diamond - strong, radiant, and precious. I treasure our deep talks, lighthearted laughter, and mother-daughter escapades. But mostly I cherish *you*–your wisdom, your guidance, your elegance– you are my forever role model and I love you forever!

Thank you to my wonderful father, whom I just got to spend quality time with during our long (and successful) trial. Dad, I'm so grateful for you - you've instilled in me the power of setting my mind to something, getting laser-focused, and accomplishing it. You taught me to never give up, to always find an angle, and a way to win. Your brilliance, tenacity, and unparalleled work ethic have been both an inspiration and a blueprint in making my dreams a reality. I love you always!

To Cheryl Benton, my amazing (and patient) publisher. Thank you for helping bring my vision to life! You waited "judgment-free" for my final edits, which took months due to that long trial. You helped make this process seamless and effortless, even when I dragged it out, made constant changes, and kept you waiting. And on the heels of that trial-or rather stilettos-you finalized my book into this bundle of magic.

To Patricia Kara, for being a great friend who is the epitome of raising up other women. During your own book publishing process, you took the time to make sure I was taken care of, always checking in, sharing your valuable info, and especially introducing me to our wonderful publisher! Love you!

To Rachel McCord, an angel sent to me from up above. Thank you for not only writing my Foreword (what an honor to me) but for being there in the very darkest hour of my life. You are such a light, and I adore you!

To Nancy Steiner, thank you for editing this book. Thank you for being my executive coach. But more than that, thank you for being there in more ways than I could thank you for. Grateful for you!

To my family and friends ... so many to name ... but I hope you all receive this. Thank you for being on this journey with me - the journey of life, drama, and this book ... whether it was to read a passage, opine on the cover, listen when I was melting in drama, or just being there to cheer me on. And especially to my inner circle - you know who you are. Thank you for being my "venting vault." I appreciate you all so, so much!

A special thank you to my SiStar Niesa Azran who has been my official "unofficial" PR person throughout this process! I love you!

To Dragana Ognenovska, my amazing coach (and friend) throughout the years, I appreciate you immensely. Thank you for encouraging me to start my journey many years ago which led me to this moment ... I am so grateful for you.

To my A3 - Alexander, Aaron, and Arabelle. You are my why. You inspire me with your curiosity, your spirit, and your being. And I hope that I inspire you to keep living with curiosity and push your own inner limits, to keep following your spirit and live freely and passionately, and to keep coming back to your being so that what you are "doing" aligns with your why. I'm so proud of each of you–all your wit, grit, and humor. Thanks for lightening all my drama-filled days, even when you may have been the source of my drama! And thank you for giving me sound advice when I was dripping in drama. I am beyond blessed to be chosen as your mother and I love you endlessly...

To my husband Russ, my love, my partner, my best friend, my twin flame, my tech support, my comic relief, my book cover designer, my everything. Thank you for being the mirror–my safe mirror–reflecting back all my fears, my doubts, my self-imposed limiting beliefs ... and for making sure it didn't shatter even when my world felt shattered. Thank you for always "Russtifying" things to make sense when my world seemed upside down. Thank you for believing in me when I wouldn't believe in myself. Thank you for holding my hand through every plot twist, for always dancing with me– literally and figuratively–and for making me laugh when I took life too seriously. Most of all, thank you for loving me through the light and the dark–I couldn't do this story without you. Our story is the reason I believe that *love always wins*. I love you always and forever ... and a day.

To you, my cherished readers, thank you for entrusting me to fill your time, space, and mind with words and energy near and dear to my heart. I hope we stay in touch, and I am so grateful to have you on this journey with me. I am so thankful that I get to be on this journey with you.

Cheers to a Drama Lite Life! xo

ABOUT THE AUTHOR

Lisa Stuart is a multifaceted powerhouse who turned her journey from *Drama Magnet* to *Drama Ninja* into a movement of radical self-empowerment. A seasoned attorney by profession, she combines sharp legal acumen and soulful storytelling, creating a voice that resonates far beyond the courtroom. But she's not just a lawyer—she's a speaker, author, songwriter, drama dietician, and unapologetic overthinker.

With her core belief that the most powerful L.A.W. is that *Love Always Wins*, Lisa helps others navigate with fear, but lead with love. She demonstrates how to embrace the full spectrum of life—light and shadow, faith and fear—guiding them to rewrite the stories that no longer serve them. Her signature approach, *The Drama Diet*, offers bite-sized, digestible tools to release emotional weight, reconnect with inner clarity, and lead with authenticity. Lisa's voice is equal parts wise and witty, grounded in the belief that in order to F.L.Y.–*First Love Yourself*–you must be willing to fall (and fail) on your way to rising, as it's all part of the journey.

Outside of her mission-driven work, Lisa wears many hats: she's a proud mom of three, wife, dog mom, workout enthusiast, and lover of clean food, coffee, and chocolate. Above all, she's an advocate for living a bold, judgment-free, and drama-lite life—where you don't just avoid chaos, you embrace it and dance with your darkness... but let love take the lead.

Lisa is also the host of The Drama Diet Show.

www.ingramcontent.com/pod-product-compliance
Lightning Source LLC
Chambersburg PA
CBHW070613030426
42337CB00020B/3787